Models of Literacy Instruction

Terry Salinger
Educational Testing Service

Merrill, an imprint of
Macmillan Publishing Company
New York

Maxwell Macmillan Canada
Toronto

Maxwell Macmillan International
New York Oxford Singapore Sydney

Cover art: Martie Husted
Editor: Linda James Scharp
Production Editor: Julie Anderson Tober
Art Coordinator: Peter A. Robison
Photo Editor: Anne Vega
Text Designer: Jill E. Bonar
Cover Designer: Russ Maselli
Production Buyer: Pamela D. Bennett
Electronic Text Management: Ben Ko, Marilyn Wilson Phelps
Artist: Jane Lopez

This book was set in Zapf Book by Macmillan Publishing Company and was printed and bound by R. R. Donnelley & Sons Company. The cover was printed by Phoenix Color Corporation.

Macmillan Publishing Company
866 Third Avenue
New York, NY 10022

Macmillan Publishing Company is part of the
Maxwell Communication Group of Companies.

Maxwell Macmillan Canada, Inc.
1200 Eglinton Avenue East, Suite 200
Don Mills, Ontario M3C 3N1

Library of Congress Cataloging-in-Publication Data
Salinger, Terry S.
    Models of literacy instruction / by Terry Salinger.
        p. cm.
    Includes bibliographical references (p.) and index.
    ISBN 0-675-21328-2
    1. Reading (Primary) 2. English language—Composition and
exercises—Study and teaching (Primary) 3. Children—Language.
I. Title.
LB1525.S25 1993
372.6'23'044—dc20   92–31881
                                                              CIP

Printing: 1 2 3 4 5 6 7 8 9   Year: 3 4 5 6 7

All photos by Robert Finken.

For Richard Cole

Preface

Many years ago, a student in a developmental reading class told me that although she had learned a lot from my teaching, she was distressed that I had not "told the class exactly how you are supposed to teach reading." I tried to explain to her that my point all semester had been that there is no single, foolproof way to teach students to read—or to write; but she went away, off to her student teaching, not quite understanding. As a new college teacher, I took her words and her dismay to heart and began the same class the next semester by saying something such as, "I'm not going to give you exact steps and procedures to teach children to read; I'm going to give you possibilities for helping them acquire literacy."

That experience is many years in the past. More recently, we have expanded our awareness of what "learning to read" actually means. Researchers have provided significant insights into what happens as students initially investigate and gradually become competent in both reading and writing behaviors. We now talk about "literacy" and expect reading and writing to be taught and practiced together. But many teachers are still looking for the formulas and gimmicks, the one or two exact ways, to get students to become literacy users. Teachers sometimes talk about "doing" whole language or turn to real literature only as long as there is a teacher's guide to help them know what to do with the books. Often, teachers' motivations are quite genuine. Aware that acquiring literacy is hard work, they want to make sure that their students have the best possible advantages in this important endeavor. These teachers simply may not be confident enough about their own abilities as decision makers to structure their classroom and their students' activities to foster literacy growth.

This book maintains that teachers must take control of the literacy curriculum in their classes—and that they can do this successfully. Teachers must draw upon their understanding of how reading and writing "work" if they are to help students acquire these skills; they must model reading and writing and "think aloud" about the processes they use as they engage in literacy behaviors. They must provide ample, enticing reading materials and opportunities for real writing. And they must watch their students, take cues from them, and continually be ready to modify, rethink, and adjust their curriculum.

None of this is easy, but taking part in children's literacy growth can be among the most satisfying aspects of teachers' interactions with their students. Without saying "exactly how to teach reading," this book makes suggestions for various models of interaction between teachers, students, books, and literacy.

Acknowledgments

This book maintains that learning to read and write is very much a social activity. So, too, is writing a book about literacy learning, and I must acknowledge the many colleagues and students who have shared ideas and experiences with me over the years. These people are too numerous to mention all by name, but their voices, enthusiasm, and even work samples are reflected in this book. I would like to thank the following individuals for reviewing this text: Gloria T. Blatt, Oakland University; Bonnie Chambers, Bowling Green State University; Kathy Danielson, University of Nebraska at Omaha; Edward J. Earley, Kutztown University; Ramona S. Frasher, Georgia State University; Robert Pehrsson, Idaho State University; Timothy V. Rasinski, Kent State University; Sam L. Sebesta, University of Washington; Marilou R. Sorensen, University of Utah; Richard B. Speaker, Jr., University of New Orleans; Maria J. Weiss, University of Nevada—Las Vegas. I also thank Linda Scharp and Julie Tober at Macmillan and copyeditor Mona Bunner for their collective and considerable skills in bringing my manuscript to print.

Finally, I am very grateful to certain friends and colleagues—Georgia Connor and Kelli Slaughter for technical expertise; Nancy Rosenberg, Miriam Grosof, Nancy Mead, and David Wright for wonderful friendships; Ted Chittenden for friendship, thought-provoking conversations, and nonstop musing about children's learning; and Dick Cole for his interest in what I do.

—T.S.

Brief Contents

Contents

A Brief Background on Literacy Research and Instruction

This book begins with a brief overview of the history of literacy research and instruction during this century. This overview suggests that traditional practice has not always been totally supportive of children's pursuit of new learning. In the name of "scientific" approaches, commercial materials and instructional methodology have frequently stymied children's curiosity and natural impulses to explore literacy.

This first chapter traces changes and constancy in the ways educators have envisioned children's progress in literacy, from first discoveries of print to joyful participation in communities of readers and writers. The chapter also discusses some of the recent research in children's acquisition of literacy skills and the instruction that this research has generated.

CONFLICTING THEORIES

The 1920s were a time of intense educational research, much of which concentrated on reading issues (Smith, 1965; Shannon, 1989). Emerging from the research and the debate it engendered were the development of standardized testing, a proliferation of structured commercial instructional materials, and the codification of two conflicting theories to explain reading. These two theories are examined in the following section.

Theory One

Around 1925, the educational community was introduced to "scientific" methods of measuring reading achievement, methods that seemed to offer ways to quantify rather than merely describe children's reading behavior. Most early assessment methods (many of which are still widely used) depended primarily on counting children's errors in oral reading or eliciting nearly verbatim recall of what was read silently. The result was a score on a test, from which information about instruction was supposed to be derived.

Also introduced at this time was a theory about reading, which maintained that children gain proficiency through repeated practice of sequential skills as a part of carefully planned and structured lessons. This theory, which still drives much classroom practice, was based on the assumption that children are "empty vessels" who learn from material and information outside themselves. The basal reader series came into prominence at this time; it is a complete instructional package, designed with the intention of making teaching easier and more efficient. The introduction of basal readers neatly complemented the developments in assessment because both were based on a definition of reading as the accumulation of numerous, discrete skills that could be identified, taught, and assessed virtually independently of each other. Much of the essence of basal readers is captured in the following description of a classroom in which a writer observed for one year.

> [The basals] were more than reading books. They were mountains of equipment, big charts for teaching what was called "skills lessons," and big metal frames to hold these charts erect, and workbooks for the children to practice those skills, and readers full of articles and stories that did not fairly represent the best of children's literature, and for each grade level, a fat teacher's manual that went so far as to print out in boldface type the very words . . . any . . . teacher anywhere should say to her pupils so as to *make* them learn to read. (Kidder, 1989, p. 29)

Two approaches to teaching reading have dominated the basal reader market and shaped the commercial material available for classroom use: (a) sight- or whole-word approaches and (b) phonics instruction. The *sight-word approach* starts with the visual representation of whole words so that children develop a "sight vocabulary" that enables them to read simple material almost from the beginning of instruction. Memorizing an initial vocabulary *at sight* helps children generalize skills for independent "word attack" so that they can figure out unfamiliar words. Knowledge of symbol-sound correspondences emerges from children's generalizations. Children gain assurance that the letter *b*, for example, makes a particular sound after numerous encounters with words in which use of the anticipated sound produces positive results. Students test the rules for symbol-sound correspondence and see if their effort produces a recognizable word. These generalizations, of course, do not help when a child encounters a word such as *lamb* for the first time; but, the theory maintains that because children have been reading meaningful material, they should have acquired other word attack skills to help figure out the word. The method encourages reading from the start but limits the vocabulary and syntax in early readers to a low, "controlled" level. Reading material, then, lacks the vibrancy of children's spoken language or the expressive language encountered in good children's literature.

Phonics instruction, on the other hand, stresses the importance of children's thoroughly learning symbol-sound correspondences in order to sound out words as they begin to read. Although usually considered inappropriate, some phonics programs have even recommended that beginners learn sounds in isolation from words, that is, that children learn the sounds of letters before being introduced to even a simple beginning vocabulary of words with clear-cut letter-sound correspondences. Having mastered symbol-sound correspondence, children are supposed to be able to make connections between letters and their sounds automatically and blend sounds appropriately when they encounter letters embedded within the context of words. Thus, seeing the graphic images *cat, CAT,* or cat, or *cat*, for example, a child is supposed to figure out the individual sounds, blend them to form a word, recognize the word, and realize that she knows what the word means.

Often, most irregular "sight" words are introduced only after the majority of sounds have been learned, so material that children encounter has to be simple, and is, therefore, often painfully dull. Thus, children may read, "Nat, the fat cat, sat on a mat" or similar texts. Children's motivation could easily wane before they are able to develop a usable storehouse of phonics rules to allow them to read interesting stories. In addition, many children become confused as they begin to encounter words that follow "irregular" rules (such as *lamb* with its silent *b*) because the rules that they have so faithfully learned do not work. The resulting lack of cognitive "clarity" often leads to children's turning off to the complex and strenuous task of strengthening their literacy skills (Downing, 1979; Johnston & Winograd, 1985).

In both sight-word and phonics-based approaches, students often spend more time completing exercises than actually reading (DeFord, 1981). This imbalance reflects the "myth . . . that reading instruction should consist exclusively of teaching phonics, vocabulary, and grammar. . . . [Reading should be] a way into worlds unheard of and undreamed, the worlds of Maurice Sendak and Dr. Seuss, of Snow White and E. B. White, even of the comics and the television advertisements" (Bruner, 1984, p. 194).

When students do read in a basal reader series, they often encounter texts that "look like real language and yet . . . do not correspond to any real language form. . . . They also sound like real utterances in spite of transmitting no information and lacking any communicative content" (Ferreiro & Teberosky, 1982, pp. 274–275). Such texts convey a false idea about what reading actually is and offer little insight into the satisfaction and joy that real books can provide. If children are accustomed to the richness of literature, basals, in comparison, are disappointingly dull; many children may wonder when the exciting words and ideas they have encountered elsewhere will be laid before them. Even "whole language" basals that use children's literature may offer stories that have been excerpted or even rewritten to fit a traditional basal reader model (Routman, 1988).

It is not only the student who can be shortchanged by the basal reader series. Recent retrospective analyses of reading instruction have suggested that the introduction of basals and their accompanying manuals marked a movement to "deskill" teachers, that is, to take from them the creative, dynamic interaction with children that can truly support and nourish growth (Shannon, 1989).

Theory Two

Influenced by Huey's *The Psychology of Reading* (1908), the work of John Dewey (1900, 1916, 1963), and other leaders of the Progressive movement in education, the second theory contended that children seek meaning from the world through cycles of experimenting, hypothesizing, and testing their ideas (Cremen, 1961; Smith, 1965; Shannon, 1989). Such experimenting extends beyond investigation of concrete aspects of the world to more abstract issues, such as trying to discover how the tasks of reading and writing are accomplished. As early as 1908, Huey proposed that the search for meaning should dominate reading and that from the beginning, children should be taught with meaningful material. Reading, he maintained, begins with what is inside each individual child and is strengthened by building upon what children care about, are curious about, and already know. Language in all its forms was considered an expressive medium, much like art, and children were thought capable of acquiring reading and writing through their diverse interactions with other content areas (Antler, 1987; Shannon, 1989).

Because the centerpiece of this model of reading acquisition was children's experiences and concerns, an approach was recommended in which children's own stories, dictated by students and transcribed by teachers, would become the basal material for beginning reading. As skills increased, children would write their own stories and use them, along with children's literature, as part of their reading material. *The Twentieth Yearbook of the National Society for the Study of Education*, published in 1926, gave this approach a name: the Experience Approach. Throughout the next decades, commercial basal material continued to predominate but "progress had been made in evolving the idea [of an experience-based approach, which was] . . . a radical departure from traditional instructional approaches" (Smith, 1965, p. 94). Recent movement toward curriculum change in reading and writing instruction has in many ways reflected some of the earlier, positive practices.

RECENT RESEARCH

Much educational research and classroom practice have continued to reflect these two divergent theories. Yet, some researchers have re-evaluated the traditional view that most children learn to read and then write in relatively sequential steps, in response to materials that meter out small doses of carefully planned, often scripted, instruction. Attending to the research on child language development and cognitive psychology, they have focused on children's active processes for the following:

- gathering information about language
- developing and testing rules for language functioning and use
- refining these rules as feedback is received from proficient language users
- reconstructing meaning from text by reading and constructing meaning in text by writing

Rather than concentrating research energies on controlled experiments to see what works or on analyses of reading and writing products such as standardized test scores or timed writing samples, many researchers have recently used the power of ethnography to become "kidwatchers." Essentially, they observe children as they learn, especially in environments that invite investigations of literacy (Y. M. Goodman, 1985). Researchers have attempted to get inside children's minds to discover the processes they use to gain meaning from literacy behaviors they see around them and the strategies they accumulate as they gain competence in reading and writing. Researchers have also studied the actual products of children's reading and writing work—scribbles, drawings, stories, oral readings, and so forth. Analysis of these products provides insight into the processes children use to create the products, the assumptions that drive children's behavior, their conceptions and misconceptions, and the ways in which they take ownership of what they are taught.

Hubbard (1989) presented an excellent example of how researchers have expanded their inquiry to try to figure out what children actually are doing as they work with literacy tasks. As she watched a first grader, David, write C - A - T eight times, Hubbard feared that he was using inventive spelling and avoiding drawing, and "was returning to the safety of a known word, written over and over again, meaninglessly" (p. 119). When Hubbard asked him what he was doing, he replied, "I'm writing and thinking about all the different cats I know" and went on to discuss each one. Hubbard mused, "What I would have missed if I had focused only on David's product!" She stressed that as teachers and researchers, we need to "begin to get past [our] ego-centric—or perhaps adult-centric—view of [children's] processes" (p. 119). The process of watching another David, also a first grader, is presented in Table 1–1 (Salinger, 1988).

Kidwatching requires respect for the intellectual efforts that children bring to self-motivated investigation of reading and writing. Researchers often have to make educated guesses or inferences about why a child performed a specific act, made a specific statement, or asked a specific question; and by observing many children, often over long periods of time, they have identified patterns of behavior that substantiate their inferences. Of course, knowledgeable teachers do this all the time in much less formal ways. As will be stressed throughout this book, validating these important teacher observations has been part of the current thrust to change literacy instruction.

Much recent work has also emphasized that teachers are decision makers who shape the classroom environment, respond to children, and reflect continuously on the results of their decisions (Shulman, 1986; Bussis, Chittenden, Amarel, & Klausner, 1985). What teachers *do* affects what children will in turn do in the classroom and by extension what they will learn; what teachers *think* and *believe* is equally important. This strand of research has focused on teachers as crucial elements in children's learning. Teachers' thought processes and decisions have become a primary unit of analysis, the analysis branching out to the complex interactions between teachers and students, between students themselves, and between people in a classroom and the materials they encounter. The recent book *Among School Children* (Kidder, 1989) has enriched the lay public's understanding of this complexity.

IMPORTANT FINDINGS

Researchers working in the areas of education and cognitive psychology have added tremendously to our understanding of how students learn to read and write. They have deemed the following issues particularly significant:

- the role of background knowledge in literacy behaviors
- the social nature of literacy learning
- the interrelation of reading and writing skills

Background Knowledge

Background knowledge has been identified as a key variable in children's successful acquisition of literacy skills (Langer, 1984). As will be discussed throughout this book, instruction can be most meaningful when teachers help students access or tap into and then build upon what they bring to their literacy tasks. When students know about the topics they encounter in their reading, they achieve higher levels

Table 1–1
A Long-Term Example of Kidwatching[1]

David entered my combined first- and second-grade classroom at the beginning of my fifth year of teaching. I had had his older brother the previous year and knew and respected the family. The brother had been a model student—well behaved, motivated, very creative, and confident. David, the mother told me, was virtually the opposite, except for his high intelligence and sense of being part of a loving family.

Among the first things I noticed about David was the power he held over the children who had known him in kindergarten. They seemed to be afraid of him or at least in awe of his energy. David seemed to realize that he had power and was determined to get control of the classroom as soon as possible.

The first few weeks of school, David and I battled too much for me to watch him extensively. He tried to terrorize the children through noise and aggression, and I fought back the dreaded words, "Why can't you be more like your brother?" The best way to keep him under control was to keep him close to me, and he became my shadow—holding my hand, sitting next to me, even eating lunch with me. Rather than resenting this attention, the other children seemed to realize that they were being protected. David especially liked to be near me during storytime so that he could see the pictures and print close up.

David refused to do much of the independent classroom work, so he stayed close by during all small-group instruction. My rationale was that he would learn through repeated exposure to the material and that he would not be on the loose to bother others. As I finally was able to begin to watch this fascinating child, I noticed his intense interest in whatever the children said and did. Because the class was a combined first and second grade, David was bombarded with instruction. He followed along with all the lessons, contributed to story dictation, and even began to volunteer answers to questions. The twinkle in his eye as I handed him a book to "look at" was heartening; he clearly was more interested in real reading than in the readiness work some of his peers from kindergarten were doing.

After about a month, David began to write notes for me. He "delivered" his first note by crumpling it into a ball and hurling it, like a baseball, onto my desk. I can't remember what the note said and didn't keep that first effort. But I remember his control over invented spelling and my vow to watch him more closely.

David obliged my interest by writing profusely. He continued to sit close to me through all instruction, participating when he wished and doing an increasing amount of independent seatwork, silent reading, and writing. Throughout the year, he loudly maintained that he couldn't read, but frequently he curled up in the library corner, just looking at books. On the test at year's end, he scored considerably above grade level in reading.

David taught me a tremendous number of things, not the least of which was the value of looking very closely at children's behaviors. He reinforced the idea that the environment plays as much a part as (and maybe a stronger part than) direct instruction in students' learning. By watching David and by studying the work he did, I discovered new dimensions of children's learning strategies and did, in fact, refine my approaches to literacy instruction.

[1]From *Language arts and literacy for young children* (pp. 70–71) by T. Salinger, 1988, New York: Merrill/Macmillan. Copyright by Macmillan. Adapted by permission.

of comprehension than when they read about unfamiliar topics. There are numerous strategies designed to help teachers assess students' background knowledge, to help students access the knowledge they possess, and to build knowledge prior to reading and writing tasks. These strategies will be discussed in subsequent chapters.

Literacy Learning as a Social Activity

Infants, toddlers, and preschoolers learn through social interactions with people around them. A specific subset of these social interactions has caught the interest of researchers of early learning, who have directed attention at what are called literacy events. *Literacy events* are planned or spontaneous situations in which children ask about or observe some aspect of literacy, discuss reading or writing with a literacy user, or participate in some event that requires reading or writing. Initiated by either adults or children, literacy events strengthen children's conceptualization of literate behaviors (Harste, Woodward, & Burke, 1983; Y. M. Goodman, 1990). Essentially, children, as literacy "novices," are turning to literacy "experts" for information, clarification, and informal instruction that address immediate concerns, needs, and questions. The props and situations for literacy events are varied and by no means limited to the bedtime story reading sessions that have so enriched countless numbers of children's lives (Holdaway, 1979). Any time an adult and child share some artifact of literacy in a way that clues the child to the usefulness or processes of reading and writing, the child's emerging sense of literacy is expanded.

The social nature of literacy events and the benefits gained from these interactions very obviously extend into beginning literacy acquisition. Young learners need to talk about what they are doing as they acquire literacy, and they need to talk with their teachers and their peers, and indeed with themselves as they work their way through reading and writing tasks (Dyson, 1986, 1988). Teachers shape much of this discussion through strategies called scaffolding, with which they provide young learners the basic outline or framework of the cognitive processes they are learning (Cazden, 1983). Scaffolding is not lecturing; it is often merely conversational, informal, and thereby social discussion. Within the context of immediate literacy tasks, teachers are "letting children in on" the steps and strategies to make using literacy easier. Small-group lessons and individual conferences provide the context for this instructional socializing. As with family-based literacy events, teachers and students assume an expert-novice relationship in a kind of apprenticeship that provides information and skills in a supportive environment.

Social interactions in literacy learning remain important throughout the elementary grades. In many classes, however, the emphasis is on a balance of teacher instruction and silent, independent student work. Ideally, as students gain competence in reading and writing, a literacy-focused social transaction should emerge between them and their peers and between them and the authors of the texts they read (Resnick, 1985). These social transactions provide pleasure, satisfaction, and information in terms of both the procedural and declarative knowledge that can be gained. Although approaches like reciprocal teaching, cooperative learning, and reading-writing workshops do encourage social interaction, all too often students seem to read primarily to pass tests or to complete assignments in classes where teachers are cast as authoritative evaluators, rather than as experts who willingly take on literacy "apprentices."

Reading and Writing as Interrelated Skills

The ways in which reading and writing are complementary have also interested researchers. The two behaviors have come to be considered part of a total developmental continuum. Children learn first to communicate with gestures, then with oral language, and finally with print. The traditional reading programs discussed earlier in this chapter would never recommend combining reading and writing instruction because such programs rest on the tenet that children must master reading before they can tackle writing. In reality, many children begin to write before they show any interest in reading; in fact, they can actually express themselves well in what has been termed "invented spelling" (Clay, 1979; Harste, Woodward, & Burke, 1983). Critics of basal readers stress that even in older grades, children do little writing in most reading programs and may merely circle words or fill in blanks in the "expressive" portion of their reading work. Yet, in classes at all levels, when children are encouraged to read and write and there is no implication that these are two separate subject areas, the children achieve more success in all language skills.

WHAT RESEARCH SUGGESTS ABOUT THE CLASSROOM

Research findings have a way of filtering into schools very slowly, a phenomenon that is especially sad when findings could lead to dramatic improvements in instructional practice. A good deal of the recent research has focused on young children, and, as a result, many early childhood classrooms have been transformed into exciting places where children can "play" with emerging literacy skills. But this is not enough. As researchers uncover more about the processes all children use as they engage in literacy learning, findings should impact all grade levels. There is no one point in a classroom when interactions with literacy should change dramatically from those that center around exploration and involvement to those that are less flexible and more linear. Nor is there one point when children's curiosity about literacy wanes and classrooms must become "traditional" if children are going to learn. In fact, reading and writing develop as processes of "emerging expertise" (Pearson, 1991). In exciting classrooms throughout the primary and middle grades, children continue to experiment with conventions of literacy as they seek out information and pleasure from reading and find their own voice through writing. The experiments become more sophisticated, even more daring, over time because children draw upon increasing amounts of information and feedback from previous efforts to understand and use literacy.

To encourage growth of literacy skills, classrooms should become literate environments—"alive with print, displaying all its functions, from things as simple as signs and labels right through to literature" (Holdaway, 1979, p. 71). The purpose of this lively display of print in early childhood classes is probably obvious but in upper grades may be less clear. Pencils, crayons, pens, and other writing equipment, including computers, allow children to explore composition.

Classes must become a community of readers and writers, individuals who share their enthusiasm for and use of print in many different ways. When varied kinds of print are displayed, students sense their own place within the literacy community and feel more motivated to master the skills that allow them to gain full membership in that community.

Literate Environment: Interpersonal Components

No matter how full of books and print their environment is, learners need contact with other literacy users in a warm, supportive learning climate. "A climate that is good to live in can also be a climate in which learning flourishes; certainly a learning climate needs first to be a living climate—because living and learning are not distinct activities" (Torbe & Medway, 1981, p. 141).

Throughout the elementary grades, students need opportunities to talk about what they are reading and writing and also to discuss the strategies they are using to perform these skills. Peer response groups, book talks, authors' chair sessions, teacher-student conferences, and other groupings of students and teachers approximate the immediacy of interaction that, ideally, supports children in the home. These interactions take time, but they enhance children's learning, metacognition, and self-confidence.

Teachers' attitudes may be almost as important a variable as time. When teachers demonstrate that they value literacy and that they support and appreciate their students' experiments with literacy, students gain ownership of literate behaviors in lasting and satisfying ways. If teacher "experts" welcome student "novices" into a kind of "apprenticeship" for learning, children sense that they have freedom to experiment and make mistakes; they know that their teachers will focus on their efforts rather than on merely bestowing grades. Indeed, teachers must recognize that "that highly structured instructional system that focuses on mastery of one rule or skill before another loses sight of the complexity of learning written language. It oversimplifies what children really do learn and focuses some insecure children on insignificant and often erroneous principles about learning" (Goodman, Y. M., 1984, p. 109).

In addition to modeling skills for students, teachers can become literacy role models by demonstrating that they value and appreciate the benefits of being able to read and write. When students see their teacher writing to communicate, turning to a book to look up information, or even merely carrying a newspaper in the morning, they realize that the teacher uses literacy as part of his or her daily life.

Purposeful Tasks in a Literate Environment

Looking closely at successful literacy learners, researchers have concluded that students acquire reading and writing skills most readily through authentic, purposeful literacy tasks such as self-selected reading and writing about personally relevant topics. Obviously, literacy tasks that students find purposeful will enhance their learning, but the tremendous faith lodged in commercial materials such as basal readers and workbooks has obscured this important fact, which Huey and others stressed so long ago.

As researchers and teachers have recognized the need to provide purposeful tasks, the focus of instruction has changed. Language arts is a good example. Children are expected to write throughout the elementary grades rather than "learn" about writing in discrete instructional units in a language arts text. One researcher explained this change:

> The revolution in writing instruction started with a simple realization: to learn to write, students must partake of the process. For many years, when we claimed to offer writing instruction and writing practice, . . . we actually offered something else—instruction and practice in grammar, most often, or in diagramming sentences, reading literature, or speaking correctly. . . . Time for the process of composing was not so common. Teachers and researchers have come to realize that there simply must be time in the classroom when students write, not perform some other activity that stands for writing, and that students need to have writing represented as a process. (Hull, 1989, p. 121)

The integration of reading and writing, along with emphasis on listening and speaking skills, is sometimes referred to as the *whole language approach.* Many books and articles have been written about whole language—as an approach to instruction, as an attitude toward children, and even as a philosophy (see Appendix A for additional readings). This book is not specifically about whole language instruction *per se*; it is instead about different models that teachers can use to structure their interactions with students in order to bring about optimal learning. Some of the models are close to many theorists' definition of whole language; some are a bit farther away. None of the models veers toward a subskill approach; instead, all focus clearly on students' active construction of personal meaning of literacy. Two sets of assumptions underlie the book, one about students and one about teachers. They are presented in Table 1–2.

SUMMARY

Research in education and cognitive psychology strongly suggests that the real impetus for literacy learning lies in children's interests and needs to expand their range of communication abilities. Impetus does not lie in methodological considerations like basal reader series, workbooks, or ditto masters. When they begin school, most children want to be able to express themselves in writing and to gain information and enjoyment from books. The enthusiasm and motivation that chil-

Table 1–2
Assumptions About Teachers, Students, and Context

Teachers

1. Teachers are decision makers who fine-tune instruction many times each day to meet the needs of their students.

2. Teachers are thinkers who possess and draw on a vast knowledge base that includes information about child development, content areas, teaching methodologies in general, and pedagogy specifically related to the teaching of reading and writing.

3. Teachers can make informed choices about materials, pedagogical methods, and pacing of instruction in order to help each student live up to his or her full potential.

4. Teachers can evaluate students as fairly and objectively as external measures, such as standardized tests, and in many situations, they can provide evaluations that are more valid and useful.

Students

1. Students in any one class are individuals who will learn at individual paces and in individual ways.

2. Students attempt to make meaning from all their activities, including their literacy-related schoolwork.

3. Students are capable of thinking about their schoolwork and need intellectual challenges to learn best.

4. Students learn best when materials and tasks are purposeful and authentic, not contrived.

5. In many circumstances, students are capable of selecting their own materials and activities.

Context of Learning

1. The classroom offers many different opportunities for reading and writing.

2. The teacher demonstrates the value that he or she places on literacy and encourages students to similarly value literacy.

3. Tasks and assignments are authentic; students are offered considerable choice in what they do.

4. The environment is warm and accepting; it invites students to take the kinds of risks needed for growth.

dren bring to school can continue throughout the elementary grades if students are given real opportunities to practice literacy skills in meaningful tasks. By responding to what children are trying to do as they seek mastery of reading and writing, and by providing literacy practice in meaningful contexts, teachers can support children's growth.

QUESTIONS AND TASKS FOR INDEPENDENT OR COLLABORATIVE WORK[2]

1. Be sure that you understand these terms:

    a. literacy "novice"

    b. phonics

    c. scaffolding

    d. whole word/sight word

2. This chapter states that reading and writing develop as processes of "emerging expertise." Write down what you think that construct means. Be as clear as you can be in your discussion because you will be asked to refer to your initial thoughts again as your own expertise emerges. In many ways, thinking about this term will help you identify and refine your own theoretical base about how children acquire literacy.

3. Find some reading and language arts instructional materials from the 1940s, 1950s, 1960s, 1970s, and/or 1980s. Compare the material against the assumptions in Table 1–2. What changes do you see over time? What has remained the same? Do the reading and language arts complement or contradict each other? How? Would you like to teach with these materials? Explain.

4. With one or more of your fellow students, brainstorm ideas and recollections about how you learned to read and write. Compare your ideas and try to place them within one of the theoretical perspectives discussed in this chapter.

5. Begin to keep a log of your responses to readings, lectures, and discussions that take place in this class. You will be asked to make specific entries in it from time to time. Also, select one of the books listed in Appendix A as supplementary reading for this course. As you read it, keep track of your reactions and the ideas that the book engenders in a reading log. If one or more of your fellow students are reading the same book, form a reading circle to discuss the book together.

---

[2]Questions and Tasks appear at the end of each chapter. Some are to be done independently; others should be completed in collaboration with others.

Classroom Organization and Management

Make a quick mental comparison between two words: *classroom* and *workshop*. What definitions result from your musings? The latter word, *workshop*, may invoke a picture of an environment in which students engage in many different activities and in which there is ample give-and-take, learning through practice, and perhaps a novice-apprentice relationship between learners and their teacher. In a workshop, teacher-student relationships "are based on expertise and knowledge *to be shared or developed* rather than held by the authority and on the *desire to help individuals acquire or construct knowledge.* [Teachers in such] learning settings attempt to pass on rather than to retain their expertise" (Marshall, 1988, p. 14).

This kind of classroom will be discussed in this chapter. Subsequent chapters detail specific models of literacy instruction, all of which are based on the management principles discussed here.

GENERAL CHARACTERISTICS OF A WORKSHOP ENVIRONMENT

There is no one way to describe a workshop environment and no one set of directions to follow to establish one; but there are commonalities among successful literacy workshops at all grade levels. Some of the common characteristics are attitudinal, and some are more managerial and structural.

Teachers who elect to involve their students in a literacy workshop often share certain beliefs and attitudes. Beliefs about reading and writing and about how students acquire literacy are important variables in how they will teach and how successfully their students will learn. Equally important is how "the teacher views and treats children. Trust, responsibility, support, and high expectations must be generously and genuinely present for all children" (Routman, 1988, p. 27). Table 2–1 lists some of the assumptions that underlie a successful literacy workshop in an elementary classroom.

Teachers who establish workshop environments want their students to develop positive attitudes about themselves as learners and as literacy users. Throughout the school day, students work independently, directly with their teacher, and in small and large groups. They interact with print through varied, purposeful tasks, both in books and in their own writing. Completing these tasks furthers learning because students recognize their importance and can relate them to their own emerging sense of competence. Teachers know that, because merely "doing assigned work" does not guarantee learning, students should be encouraged to develop pride in their school-related activities, just as novices' emerging skills at a chosen craft are paralleled by their growing pride in competence (Marshall, 1988).

In a workshop environment, teachers work to develop a common language with which they and their students can talk about instruction. Learning to read and write, and indeed reading and writing themselves, become *objects of study*, not just subjects to study. Because teachers and students talk about the processes used to read and write, the cognitive activities undergirding these behaviors become as visible as possible. As children work, they come to perceive "literacy . . . [as] a dynamic, complex multi-dimensional phenomenon that is transformed through the interdependence of activity and setting" (Taylor, 1989, p. 190).

Workshop teachers are more interested in the processes of reading and writing than in the "products" represented by correct answers and neat assignments. Students—the novices—are not afraid to make mistakes because they sense that the teacher—the expert—recognizes that mistakes are essential for learning. Indeed, teachers use students' mistakes diagnostically and fine-tune instruction accordingly.

Table 2–1
Assumptions About Literacy Learning That Provide a Foundation to the Workshop
Approach

1. Reading and writing are both interactive processes that invite readers' construction of meaning from
   - the print they encounter
   - the writing they themselves create

2. Readers draw upon the following three cuing systems:
   - semantic
   - syntactic
   - graphophonemic

3. Reading and writing are reciprocal processes. Growth in one can reinforce growth in the other; reading and writing should be taught and practiced together.

4. Students learn reading and writing most effectively through purposeful, authentic tasks; practice with artificial activities, such as workbook exercises or "story starters" will not foster real growth.

5. Readers and writers learn by practicing reading and writing, not by completing exercises that fragment or isolate the skills.

6. The context in which students read and write is important; students should consider the purposes for which they will read and write, as well as the time and place of their literacy activities.

7. Reading and writing are social activities, and students should be encouraged to talk to each other.

8. Both reading and writing are thinking activities; students must learn to think about and to express their thinking about their literacy endeavors.

9. Teachers should model and explain many strategies for identifying unfamiliar words, monitoring comprehension, and clearing up any miscomprehension; students should be helped to understand how, when, and why to use these strategies as part of their own reading behavior.

10. Students must be given opportunities to read and write for fun, to learn to value literacy in their lives, and to appreciate the many opportunities they have to use reading and writing.

TEACHERS AS DECISION MAKERS, KIDWATCHERS, AND RESEARCHERS

Teachers' roles are complex in any environment, especially in classrooms where students engage in many different tasks at any given time. Britton expresses this complexity:

Teaching consists of interactive behavior. . . . In the course of interacting with individuals and classes, a teacher must make a hundred and one decisions in every session—off-the-cuff decisions that can only reliably come from their inner conviction, that is to say, by consistently applying an ever-developing rationale. This requires that every lesson should be for the teacher an inquiry, some further discovery, a quiet form of research, and that time to reflect, draw inferences, and plan further is essential. (Britton, 1987, p. 15)

Of particular relevance to this chapter are three roles of the teacher: decision maker, kidwatcher, and researcher.

Decision Making

As Britton stated, teachers in all sorts of classes make many decisions. Teachers who think of themselves as decision makers begin each school year by deciding about the structure of their classroom, the activities they hope to offer students, and the curriculum. These decisions do not negate the existence of mandated curricula but instead reflect how teachers align their own styles, goals, experimentation, and indeed, research, with whatever guidelines they are required to follow. In making decisions, teachers draw on a multifaceted knowledge base that includes knowledge of reading and writing as subjects and of appropriate instructional methodology to help students construct meaning through reading and writing (Marshall, 1988). Teachers' observations of how language is actually learned heighten their awareness of what they must do to support students' growth.

Throughout the school year, teachers alter their decisions, instruction, and ways of interacting with students; but they start with a plan with which to evaluate subsequent decisions. A sampling of teachers' decisions and questions is presented in Table 2–2.

Kidwatching

The process of kidwatching involves observing children's work, behavior, affect, and accomplishments; trying to make sense of the observations; and using the information to fine-tune the classroom environment (Y. M. Goodman, 1985). Kidwatchers constantly take in information, combine it with what they already know, evaluate its importance, and make decisions about children and instruction. Kidwatching results in richer, deeper understandings of individuals and groups of children, allowing teachers to align instruction, activities, pacing, and curriculum to students' needs. "Good teachers have always been kidwatchers. . . . Mistakes, errors, and miscues provide a great deal of knowledge about a child's [literary learning]" (Goodman, 1987, p. 44–45).

Kidwatching is most productive when teachers know what to expect and act accordingly. As they observe, teachers "need the patience to stand back and watch and listen, and trust that in response to [their] patience, children will in fact reveal . . . what they know, what they are struggling with, and what they want to learn

Table 2–2
Teachers' Questions and Decisions

Teachers ask questions about students'
- readiness to participate in a literacy workshop
- previous experiences with workshops
- expectations for school
- ability to handle independence
- levels of maturity and development
- strengths and weaknesses in reading and writing
- learning styles
- previous experiences with literacy
- home support for literacy learning
- needs, especially those of mainstreamed students
- personal problems that may sidetrack learning
- interests that might be used to motivate learning

Teachers make decisions about
- the time and means by which the workshop approach will be introduced
- the amount of choice students will have initially and how students will be helped to make good choices
- sophistication of expectations for student behavior
- pairings and groupings of students
- kinds of enrichment, reinforcement, and reteaching students need
- adjustments to long- or short-term plans that become necessary through the year

---

next" (Siu-Runyan, 1991, p. 102). Teachers should have confidence in their students' ability to learn, should expect them to meet at least minimum competencies, and over time should see students taking responsibility for their own learning.

Researching

Teachers should think of themselves as researchers who actively endeavor to find out about their students. As researchers, teachers pose questions about students, explore behaviors or find reasons to answer the questions, and adjust the classroom environment or instructional offerings on the basis of the investigation. Many teacher-researchers write about their studies and publish widely in the professional literature; others share their observations with colleagues and in local, regional, and national meetings. Even beginning teachers can adopt the stance of teacher-researchers; their "quiet" research—research that is not published or shared on a large scale—will indeed enhance their growth as professionals.

Figure 2–1 illustrates the way in which these three aspects of the teacher's role intersect.

Figure 2–1
Interaction of Teachers' Roles

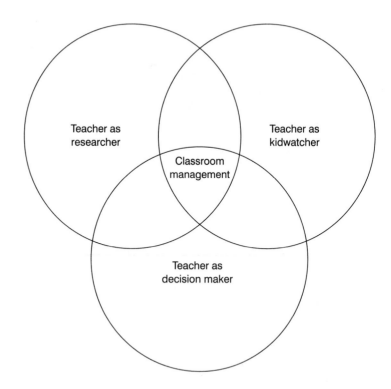

Teacher as
researcher

Teacher as
kidwatcher

Classroom
management

Teacher as
decision maker

Where Classroom Management Fits In

Within the context of the classroom environment, the essence of classroom management is the intersection of long-term decisions, immediate decisions, and kidwatching. Classroom management merges the "inner conviction" or "ever-developing rationale" mentioned by Britton, the theoretical stance about literacy, the understanding of child development, and the expertise in pedagogy that teachers bring to their work. Management strategies that conflict with teachers' ideas about how children learn or that are inappropriate developmentally for a particular group of children will not be effective. Children may be "controlled," but both students and teachers will be frustrated by the external and possibly irrelevant management plan.

Whether in a workshop or in a more traditional classroom, both teacher and students should assume that they will be respected and listened to. The first step toward this goal is to establish fair and appropriate expectations so that all members of the classroom community know their roles. In addition, teachers and students should reach consensus on the consequences for violating expectations. Posting expectations and consequences in a classroom is a common practice, one that can be helpful in reminding both teachers and students what the expected behaviors are. "Expectations define classroom management goals and guide decisions about creating, maintaining, and restoring desirable student behavior" (Good and Brophy, 1987, p. 216).

If students have not had experience with a workshop environment, they will need extensive training in and reiteration of expectations for classroom behaviors. Then, as students gain an understanding of their environment, teachers need to use their kidwatching skills to adjust their own expectations and requirements. It is also important to keep in mind the expectations that students have for teachers. Students usually expect teachers to engage in "familiar" teaching behaviors, to explain and answer questions, and to provide a variety of interesting activities throughout the day (Routman, 1991). Students' definition of what constitutes "teaching" and other teacher behaviors may be very traditional, and they will need time and support in adjusting to the teacher's role in a workshop environment.

GETTING WORKSHOPS STARTED

Teachers who want to introduce their students to a workshop approach must think carefully about several variables. Anticipating how each of these variables will be handled enables teachers to begin the workshop approach more smoothly and to make appropriate judgments when initial decisions must be changed.

Teachers' Style and Preferences

When teachers initiate a workshop approach, they demonstrate a particular view of reading and writing and a specific stance toward instruction. Still, their individual style and preferences play an important part in how they implement their program. Teachers must give up certain kinds of control in a workshop as the class becomes both student- and literacy-centered. Students select their own activities; they direct and evaluate much of their work; and they turn to their peers for learning, feedback, and collaboration. The pursuit of literacy by individuals and groups is the common thrust of the classroom. Teachers become resources, guides, mentors, models, and managers. These changes may at first violate teachers' own expectations of what "school" is as much as they violate those of students inexperienced with the approach.

While teachers in a workshop try to keep track of each student, they will not have as clear-cut and definitive an idea of what each child is actually *doing*, as compared to a class with only one or two groups of students doing similar work. Teachers will know, in a more holistic sense, how students are *progressing* in both their acquisition of skills and their attitudes toward literacy. They will gain this knowledge from daily checkups on the whole class, small-group work, individual conferences, and observational "sweeps" of the class, all of which indicate who seems to be having difficulty.

Teachers must also be willing to tolerate noise. Inherent in any kind of workshop approach is student collaboration; in pairs or in larger groups, students discuss what they are doing, seek to solve problems together, and share ideas. Restructuring the physical arrangement of the room and working with students to moderate conversational levels help to reduce noise levels.

Use of Space

A classroom in which reading and writing workshops take place is apt to look and "feel" different from a more traditional classroom, even if the basic trappings, such as a prominently situated teacher's desk, are evident. In her book *In the Middle*, Nancie Atwell (1987, pp. 64–65) listed the areas of her classroom that contribute to the success of her literacy workshop. Although Atwell's work was with seventh graders, her room arrangement ideas can be modified to work with younger learners in both self-contained and departmentalized classrooms. The basic areas of any room are as follows:

- places for conferencing
- room for group work
- room for solitary writing and reading
- room for storage
- space for display and reference

Establishing definite work areas is important if students are to understand the "traffic flow" and dynamics of the room and to share responsibility for keeping their classroom a lively and orderly learning environment. Table 2–3 elaborates upon these areas, and Figures 2–2 and 2–3 offer possible floor plans.

Atwell described a room that allowed for nooks and crannies between file cabinets and room dividers, places where students could settle down to read or write in private. Providing relatively private space for writing, reading, and thinking is important. Consider the environment that will encourage children to write:

> Significant writing, rather than the marking-of-workbook-pages variety, is a personal experience that grows best when nourished by a degree of privacy and frequent opportunities to concentrate. This is in contrast to the kind of setting where everyone is expected to produce creative writing on cue. The child who is more reflective, or who needs more time to produce, can look around at other busy pencil pushers and feel inadequate, unsuccessful, and powerless to produce. (Fromberg & Driscoll, 1985, p. 41)

Because Atwell's was a departmentalized reading-writing class, all parts of the classroom could be devoted to literacy work. Arranging many private spaces for literacy work may not be possible in self-contained classrooms, but teachers should strive for at least two private areas: one for writing and one for reading. The reading area may be a library corner with a published schedule that indicates time for browsing and talking about books and other times for silent reading. Alternately, corners in the room may be designated as private reading spaces during workshop time, and students can bring pillows, chairs, or rugs to the areas to use as they read independently. When literacy workshop is not in session, the areas are used for other purposes. If teachers sharing a common hall are all using a workshop approach, the hallway can be declared a quiet, private workspace.

Table 2–3
Use of Space in a Workshop Environment

Places for conferencing:

Needed because conferences should be held in relatively private places where normal conversational tones can be used

Possible locations:
- by the teacher's desk
- in a corner
- at a worktable separated from other work areas
- in a hallway

Room for group work:

Needed because many groups, both large and small, will be working together during workshop time

Possible locations:
- around tables in several parts of the room
- in learning centers or library corner
- in hallways

Room for private reading and writing:

Needed because students need time to work quietly by themselves

Possible locations:
- in corners of the room or library corner
- at a specially designated table
- in nooks and crannies created by file cabinets or bookcases
- in a hallway

Room for storage:

Needed because many books, print material, and other supplies are essential to learning; students will produce many different kinds of work, including journals, papers, projects, and so forth

Possible locations:
- file cabinets
- closets
- bookcases and revolving book racks
- students' desks or cubbies
- bins for workfolders or portfolios
- "in" and "out" baskets for work

Room for display and reference:

Needed because students' work should be "published" for classmates to see; students benefit from prominently displayed references to aid their work (e.g., editing marks)

Possible locations:
- bulletin boards
- chalk boards
- hanging from the ceiling

Figure 2–2
Classroom Floor Plan for Literacy Workshops: Primary Self-contained Classroom

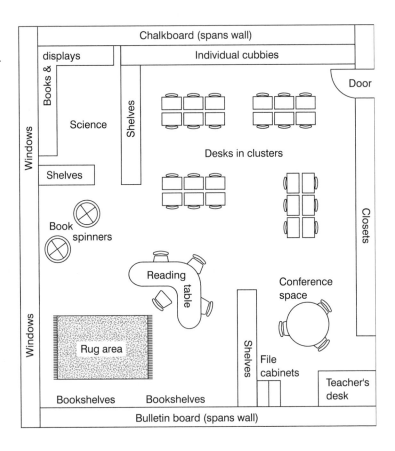

Atwell's room arrangement featured a separate table for quiet writing: "In the front of the classroom, as far from the hurly-burly of the workshop as we could put it, stands the table kids call 'No Man's Land.' Writers work here, their backs to the room, when they want solitude and no interference; pulling up a chair at this table is a signal to friends and me that a writer doesn't want to confer" (p. 64). Needless to say, a writers' table in a self-contained classroom can serve many purposes before and after literacy workshop sessions.

Also important is adequate storage and display space. Storage space must be both accessible for books and private for students' work folders and portfolios. What may seem like an ample amount of storage space at the beginning of the year is soon revealed to be inadequate as the classroom library swells and students' folders bulge with work.

Resources

Herbert Kohl contended that "all you really need to help someone learn to read and write is something to write with and something to write on" (1974, p. 174). Kohl's idea is attractive and basically true; but the reality of trying to foster literacy

Figure 2–3
Classroom Floor Plan for Literacy Workshops: Departmentalized Language Arts Classroom

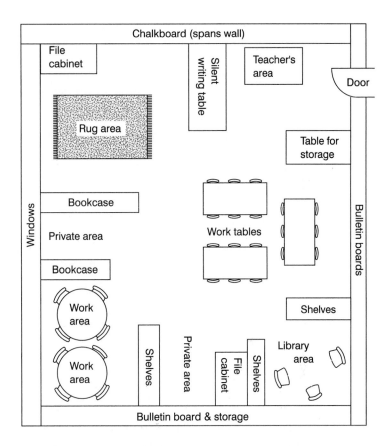

growth in a whole classroom of students demonstrates that much more is needed. Beginning teachers may not have ample supplies of books to set up their own classroom libraries, but garage and yard sales, library sales of excess books, friends and relatives, and one's own attic are all sources the beginner can use to build a supply quickly. Veatch (1968) pointedly suggests that teachers "beg, borrow, and steal" so that students have choices from the very first day of school. As will be discussed in Chapters 6 and 7, having a choice is important because it motivates students and in fact keeps them busy; but having a choice is also important because it enables students to explore different kinds of books and to develop literary tastes.

Gathering resources for writing instruction may be less problematic; schools usually have paper. Extra resources for a strong writing program include notebooks for logs and journals (which students can often provide); folders for storing drafts and finished papers; and references such as dictionaries and thesauri at appropriate levels. Having different kinds of paper can be beneficial, too. Wide-lined paper with room at the top for drawings helps young writers orchestrate their use of art and writing to tell stories; pulpy, low quality paper that rips easily discourages erasing on initial drafts and encourages students to attend to what they are trying to say; paper with lines may make some students feel more secure as they perfect handwriting skills; and colored paper or paper with a good "feel" can allow children to celebrate finished efforts that are about to be published. Pencils, pens, and erasers are usually readily available; but a computer may not be. The benefits of word processing, even for young writers, should not be overlooked.

DECIDING WHAT STUDENTS WILL DO

Along with organizing classroom space for workshops, teachers must also, of course, determine what happens during workshop sessions. A publication of the National Council of Teachers of English (Lloyd-Jones & Lundsford, 1989) offered a good description of an effective teacher:

> The teacher is an expert and authority on learning and pedagogy. . . . She is herself a skillful user of language—a reader and a writer as well as a speaker and listener. Even before children enter the classroom, she plans, organizes, chooses materials, considers teaching strategies. She sets up a structured learning environment to ensure that the desired academic and social interactions take place. . . . When the teacher works with children, [her] role is delicately balanced between that of a manager-director and an enabler-interactor with [the students] and their learning. (pp. 7–8)

Planning

Careful, thoughtful planning can eliminate many potential classroom management problems and increase everyone's chance of learning successfully. The workshop approach demands that teachers take responsibility in determining curriculum, and put "a lot of thinking and organizing . . . into planning meaning-centered, authentic literacy events. Teachers must teach, but making decisions about when to teach it, and how to teach it is difficult" (Siu-Runyan, 1991, p. 101).

In planning, teachers should be guided by several factors, the first four of which can be considered in the abstract before even meeting a group of students. The most important factors are explained in Table 2–4. These factors, taken together, encourage teachers to tailor their planning and the resulting student activities to meet mandated objectives external to their own classrooms (Factor 1), without losing sight of the uniqueness of each group of students (Factor 5) or their own strengths and weaknesses as teachers (Factor 4). Assessing and balancing the five factors marks the beginning of successful planning.

Teachers' expectations (Factor 2) begin with the knowledge base that teachers have about literacy, child development, and pedagogy. Essentially, teachers establish long-term expectations of outcomes that describe what students should do during the school year. These outcome descriptions serve several functions. First, they give teachers an idea of the knowledge, skills, and abilities to look for as they get to know a new group of students. Teachers can ask themselves how ready students are to undertake the learning they, the teachers, have envisioned, and they can then determine what instruction in skills and behaviors must be provided at the onset.

Table 2–4
Factors That Influence Planning a Literacy Workshop

---

1. External requirements

These include grade, school, district, or state curriculum guides and mandated standardized tests that (however inappropriately) determine promotion.

2. Teacher expectations for curriculum

Teachers draw upon their ideas about what prior knowledge students should "bring" to class and what they should learn in any grade.

3. Resources

Included here are those resources available in the classroom and those that must be donated, purchased, or "scrounged up." At a minimum, a classroom should have a varied, multilevel library of books and other print materials, and ample writing supplies.

4. Time

A major advantage of the literacy workshop is that students can pursue their work in extended blocks of time, as long as such blocks are available. Teachers should allow 1 1/2 to 2 hours for workshop activities. It is probably better to have a long workshop three times a week instead of a short one each day.

5. Teachers' own style, tolerances, and interests

Teachers must ask themselves how much control they are willing to relinquish and how much noise and apparent confusion they will be able to tolerate.

6. Nature, needs, and interests of students

Even more than in a traditional setting, workshop teachers must attend to individuals' personalities, needs, and interests to help students achieve their maximum potential. The individual and small-group interactions common in a workshop enable teachers to get to know their students and to meet individuals' needs successfully.

These outcomes also give teachers a basic sense of the kinds of instructional and independent activities that students might engage in for learning to occur. This basic sense is refined as teachers get to know their students. An example might be the teacher who has planned to require extensive independent work so that she can work with small groups. By the second week of school, she realizes that her students are very dependent and unfamiliar with this method of working, and cannot understand what is expected of them. Because the teacher has thought through why she values and wants an independent work environment and has anticipated how such an environment can be brought about, she is able to tailor activities during the initial weeks of school to help ease students into a new work orientation, new patterns of interaction, and new sets of expectations for themselves and their teacher. The teacher's plan does not have to be abandoned because the students are "not right," "too immature," or "too undisciplined"; and neither do the students have to undergo the frustration of trying to figure out a classroom structure for which they have had little or no preparation.

Teachers must, of course, also develop plans for shorter periods of time, such as a class period or a day. In a workshop, where students often work independently on self-selected tasks, planning can serve a dual role. Teachers use plans to guide students to logically sequenced, purposeful activities and also to keep track of students' activities and progress. Prototype plans are presented in Appendix B. The specific activities in the plans are discussed throughout the remainder of the chapter.

Grouping

Teachers in literacy workshops make good use of groups, but they are different groupings than those determined by placement in a basal reader series. The social nature of literacy learning is the major reason for grouping students: students will learn from each other. Criteria for grouping students include immediate academic need, perceived readiness for instruction, and shared interests. Table 2–5 contrasts the different kinds of student groups that are used in a literacy workshop classroom.

ACTIVITIES FOR THE LITERACY WORKSHOP

Reflective teachers—ones who have thought about their own style, needs, and interests—approach instruction as a practical and ongoing exercise that parallels their emerging knowledge about the individuals in their classes. In a workshop or similar environment, students are encouraged to progress more or less at their own pace. Teachers offer instruction and support as needed to foster skills acquisition and to nudge students to each successive developmental level. This does not mean that teachers produce lesson plans for each student. Instead, teachers rely on their sense of what students should learn (their expectations of learning outcomes) and on their records of how each student is progressing (see Chapter 3 for details about portfolios, checklists, and observations). Teachers' interactions with students include three kinds of behaviors:

1. Conducting "mini-lessons" to offer brief, focused instruction to the whole class

2. Offering individual instruction in both planned and spontaneous conferences

3. Providing small-group instruction to students brought together to work on a specific skill or ability

Table 2–5
Student Groupings in a Literacy Workshop

Whole-class interaction
- *Advantages:* develops a sense of community, cohesion, and sharing; teachers and students get to know each other; provides efficient means of communicating procedural information and focused instruction; allows teacher to check quickly on progress of all students
- *When used:* at the beginning or possibly the end of class

Small-group interaction
- *Advantages:* allows students who share interests or needs to work together; builds collaboration and sharing of literacy knowledge; fosters use of oral language in literacy learning; helps students develop awareness of and sensitivity to multiple perspectives
- *When used:* during workshop period
- *Who:* students assigned by the teacher or self-selected; teacher may or may not participate
- *Activities:* group reading, conferring about writing, working on projects, etc.

Pairs of students
- *Advantage:* "two heads are better than one" in solving literacy puzzles and completing work
- *When used:* during workshop period
- *Who:* usually students who have elected to work together
- *Activities:* most often working on projects of mutual interest; conferring about writing; shared reading

Students working alone
- *Advantage:* student can focus on his or her own interests or needs
- *When used:* during workshop period
- *Who:* single students who have elected to work alone or who have been given assignments by the teacher
- *Activities:* working on individual projects; reading or writing; conferring about writing with teacher; shared reading

---

Mini-Lessons

Nancie Atwell (1987) and others recommend mini-lessons as the core of a workshop structure. Usually presented first during a class session, they are always brief. At the beginning of the school year, teachers use the mini-lesson time to build consensus about classroom expectations and routines. Gradually, the mini-lessons become more academic, although teachers still use the time to check on students' progress and clarify behavioral expectations.

During a mini-lesson, which may be as brief as five minutes, teachers present a short, focused, *single-topic* lesson. Atwell recommended three distinct topics for mini-lessons:

1. Procedural information and rules about life in the classroom
2. Instruction in specific skills and strategies
3. The craft of writing or author's craft

Elaboration and examples of these three topics are presented in Table 2–6.

Mini-lessons can be part of a teacher's overall assessment program. Atwell recommends asking students to state briefly what they plan to accomplish each day. This information is recorded on a "status of the class" report, which the teachers can check each day. This kind of report is merely a grid with students' names down one side and the days of the week across the top, creating a box for each student for each day. During the mini-lesson, students state quickly what they will work on and teachers record this information in the appropriate boxes. Teachers can then easily check up on progress and changes in plans. They can also determine who may be abusing the relative freedom of a workshop environment by not committing themselves to particular tasks. This overall summary of what students plan to do can be compared periodically with what they actually accomplish, and discrepancies can be attended to.

Conferences

As will be discussed in subsequent chapters, conferences between teachers and individual students provide fertile ground for focused instruction that is immediately useful, and for skill modeling. Teachers should schedule frequent conferences with every student and expect students to come to the conference prepared. For writing conferences, students might be asked to have a draft paper to share; for reading conferences students might prepare a selection to read. Students who do not come prepared should lose their opportunity to confer privately with the teacher, although, clearly, if such behavior continues, the teacher should intervene to discover why. In addition to scheduled conferences, teachers conduct impromptu conferences as they circulate around the room conferring with students as they work independently on reading or writing tasks.

At either planned or spontaneous conferences, discussions may concern a topic for writing, a difficulty encountered in attempting to write a piece, a draft or a finished piece of writing, the selection of a book to read, a book that the student has actually read, a project or activity to extend the study of a topic or book, or other pressing matters. While in a conference, teachers check up on a student's progress. They may uncover difficulties a student is having with literacy and teach to that particular difficulty, make suggestions for further growth, suggest reading or writing topics, and generally encourage the student to take risks to improve skills. Conferences need not take long, and teacher record keeping about conferences need be little more than notations. Because teachers know their students well, simple notes can be meaningful shorthand for whole narratives of frustration, progress, and effort.

Students should feel comfortable, not threatened, during a conference. Having a quiet, private space is important for teacher-student rapport and communica-

Table 2–6
Mini-Lessons in a Literacy Workshop

Procedural information and rules about life in the classroom
- *When used:* primarily at the beginning of the year; throughout the year for re-orientation as needed
- *Purposes:* to orient students to teacher's expectations, give students opportunities to voice their own expectations, and suggest consequences for violating expected behavior
- *Content:* procedural information
- *Advantage:* encourages students to take ownership of expectations for behavior

Instruction in specific skills and strategies
- *When used:* throughout the year
- *Purposes:* to present focused instruction on skills or strategies that teachers think students need to know
- *Content:* reading, writing, or thinking strategies that will be helpful to *all* students in their work; instruction in use of the library and reference materials; information that will help students build background knowledge; strategies or skills in which some students seem deficient and that other students can meaningfully review.
- *Advantages:* creates a sense of instructional unity that fosters cooperation rather than competition; provides efficient means to introduce, review, and reteach skills and strategies

Instruction in author's craft
- *When used:* throughout the year
- *Purpose:* to show students the craft of writing
- *Content:* any of the techniques that writers use—for example, methods for thinking of ideas or opening sentences; editing strategies; editing marks; use of specific conventions such as descriptive language, direct or indirect quotations, etc.; paragraphing; structure of different kinds of discourse; letter writing, and so forth. Teachers may also use a piece of writing to demonstrate revision strategies. In short, the content will be determined by students' abilities and needs. There will be much overlap with mini-lessons on skills and strategies, but the focus here is primarily on writing.
- *Advantages:* Instruction is focused on one particular aspect of writing. Students can put what they learn into practice immediately.

---

tion. It is important also that teacher and student confer sitting at the same level, next to each other, for example, at the teacher's desk.

Small-Group Instruction

Teachers in a workshop often pull together small groups of students who seem to have specific needs or interests. These groups, always flexible and shifting in membership, may meet once or twice a week, or even more frequently. In direct response to students' questions and needs, teachers can offer instruction, encouragement, and feedback immediately. Students who have mastered a particular skill do not have to be bored by additional "practice" instruction, and students who need this extra practice can receive it in a quick and focused way. In small-group instruction that concerns students' immediate needs, teachers can gain deeper understanding of the strategies and attitudes students bring to learning than they ever can through large-group instruction, and they can further gain insight into how students interact with their peers in different instructional settings. Furthermore, students feel that their needs are in fact being recognized and met, so that they can get on with the tasks of mastering reading and writing skills.

Teachers identify group membership by carefully collating various data sources, including the assessments they have made during individual conferences, the students' written work, and the students' expressed attitudes and interests. Thus, one small group may meet to review some particular grammatical principle that is causing difficulty, another may meet to plan an extended unit of study about a common interest, and a third may meet to get additional help in applying a reading strategy.

Because small-group instruction addresses students' immediate needs, teachers cannot anticipate exactly the number of groups they will meet with each week or the length of each session. In conjunction with the mini-lessons discussed above, a balance of planned individual conferences, spontaneous conferring as teachers walk around the room, and small-group instruction enables teachers to provide the best possible instruction to any group of students.

Students' Independent Work

Following the mini-lesson that begins a workshop session and while the teacher works with individuals or small groups of students, the rest of the class works on their own assignments. Students may work alone or with one or two classmates, but they should work in an independent, self-directed way. To do this, of course, they must have a strong sense of what independent work is in general, and they must know specifically what they are supposed to do each day.

The success of the workshop approach depends to a large extent on the characteristics of the work students do independently. Independent assignments must have clear directions, and students must be able to see how they will contribute to learning. Teachers should provide a balance of independent and collaborative assignments, as well as a variety in type of tasks and methods for fulfilling requirements. Students should also have time to read and write for pleasure. Routman (1991) suggests giving students lists of required assignments, along with suggestions for other work that students are invited, but not required, to do. Students must understand that "assigned" equals "required," and that their first responsibility is to complete the required tasks. Samples of such lists are presented in Appendix B.

Checking up on students with a "status of the class" report and notes, conferences, and impromptu conversations helps teachers keep a paper trail of students' academic progress and compliance with classroom procedures. This paper trail also allows teachers to determine if students are doing a variety of tasks or merely repeating the same kinds of work over and over. Finally, teachers are able to assemble numerous kinds of data and identify early on any students who use the workshop as a means of avoiding essential schoolwork. One such student, described in a recent article, "used the workshop time to dance, twirl, leap, and stroll among his classmates, moving restlessly to rhythms often expressed in drumbeats on desk tops or recitation of rap music. Through these activities, [the student] avoided his inability to write more than simple sentences and very short stories" (Gomez, Graue, & Bloch, 1991, p. 624).

The activities students *should* be participating in include attending to reading and writing assignments of all kinds, performing content area work that requires literacy, collaborating with classmates, and even just reading or writing all by themselves for fun. Appendix B should serve as a reference with sample schedules and assignment sheets. What is not included are the daily goals that teachers set for and with individual students. By communicating information about goals to students and enlisting their help in setting them, teachers help students take responsibility for their own learning and for the success of the workshop.

SUMMARY

Teaching is hard work, and teaching in the context of a workshop environment is especially difficult. But through careful planning, thoughtful organization of time and resources, and respect for students and their own abilities as literacy users, teachers can bring about a successful literacy workshop approach. The benefits that result from this effort are tremendous, both in terms of students' learning and teacher satisfaction. The real secret to initiating a workshop is to go slowly at first, and to progress in measured, thoughtful steps, so that students understand and value their role in this classroom approach. Going slowly also allows teachers time to reflect on what they are doing and to make necessary adjustments to the environment and to their instructional planning.

QUESTIONS AND TASKS

1. Be sure that you understand these terms:
   a. expert-novice relationship
   b. kidwatching
   c. mini-lesson
   d. teacher as decision maker
   e teacher as researcher
   f. workshops

2. Working with one or more classmates, draw a series of floor plans for classrooms at the early childhood, primary school, and middle school levels. Discuss the advantages and disadvantages of various ways of arranging furniture and of providing space for storage, privacy, display, instruction, and conferences.

3. Observe two or three teachers who have developed a workshop approach in their classrooms. Look especially for evidence of their awareness of their own personal styles and needs. Look also for evidence of an expert-novice relationship between teachers and students. What signs of each of these considerations have you seen?

4. Draft a list of expectations for teachers and students at the grade level you want to teach. Analyze the list for reasonableness in terms of child development and pedagogy. Compare your list with those of others in your class to try to develop a workable master list. In what ways do master lists differ at different grade levels?

5. Develop a definition of teacher research based on your knowledge of schools and teachers' tasks. Update your definition as you think more about the teaching of literacy.

Assessment of Literacy

F ew educational issues are more volatile and controversial than assessment. In its most global sense, *assessment* refers to both formal and informal means of gathering information about students; few parents or educators disagree that there is a need for some mechanism to accomplish this task. What most frequently causes ire is standardized tests, for they have become a routine part of the processes used to make decisions about students. Preparing for and taking standardized achievement tests take up considerable classroom time, and the tests themselves increasingly do not reflect the kinds of authentic literacy activities in which students engage. "Formal [standardized] testing, by its very nature, has treated the complex task of assessment of reading and writing abilities as if it were simpler than it really is, and in so doing, has artificially neatened the process of language arts assessment. Such neatening has resulted in the misrepresentation of children's ability to read and write" (Tierney, Carter, & Desai, 1991, p. 30).

Standardized tests provide specific kinds of information, but rarely is it of the sort that teachers can put to immediate use in fine-tuning instruction. Indeed, by projecting specific definitions of mastery, such tests may actually force teachers out of the process of evaluating student progress (Pearson & Valencia, 1987). Still, because so many educators and lay persons place such confidence in these instruments, their specifications and content often strongly influence curricula. Essentially, what will be measured becomes what is taught (Hiebert & Hutchison, 1991). Creative teaching, response to students' interests, intellectual diversions, and flights of fancy suffer, test critics maintain, in the face of "teaching to the test." Even when testing specifications do not "drive" curricula, problems can arise because the scope of instruction and the demands of testing contradict each other. Such contradictions are especially prevalent when literacy curricula have moved beyond dependence on basal readers, workbooks, and subskill or scope and sequence lists to more dynamic, student-centered learning.

Basal reader end-of-unit tests can also present problems because they often dictate the shape and scope of students' reading experiences and determine students' progress through a reading series. While ostensibly tied to the reading instruction and reading experiences students encounter, these tests frequently reflect a narrow definition of reading, one based on the assumption that mastery of individual enabling skills in a specific, predetermined order *automatically* signifies reading competence. This definition neither takes into account the many, broad reading experiences children should have, nor credits the importance of writing as a mutual support for reading growth. Thus, a student who writes fluently and reads prolifically in self-selected books might not do well on a test that isolates specific enabling skills and fragments the holistic literacy behavior that the child is striving to master. This child could be falsely labeled a disabled reader.

Because of their artificial nature, then, the tasks on basal end-of-unit tests can stymie students' abilities to demonstrate what they actually know and can do. When these tests are imbued with too much importance, as when they are the sole criterion for advancement within a reading series, they can be harmful to students' progress. Used as rough indicators by teachers who draw upon and give at least equal weight to other sources of information, they can serve as a narrow indicator of students' progress. But they must be used judiciously, with a realistic view of what they can and cannot add to teachers' assessment of student progress (Lipson & Wixson, 1989).

Table 3–1 summarizes information about both standardized tests and the alternative methodologies that are discussed in this chapter.

Table 3–1
Information About Standardized Tests

KINDS OF TESTS

Norm-referenced tests

- comparison of individuals to one another or to groups; comparison of groups to other groups
- comparisons made with *norming tables* that are developed from extensive administration of tests nationwide to various groups of students
- foundation of comparisons made through commercially developed tests
- some comparability within tests but comparisons can break down across different tests and different test manufacturers

Criterion-referenced tests

- based on a set of objectives or standards tied to instructional sequences
- frequently used as pretest, followed by instruction, then followed by posttest to determine mastery of objectives included in instruction
- not used to compare students to each other; instead compare against standards for instruction
- may be teacher-made or commercially developed

Standardized tests

- only available from commercial test developers
- can be survey or diagnostic
- group or individually administered
- usually norm referenced
- primarily for program evaluation or comparative purposes
- individually administered tests may have oral component

Informal reading tests

- usually teacher-made, although commercial ones are available
- generally considered diagnostic, in that their purpose is to provide specific information to make immediate decisions about students
- frequently administered one-on-one
- criterion referenced
- usually not standardized
- frequently administered orally

CLASSROOM-BASED MODES OF ASSESSMENT

Standardized and basal reader tests, no matter how well constructed, originate in a relative vacuum outside of the classroom. The majority of assessment procedures should develop from what takes place inside the classroom, under the teacher's control, and include input from the students themselves. In this way,

Table 3–1
continued

TERMINOLOGY

Scores

Raw score: the number of items an individual has answered correctly

Scaled score: a score for separate subtests within a test battery. Statistical comparisons across various forms of a test are possible with scaled scores. However, they may not be comparable within a test, so that a scaled score on a decoding subtest might be a higher number but actually might not be as good a score as that obtained on a comprehension subtest. For this reason they can be misleading to teachers and parents.

Grade equivalency score: a score that provides information about how a student compares to students in other grades. A grade equivalency score for a particular grade represents average performance (e.g., 3.4 means average performance of a child in the 4th month of 3rd grade). Although useful for comparisons, grade equivalencies can be easily confused with the instructional level of material appropriate for students, especially when a child achieves above or below his or her grade level placement. Thus, a third grader scoring at the sixth-grade level might erroneously be thought to be ready to read sixth-grade readers or textbooks, a false idea because the child might not have the background knowledge, experiences, concepts, or vocabulary to handle the more advanced material. The International Reading Association has strongly advised against the use of this kind of score.

Test characteristics

Reliability: whether or not a test will produce the same or similar results at numerous administrations to the same individuals; whether or not two or more tests supposedly measuring the same construct will, in fact, produce similar scores.

Validity: whether or not a test is measuring what it claims to be measuring. For example, does a reading test measure reading ability or background knowledge held by only a small number of the test takers, who subsequently score better than others on the test? Likewise, a math test that involves many complex word problems may measure reading skills to a greater extent than it measures mathematical ability.

Test bias: whether or not a test discriminates groups of test takers on the basis of something other than the construct being measured. For example, a test of reading

---

assessment can actually reinforce sound teaching practices, and students can gain a sense of ownership in the evaluation process. In taking part in assessment procedures, students get to tell their own stories about their progress.

This merging of assessment and instruction results in a focus on the *processes* students use rather than merely on the product or end result of their learning. To make sense of processes, teachers must continuously observe students and carefully analyze work samples to document their observations. Such actions give

Table 3–1
continued

comprehension that has numerous passages about sports may discriminate against test takers, not on the basis of reading skill, but on the basis of familiarity with the terminology and concepts involved in understanding the passages, and also on the basis of motivation and interest in sports. Such a test would then be considered biased in favor of sports enthusiasts.

Other terms

Portfolios: collections of student work that demonstrates progress and variety of accomplishments

Product measures of reading: multiple choice and matching tasks, oral or written responses to questions requiring recall of stories, or other demonstrations of the *product* of comprehension. These measures usually involve either recognition of correct answers or recall of information from what has been read.

Process measures of reading comprehension: miscue analyses, preparation of graphic organizers, completion of cloze exercises, free response exercises, and other activities that measure how students construct meaning rather than the actual form the meaning may take. These measures provide insight into the processes students use to gain comprehension and reveal both strengths and weaknesses in strategies used.

Metacognitive measures of reading comprehension: think-alouds, log entries that discuss strategies used, error detection tasks, and other activities that invite students to externalize their strategies for constructing meaning, thus providing measures of comprehension. These measures overlap with process measures.

Constructed response items: also called "open-ended items"; questions that ask students to think about, hypothesize, and interact with what they read; answered orally or in writing but do not have one correct answer. Students' background knowledge and inferences are displayed in their responses.

Scoring rubrics: possible answers to constructed response items, listing all possibilities that have occurred to teachers or scorers and ranking them in levels of correctness. Rubrics may include descriptions of the levels of elaboration and mechanical correctness necessary to obtain specific scores.

teachers' assessments validity and reinforce the basic contention that teachers are professional decision makers who should guide the curriculum in their classrooms. Observation and analysis lead teachers to refine their instruction to better meet students' needs and interests.

Accepting classroom-based assessment methods requires accepting four principles, all of which can highly empower both teachers and students (Valencia, McGinley, & Pearson, 1990). The first principle is that assessment is *on-going*:

Whether teachers recognize it or not, they assess students constantly, and because they know their students and their classrooms, their assessment is highly valid and reliable. Yet, this ongoing assessment does not always result in grades—nor should it. It results in information that is useful for teachers and students alike.

Second, assessment should be *collaborative*, in that students should be included in the process of assessment. They should be asked what they think will show their expertise, invited to suggest methods for demonstrating mastery, required to keep some of the records that document their progress, and encouraged to participate in and share self-evaluation and reflection. They must also be thoroughly informed as to what constitutes good and substandard performance. They should understand the criteria upon which evaluation will be based so that they can engage in purposeful self-evaluation (Wiggins, 1989).

Third, assessment, as performed by teachers, should be grounded in two kinds of knowledge: context-specific and content-specific knowledge. Teachers' *context-specific knowledge* is what they know of their students, their classrooms, and their curricular goals and objectives. Teachers' *content-specific knowledge* is what they know about the structure of content areas they are assessing and the specific pedagogical principles appropriate for each area. Externally imposed testing ignores the multifaceted knowledge base teachers possess and often fails to recognize that there is more to students' learning than can be measured by a single test.

Finally, assessments must be *authentic*. Many tests, whether commercial or teacher made, are artificial—unless all that students do in class is answer multiple choice questions, circle answers, or complete matching exercises! If students are reading and writing for real purposes and exploring the many dimensions of literacy, they should not be assessed by instruments and activities that reduce reading and writing to simplistic, artificial tasks. For example, the task of using context to find word meanings appears on many reading tests, but the "context" presented is often no more than a single sentence. In real reading, students can draw upon more extensive chunks of context and, often, upon picture clues; thus, the test does not really assess students' true grasp of this reading behavior (Hiebert & Hutchison, 1991).

Many methods have been recommended as classroom-based alternatives to traditional assessment. They depend on the collection of various kinds of evidence that can be used to document what students are trying to do and what they have accomplished. This evidence may be of two main types: teachers' records of observations, conferences, and interviews with students; and "artifacts" of student work such as work samples selected by the students, pieces of work assigned by the teachers, audiotapes, drawings, or other records of accomplishments (see Table 3–5). Even traditional evidence such as test scores can be included as long as students understand their meaning and significance. Keeping track of so much information may seem monumental; in truth, establishing a mechanism for alternative assessments initially takes a large commitment of time and energy. The key is to think of a system and a timetable, a routinized method for collecting, storing, evaluating, collating, and synthesizing information about students' reading and writing. This chapter will present ideas for developing both a system and a timetable, with the strong caveat that teachers must tailor any methodology to fit their own teaching situations. The order of discussion will reflect practical considerations: (a) finding time, (b) observing, conferencing, and interviewing students, and (c) maintaining portfolios to keep everything together.

Finding Time for Classroom-Based Assessment

When teachers take on more responsibility for assessing students, they must find the time to accomplish their goals. As the chapter on classroom management stressed, the workshop approach to literacy instruction allows teachers more time to observe and conduct conferences with students. If the results of these efforts are to gather information for assessment, teachers must use the time efficiently and take careful notes to document what they see and hear.

Thinking through an effective timetable is among the first steps teachers should take in establishing a classroom-based assessment program. The constraints of a school grading period will probably influence the timetable, but a definite period of time for assessment should be decided upon. Eggleton (1990) recommends an eight-week evaluation/monitoring cycle. Although the cycle is designed for use in primary classes, it can be equally effective with older students. Table 3–2 incorporates some of Eggleton's ideas into a suggested sequence for conducting classroom-based assessment.

Within any given cycle, teachers will use three different levels of assessment: (a) checking up, (b) keeping track, and (c) finding out (Chittenden, 1990).

Keeping track is what teachers do all the time as they watch students and interpret behavior, noting which students to nudge forward, which students to help on the spot, and which students to help through reteaching. Often, teachers carry this information in their heads, although they should make a brief record in some useful format as part of the overall assessment procedures (Lamme & Hysmith, 1991).

The process of *Checking up on* students is more structured; it includes all the activities and procedures that result in the accumulation of primary data that document students' progress. As teachers talk with students in conferences, look at their work, listen to them read, or review quizzes, they are checking up—accumulating vast quantities of information that can be thought of as primary data about each student in a class. Engle (1990) wrote, "An ongoing collection of primary data is, like a baby book [which parents might keep], descriptive, affirming and relevant, a rich mine of sequential material which enables learning and can inform teaching. It is also, however, unwieldy and at some point it calls for review and interpretation . . . the [next] level of evaluation" (p. 11).

The final level—*finding out*—involves interpretation of accumulated data. To perform this kind of assessment, teachers may pose specific tasks, such as collecting running records by using the same book for several students (as discussed in the following section) or asking all students to write on an assigned topic for a specific amount of time. Likewise, teachers may direct their attention to a detailed analysis of existing documentation, such as their accumulated notes about stu-

Table 3–2
Sequencing of Classroom-Based Assessment

This schedule is based on a six-week cycle but could easily be modified to suit time frames specific to individual classes. The teacher integrates these classroom-based assessment strategies into the classroom day by balancing instructional and assessment time and by using some of the instructional interactions with students as part of the assessment cycle.

CYCLE FOR EARLY CHILDHOOD CLASSES

Week 1: Observation

The teacher observes students as they work and interacts with them informally. The foci of observation should be on students' understanding of what they are doing, their ability to talk to each other and to the teacher about their work, and their level of confidence in and ease with their work. The teacher may hold impromptu conferences with students as they work. The teacher takes notes on observations and collates them for future use.

Weeks 2 and 3: Reading

The teacher concentrates on assessment of reading by collecting running records, interviewing students about their reading, and holding reading conferences. The teacher uses instructional time to focus on specific aspects of the students' reading work, for example, by asking predetermined questions about content or strategies.

Weeks 4 and 5: Writing

The teacher concentrates on assessment of writing by collecting writing samples, holding writing conferences, and eavesdropping as students write. The teacher may sit in on peer response groups with the specific intent of gathering information on the processes students use to think and talk about writing.

Week 6: Repeat Reading

The teacher again concentrates on reading, perhaps by focusing more intently on those students identified as having problems.

dents or the contents of students' portfolios. The purpose at this level is for teachers to analyze, interpret, and often compare students' work against criteria specifying what should have been accomplished by a particular point in time. These criteria are drawn from teachers' knowledge of a logical scope and sequence for literacy skills development and from knowledge of the needs, characteristics, strengths, and weaknesses of each individual child whose work is being evaluated. Because the two sources of criteria—the structure of the content areas and the students themselves—are contextualized within the classroom, this kind of evaluation is more truly reflective of students' accomplishments than an externally imposed testing program could ever be. Indeed, it gives a broad and meaningful portrait of students' achievements.

Table 3–2
continued

CYCLE FOR UPPER ELEMENTARY AND MIDDLE SCHOOL CLASSES

Week 1: Observation

The teacher observes students as they work and interact with each other. The teacher sits in on author's circles and other interactive sessions, primarily to observe students' processes. The teacher checks up on all aspects of any long-term projects students are conducting. The teacher draws inferences about students' achievement by collating notes of these observations and follows up on any hunches in subsequent weeks of assessment.

Weeks 2 and 3: Reading

The teacher holds reading conferences and sits in on any peer reading groups. The teacher may ask specific questions about books that he or she reads to students to gather information about listening comprehension. The teacher gathers data about the various kinds of material students are reading, most specifically material they have prepared ahead of time and material they are reading "cold."

Weeks 4 and 5: Writing

The teacher holds writing conferences about works in progress, sits in on peer interactions concerning writing, and talks extensively to students about the work in their work folders. The teacher uses this time to initiate portfolio assessment and to establish the procedures for culling papers for portfolio assessments. The teacher may give a timed writing assignment during this time.

Week 6: Checkup

The teacher meets again with any students who have been identified as having difficulties. This provides the teacher with an opportunity to gather information about any remedial measures that may have been put in place as the result of previous assessment.

OBSERVATIONS, CONFERENCES, AND OTHER INTERACTIVE ASSESSMENTS

As part of their assessment procedures, teachers keep observational records, conduct focused interviews with students, and tally specific kinds of literacy activities that engage students during the marking period or school year.

Teachers should keep short, narrative notes while observing students work, interact in conversations with students, or engage in class discussions or other cooperative ventures. There are three focal groups for observations: (a) a single child, (b) pairs or small groups of children, and (c) the entire class. Because observational records for all three kinds of focal groups are valuable, teachers should schedule times periodically during class work sessions to step back from work with students in order to collect observations on all three focal groups. Notes taken during such observations should be brief but highly descriptive and written in the kind of shorthand teachers readily develop to help them remember information about their students. As teachers observe, they look for positive aspects of student behavior so that they form a record of what individual students or the class as a whole can do in a given situation. Reviewing the notes provides insight into behaviors of individual students and into the dynamics of the entire class. Patterns of behavior that emerge from this analysis contribute to instructional planning, suggest ways to regroup students, and point to further inquiry about students' learning.

Teachers might keep descriptive notes in a notebook, on cards, or on sticky-backed note paper that can later be affixed in a more permanent fashion. An alternative approach is to fill out observational record forms that have been designed to reflect the kinds of activities that will engage students and the strategies that students are to learn. As teachers use these forms, they write brief notes or check off indicators of student mastery. A word of warning is necessary, however, for teachers who plan to use checklists of any sort. The content of a checklist should parallel as much as possible what will actually happen in the classroom rather than being a mere reproduction of a generic list of behavioral indicators of literacy growth. This means that teachers should ask themselves what is an indication of growth and what kinds of behaviors will be evidence of that growth. Answers to these questions then become the content of the checklists to be used. Sample recording forms are presented in Appendix B.

To gain more information, for assessment purposes, about students' work, attitudes, and approaches to literacy, teachers may also conduct interviews with students. Interviews should be structured around a predetermined set of questions and a literacy task, such as reading a story or discussing a piece of writing (see Appendix B). During an interview, teachers may take brief notes on what transpires, but in most cases it is advisable to tape record the conversation and students' reading. The tape recording does not have to be transcribed to be useful; instead, teachers should listen to it carefully and write a brief summary of its contents.

Conferences, which will be discussed more thoroughly in other chapters in this book, are excellent means by which teachers can interact with students about an individual reading or writing task. Conferences differ from interviews in that the immediate literacy task is the focus, and teachers do not frame discussion with a predetermined set of questions. Needless to say, valuable assessment information can be obtained during conferences, and teachers should take care to include such data in records on students.

The running record is another form of a verbal interactive assessment method (Clay, 1979). A total running record is labor intensive, as suggested by the outline shown in Table 3–3; but it is invaluable because of the breadth of information that it can provide. Teachers in early childhood classes will often set aside time to prepare running records on all students as part of their assessment procedures, but upper grade teachers, whose students read silently most of the time, may ignore or not even be aware of this tool, even though it can be very valuable at their level. Running records are not needed in upper grades for students who seem to be doing well in their reading. For those students who are having difficulty, however, the running record can provide real insight into how the students go about constructing meaning. Teachers might see, for example, that a student can decode words from print to oral speech perfectly, an ability that might have let the student's emergent difficulties in other areas go undetected during early grades. However, when the student tries to retell a story, he or she has trouble, even with teacher prompting. This is an indication of comprehension weaknesses. As the teacher guides the student through reflection and self-report, patterns of weaknesses, of misuse or lack of strategies, and of misconceptions about reading become apparent. The teacher, then, has real evidence about what the student does and does not do during reading—in short, a real direction for future instruction.

STUDENT PORTFOLIOS FOR ASSESSMENT

The term *portfolio* refers to samples of a student's work and a student's thoughts about his or her work, compiled over a period of time to profile what and how the student has learned. "Thinkers and inventors often keep longitudinal collections of their ideas, drafts, and questions. They use these as a kind of storehouse of possibilities for later work, valuing them as a record of where they have been and reading them for a sharp sense of their own signatures and uncertainties" (Wolf, 1989, p. 37). Different from a work folder, a portfolio "storehouse" can also be a means of assessing student growth when teachers and students analyze and reflect on what is included in each portfolio and what its contents mean.

Deciding to Keep Student Portfolios

Assessment strategies must provide a clearly defined answer to the question "What do I as the teacher want and need to know about student learning?" With that as the focus for planning portfolio use, teachers must answer several additional questions, which are presented in Table 3–4.

Teachers who decide to keep portfolios of their students' work should meet certain "qualifications." They must know the difference between work folders and assessment portfolios. They should establish criteria and use these criteria in selecting what will go into a portfolio. Teachers should have confidence in their own ability to retell to evaluate their students' work, and gather specific kinds of information to inform that process. In addition, teachers should have confidence in their students' ability to think about their work and to select appropriate examples to demonstrate their growth. Finally, teachers must be willing to take the time to analyze and make sense of the varied artifacts of student work that can find their way into a portfolio.

Table 3–3
Simplified Procedures for a Running Record

The passage(s)

1. Select one or more passages for students to read; if there is more than one passage at the same level, students may be given a choice of what to read.

2. Determine the levels of the passages according to the vocabulary and the number and types of concepts and the extent to which prior knowledge is needed for comprehension.

3. Prepare a photocopy of the material for your use.

Initial interview

1. Talk to the student about literacy use in general.

2. Establish rapport and gain insight into how the student thinks he or she should go about constructing meaning.

Oral reading

1. Listen to the student read the selection orally.

2. Either tape the reading for later coding or transcribe it as the child reads. (The latter is easier to do with simple material.)

3. Use relatively straightforward markings to note
    *   substitutions: write in above the word
    *   omissions: circle words
    *   repetitions: indicate with right angle mark and letter *R*; write additional word student says as repetitions; use multiple lines for multiple repetitions
    *   insertions: mark with caret
    *   corrections: indicate with right angle mark and letter *C*; stop underline at the last word in the text before the correction; write in original word and circle.

In many ways, teachers who decide to keep portfolios are stating their intention to take back some of the evaluation "power" that has been wrenched from them by commercial test developers and textbook publishers. They are willing to work hard at evaluating their students and to share some of that work with the individuals they teach and assess. They are also willing to give up some of the power—or at least to share it with students (Tierney, Carter, & Desai, 1991). As Wolf (1989) has stated, "Portfolios are messy. They demand intimate and often frighteningly subjective talk with students. Portfolios are work. Teachers who ask students to read their own progress in the 'footprints' of their work have to coax and bicker with individuals who are used to being assessed [in more traditional ways]" (p. 37).

Introducing Portfolio Assessment

Who determines what will go into a portfolio can be a perplexing issue. Students must have input if they are to take ownership of the portfolio. However, given a list

Table 3–3
continued

Retelling

1. Ask the student to retell what he or she has read.
2. Aid the student as needed in
   - unaided retelling, during which the teacher may give support with words such as "Good" and "What else?" but does not provide content
   - aided retelling, during which the teacher responds to unfinished sentences, as much as possible without providing what the student should be saying
   - cued retelling, during which the teacher tells the student that there is more to say about the reading and essentially tells the student to fill in gaps.

Reflection

1. The teacher asks the student to reflect on reading, possibly by asking first, "How do you think your reading went?" or "How was the retelling?"
2. The teacher may ask more specific questions about parts that went well and those that did not.
3. The teacher returns the book and asks the student to locate specific words and parts of the story. An example is telling the student that he or she left out a particular word and asking the student to try to figure it out.

Analysis of miscues and follow-up

1. Later, the teacher will analyze the miscues to see the extent to which the student changed meaning, review the student's strengths and weaknesses, and suggest reteaching.
2. The teacher plans additional instruction as indicated.

---

and told to include certain assignments or pieces of work, students will rarely be inclined to exert the reflection necessary to make portfolio use valuable to them and their teachers. Teachers must exercise some control if they are going to be able to generalize about class achievement and growth (Salinger, in press). In addition, the purpose of the portfolio will to some extent dictate the content. For example, if the portfolio will take the place of a cumulative record folder to be passed along to subsequent teachers, the contents should be carefully controlled so that the information included communicates information about the student's literacy growth.

Whatever the purpose, it is wise for teachers to prepare a list of the basic categories of work samples to be included in each student's portfolio. Such a list is not inconsistent with student choice because it delineates what data the teacher will collect and what samples students may themselves select. Table 3–5 lists many work samples that can find their way into a portfolio and suggests whether they are selected by the teacher or the student. Given the breadth of this list, it is easy to

Table 3–4
Questions to Ask About Assessments

Questions about Purpose

1.   What do you want to find out? Why are you going to assess students' literacy?
2.   Why do you need this information?
3.   What will you do with this information? Specifically, will it be used to adjust instruction?
4.   What short-term use will the information have? What long-term use?

Questions about Context

1.   Where will you best be able to gather information? What opportunities in the course of the day will provide "assessment moments" for observing and recording students' progress?
2.   What will best show you what you need and want to know? What kind(s) of instruments(s) or procedures will you need to use?
3.   What current assessment strategies will continue to be useful or can be modified to become more useful?

Questions about Audience

1.   To whom will you report the information you gather? To students? Administrators? District or state officials? Parents?
2.   In what form(s) will the information be most useful? Will different forms be needed for each audience?
3.   In what ways can the students themselves be involved in shaping the assessment procedures?

see how teachers can specify the contents of a portfolio to suit their own assessment needs and still provide ample student selection.

Guiding principles for determining what to include in a portfolio should be clarity and breadth. *Clarity* refers to the purpose of individual work samples; the purpose should be clear so that anyone who reads the portfolio can easily identify the skills, concepts, or competencies students were grappling with as they prepared the work. This is especially important if, as will be discussed, portfolios are going to be evaluated by someone other than students' own teacher. If the purpose of a work sample is not clear and students still want to include it, they should be asked to annotate their selection, possibly by affixing a note to explain their piece and its importance.

Breadth refers to the range of samples students select and to the range of other data that might be included. Portfolios offer students the opportunity to demonstrate how much they are learning, as long as the samples included are varied and distinctive. For example, three essays, no matter how good, present only a "slice" of what a student may have accomplished in a given marking period. Samples of the student's other work must be included, even if it is less well executed than the essays. The portfolio must show a range of accomplishments if it is to be a valid assessment tool.

The majority of samples included in a portfolio will probably be paper-and-pencil work, but other sorts of demonstrations of competence are also acceptable entries. Students might, for example, want to include videotapes, audiotapes, photographs, or illustrations to accompany something they have written. Work samples such as these actually strengthen a portfolio by providing a broader view of students' accomplishments than two-dimensional written work. Students may also include evidence of the developmental stages of their literacy work, such as notes used to brainstorm topics, graphic organizers, summaries of critiques from peers, and other evidence of the processes of writing and reading. Various kinds of lists kept by students belong in a portfolio as well. Reviewing the lists from time to time strengthens students' sense of themselves as readers and writers, which is a valuable objective in itself. Students can also use the lists as points of reference in discussions with others about books and sources they have enjoyed or found useful. Such lists help students begin to reflect on their work. Appendix B shows sample forms.

In some cases, portfolios are used for accountability, even to the extent of replacing report cards and cumulative records. Teachers who use portfolios in this way should include specific kinds of information to supplement student-selected work samples. Running records of reading behavior, periodic criterion-referenced mastery tests, summaries of conferences, reviews of error analyses, or student retellings of what they have read deepen the portrait of each student. Prompted writing samples—responses of all students to the same topic within a time limit—and standardized test scores can be useful portfolio entries. These documents may seem more like tests than work samples, but summarizing and explaining them during a private, focused teacher-student conference can help students understand the strategies they use successfully in reading and writing and those that they must build to higher levels of mastery. If teachers want students to be aware of their processes for constructing meaning, they must be willing to discuss observations about strengths and weaknesses and buttress these discussions with concrete suggestions for improvement. By doing this, teachers are inviting students into the assessment process, giving them insight into learning, and passing some of the responsibility for learning over to the learners themselves. Conducted without judgment or criticism, such discussions can propel students to new levels of independence.

Collection Periods

The actual compilation of work for a portfolio should take place several times a year, depending on when contents must be summarized for report cards, for conferences with students or parents, or for other reports of student progress. This process will not be a mad dash to find things to include if teachers have encouraged students to keep an ongoing, cumulative folder of work. In preparing students to make their selections, teachers should periodically suggest the kinds of

Table 3–5
Possible Entries for a Literacy Portfolio

Responses to literature
- literature log
- report on reading (summary, drawing, report, etc.)

Use of revision in writing
- efforts to improve informational writing
- efforts to improve literary writing (nonfiction, poetry, essay)
- best example of use of revision, with first and subsequent drafts of piece of writing

Other writing samples
- freewriting used to generate ideas
- research paper
- functional writing efforts
- graphic organizers
- writing done outside of class
- imaginative writing

Examples of writing in content areas
- any writing sample to demonstrate content learning
- graphic organizers

Log entries
- freewriting in logs
- dialogue journal entries
- learning log entries
- literature log entries

work that *might* be included; also they may specify early in a term certain evidence that *must* be included if the portfolio is to be considered complete (Salinger, in press). Teachers should discuss criteria by which students will evaluate their own work. These discussions will undoubtedly echo the language of teacher-student conferences and of instruction. The process of selecting entries for a portfolio requires student reflection. Using the criteria teachers have discussed, students evaluate their work samples and make selections.

It is often helpful for students to work in pairs on selection day, discussing, comparing, critiquing, and possibly defending their individual choices. As students think about and apply the criteria for selection and measure their work against them to find representative samples, their choices may be idiosyncratic; that is, their decision about what is their best paper or the one that shows the most effective use of revision may differ markedly from what the teacher would select from the folder of work. This does not mean that the selection is wrong or that the stu-

Table 3–5

continued

Artwork
- pictures about what students have read
- pictures about what students have written

Tape recordings
- students reading what they have written
- oral reading samples

Data about reading
- voluntary reading log
- running record or other record of oral fluency
- standardized reading test scores
- basal reader test scores
- student-teacher summaries of conferences

Self-analysis and reflection
- letter to teacher about oneself as a reader, writer, or learner (at beginning and end of school)
- list of personal literacy goals
- personal profiles, outlining students' sense of themselves as literacy users
- cover letter to portfolio reader, explaining what pieces show and why they were selected

Wild cards
- any example of students' literacy learning that they want to include in the portfolio

---

dent has misused the selection criteria; it means only that the student's evaluation of his or her work has been individualistic. Because knowing *how* and *why* the student has made the selections illuminates important thought processes, students are asked to write a letter to the reader of the portfolio or to annotate individual pieces with explanations of the selection process. Initially, these letters or notes may be quite superficial: "This is my best paper because I like it the most of all I have written." But, gradually, students do reflect more deeply about their work and feel more comfortable expressing their own evaluations (Camp, in press).

For practical purposes, teachers must have some way to distill the information that can be culled from a portfolio so that individual efforts can be interpreted quickly and so that portfolios can be compared across classes. Narratives, checklists, and other recording sheets are the most efficient ways to summarize information. Checklists must be well focused and tied to the specific purpose of the portfolio and to the work students have done throughout a grading period or full year.

Developing the very first portfolio-evaluation checklist may be the hardest task in establishing a portfolio assessment system. This task requires looking very closely at numerous portfolios to determine the range of performances that are represented and clarifying what evidence really constitutes mastery. Teachers should anticipate that initial checklists will go through numerous drafts, especially if they are to be used in several classes and if their development is a group project. Table 3–6 outlines procedures for this task. Sample checklists are presented in Appendix B; they are "bare bones" checklists that teachers should personalize to meet their own assessment purposes.

Table 3–6
Steps for Developing Checklists to Evaluate Portfolios

1. Decide what you *want* to see.
   - Make a first guess about the information that would be useful.
   - Determine if the portfolios will be used to evaluate the class as a whole or individual students or both.
   - After determining information and purpose, help students understand the criteria for selecting entries for the portfolio.
2. Schedule a selection day.
   - Because students have been keeping work folders, they should have ample supplies of work from which to select.
   - Exert as much structure on the selection process as seems appropriate for the maturity level of the students and your evaluation purposes.
   - Let the students make selections, include whatever evidence of work you have decided must be included, and gather the portfolios together.
   - Make sure students write a "Dear Reader" letter to provide insight into their application of selections criteria.
3. Read the portfolios.
   - Read through a sample of the portfolios to see what students actually selected. Make notes about the kinds of work samples students selected, such as essays, graphic organizers, lists of ideas, and so forth; and the kinds of reading and writing behaviors they have demonstrated, such as thinking and writing about what they have read, attempting to explore different "voices" in their writing, adopting a different point of view in examining an historical event, and so forth
   - Compare this list with the list generated in Step 1 to determine the kinds of information actually available for evaluating students' progress. This list becomes the first checklist for portfolio evaluation.
4. Tally work samples and/or evidence of reading and writing behavior.
   - Use this tally to evaluate the effectiveness of the first selection day as a measure of students' progress.
   - If the information does not seem adequate to evaluate students' growth, restructure the selection process so that more specific kinds of work samples are included.

Assigning Scores

For portfolios to be a real part of classroom assessment, scores can be assigned as an indicator of the overall level of achievement. Such scores reflect evaluation of the entire portfolio, not the totaling of discrete grades. To arrive at such a holistic score, at least one reader goes through each entire portfolio relatively quickly to gain a general impression of its contents. Ideally, there should be two readers, the classroom teacher and one other teacher, so that two scores can be compared to gain some objectivity. Because the portfolio will have a "Letter to My Reader" and other annotations, the other teacher will have some idea of students' reasons for including certain pieces.

As readers evaluate portfolios, they use a *rubric* that describes the various levels of achievement that can be demonstrated. The points on the rubric have been carefully determined to reflect what is possible for and expected of students at the particular age, grade, and experiential level of those who have submitted the portfolio. They are also general enough to give students ample credit for what they have tried to accomplish and what they want to demonstrate they have done. A six- or seven-point rubric such as the one shown in Table 3–7 can be used effectively in evaluating portfolios in the elementary and middle school grades (Valencia, McGinley, & Pearson, 1990). If a portfolio is used to evaluate reading and writing in content area classes, the categories should be elaborated to reflect content mastery, as suggested in Table 3–7.

If the two readers disagree on the score that should be assigned, they must discuss their reasons and refer back to the work itself to resolve their differences. Ultimately, a numerical score is assigned to each portfolio. This score does not translate automatically to a letter grade but instead becomes one criterion among others that the classroom teacher will use in determining the grade for a marking term.

GRADING IN A CLASSROOM-BASED ASSESSMENT APPROACH

Grading remains an ever-present reality; in most schools, teachers must assign a grade to students' work at predetermined intervals. Totaling letter grades on quizzes, tests, and other written work has traditionally resulted in one grade to be assigned for a marking period. However, even when this grade is accompanied by a brief statement about a student's accomplishments, it is rarely enough to express the amount of effort a student has demonstrated. When reading and writing are perceived as integrated processes, when concerns in the literacy curriculum meld into each other, and when teachers invest in establishing portfolio assessment and keeping anecdotal and other written records of students' progress, the game plan of assigning grades changes dramatically. It changes because there is a paper trail of evidence to document teacher decisions. P. Johnston (1990), in using a metaphor of an "accountability audit" to discuss this decision making, writes

> the idea is to leave a trail documenting the methods, the data, and the interpretations [of student work] so that an external auditor might examine them and comment on their

Table 3–7
Rubric for Evaluating Portfolios

Outstanding Accomplishment

Writing in these portfolios exhibit the following characteristics:[1]
- Real issues are presented and dealt with.
- Writing shows an authentic "voice" and sense of audience.
- Varied, competent writing strategies are demonstrated.
- Few errors in mechanics are evident.
- Strong thinking skills are evident in drafts and final pieces.
- Students consider topics and ideas in depth.

Evidence of reading behaviors in these portfolios indicate the following:
- Students read widely or have a clear, purposeful focus in their selection of books.
- Writing about literature shows high levels of comprehension.
- Students seem to be integrating what they read in various sources.
- Running records or tape recordings indicate fluency and inclination to self correct errors.
- Running records, surveys, and other devices show awareness of multiple reading strategies and inclination to use them appropriately.

References to content area learning in these portfolios indicate the following:
- Students understand and use appropriate terminology.
- Students have grasped and can use necessary concepts.
- Students integrate information from texts and other sources and offer elaborate discussions of content areas.
- Students can interact with content material in appropriate ways, as in assuming different perspectives in writing about social studies or literature, explaining science experiments, and so forth.

Commendable Accomplishment

Writing in these portfolios exhibit the following characteristics:
- Topics are treated in a thoughtful manner.
- Evidence of thinking to some depth is present.
- Varied, skilled writing strategies are evident.
- There is a clear voice, but not as strong as in papers described in top category.
- There is a sense of audience.
- Mechanical errors are infrequent and relatively minor.

---

[1]Characteristics presented are generic; grade and students' developmental levels will determine how many of the characteristics teachers can expect to see in portfolios at each level of the rubric.

adequacy. The audit trail might be an archive of teacher logs, student portfolios, records of meetings, videotapes of instruction perhaps with accompanying comment, and other 'raw' data against which external reviewers can compare interpretation. (p. 27)

A convenient way to think about the "audit trail" and grades is to consider three sources of evidence of students' accomplishments: documentation of teacher

Table 3–7
continued

Evidence of reading behaviors in these portfolios indicate the following:
- Documentation about wide reading behaviors is presented, but it is not as strong as described in top category.
- Evidence of oral reading indicates fluency, ability to use numerous strategies, and inclination to self correct.
- Responses to literature show high levels of comprehension but less inclination to integrate reading and to refer to personal experiences.

References to content area learning in these portfolios indicate the following:
- Terminology is used correctly.
- Concepts have clearly been understood.
- There is less evidence of integration and elaboration than described in top category.

Adequate Accomplishment

Writing in these portfolios exhibit the following characteristics:
- Papers show competent treatment of and thinking about topics and issues but lack the elaboration and depth of papers described in two top categories.
- Students have clearly attempted to vary their writing strategies and have achieved adequate success in doing so.
- There are occasional errors in mechanics.

Evidence of reading behaviors in these portfolios indicate the following:
- An adequate range of independent reading is shown.
- There is indication of fluency, use of strategies, and self correction.
- There is evidence of adequate comprehension.

References to content area learning in these portfolios indicate the following:
- Grasp of content knowledge, concepts, and terminology is adequate but not elaborate.

Some Evidence of Accomplishment

Writing in these portfolios exhibit the following characteristics:
- Papers do not show deep or purposeful examination of topics, although there is evidence of competent thinking about topics.
- Writing strategies are somewhat varied and used with some effect but errors in conventions are frequent.

Evidence of reading behaviors in these portfolios indicate the following:
- Documentation of reading indicates a narrow range of interests and choices.
- Discussions of literature, if present, are superficial.

observations, analysis of student work samples, and tests and test-like information (Chittenden, 1991). Tests and test-like information are the most traditional sources of student evaluation, akin to the kinds of data gathered in the "finding out" phase of the assessment cycle. When balanced by context-rich information from the other two sources, tests and test-like data are much more meaningful. The diversity, intensity, and quality of data that teachers gather and students contribute validate

Table 3–7
continued

- Demonstrations of fluency show narrow range of strategies and disinclination to self correct.

References to content area learning in these portfolios indicate the following:
- Content area understandings are less well-developed, and gaps, incorrect ideas, and misuse of terminology may be present.

Little Evidence of Accomplishment[2]

Writing in these portfolios exhibit the following characteristics:
- Examinations of topics and issues may be superficial; evidence of thinking lacks clarity and may be flawed.
- Writing strategies are not varied or are used inappropriately.
- Lack of control of writing conventions is evident.

Evidence of reading behaviors in these portfolios indicate the following:
- Evidence of independent reading, if present, shows narrow range of interests.
- Few indications are present of ability to access and use varied reading strategies to gain comprehension or decode unfamiliar words.
- Disinclination to self correct is apparent.

References to content area learning in these portfolios indicate the following:
- Weak understanding of basic concepts, terminology, or information is apparent.
- Students show an inability or disinclination to integrate information.

Minimal Evidence of Accomplishment

Writing in these portfolios exhibit the following characteristics:
- Treatment of topics, if present, is flawed, sketchy, and insubstantial.
- Mechanical errors impede reading of papers.
- Serious handwriting flaws impede reading of papers.

Evidence of reading behaviors in these portfolios indicate the following:
- Students do not engage in much independent reading.
- Comprehension is seriously flawed.
- Students do not have battery of strategies to use in oral or silent reading.

References to content area learning in these portfolios indicate the following:
- Basic terminology, concepts, and issues have not been understood.

---

[2]Distinctions between "Some Evidence" and "Little Evidence" may be difficult to identify, especially at the lower grades. Six distinct categories are presented here as a guide, but categories can easily be collapsed to better reflect the realities of an individual class's performance.

their accuracy as the means for determining grades. Thus, if teachers who have adopted this approach to instruction and evaluation should be questioned on their criteria for grading, they can readily invite questioners to view and understand their sources, to share their insights, and to realize how contextualized data far outweighs isolated test scores as a means of evaluating students.

SUMMARY

Along with much of the rethinking of literacy curricula has come a fortunate rethinking of assessment. The responsibility for assessment is being placed again where it belongs, in the hands of teachers and students. Teacher-made checklists that gather the kinds of information needed to make decisions about the curriculum and about individual students are supplementing and in some instances even replacing externally imposed, commercial evaluation methods. Students' actual work samples, both oral and written records of what they can do, are being valued as sources of valid, reliable information about literacy growth. As teachers gain more control of the assessment process and as students become participants in the process, classroom instruction and student learning are bound to improve.

QUESTIONS AND TASKS

1. Be sure that you understand these terms:
   a. standardized testing
   b. classroom-based assessment
   c. checking up, keeping track, finding out
   d. portfolios
   e. scoring rubric

2. State in your own words the difference between *assessment* and *testing*. Compare your statement with those of other students. What ideas are consistent and what are different?

3. Many researchers and teachers refer to informal, classroom-based assessment as "authentic assessment." This implies that more traditional testing may be inauthentic. What do you think this means? Do you agree or disagree?

4. Use the questions presented in Appendix B to interview several children at different grade levels. Summarize your results. What other questions might you add to the interviews?

5. List as many advantages as you can for classroom-based assessment methods for (a) students, (b) teachers, (c) administrators, and (d) parents. What disadvantages would you anticipate for each group?

Classrooms for Emergent Literacy

Many preschoolers experiment with reading. They make up a story based on the pictures in a book, use a book for an almost word-for-word "reenactment" of a story they have heard, or even "help" an adult read a familiar book by accurately naming words they can recognize. In fact, "before school instruction begins, some children may combine memories for words, recall visual cues from text, picture clues, and their own ability to predict from the language of . . . text, and begin to read independently" (Genishi & Dyson, 1984, p. 166).

Preschoolers also experiment with writing. Starting with what appear to be scribbles, they work consistently toward conventional spelling and legible print (Clay, 1979; Bissex, 1980; Baghbam, 1984). Recently, researchers have suggested that for some children, the desire to write emerges first, while for others, reading and writing develop simultaneously and are mutually reinforcing.

Almost all young children observe and ask questions about print and about reading and writing. They attend closely to billboards, signs, labels, and other so-called *environmental print* that they see around them. It is the rare preschooler who cannot "read" a stop sign or the sign of their favorite fast-food restaurant.

From these investigations, children learn factual and procedural knowledge about literacy: they know about reading and writing as behaviors and they know a smattering of the processes that literacy users employ. The belief that reading and writing can develop simultaneously as *emergent literacy* and recognition of what children can figure out for themselves have led to dramatic changes in early childhood reading and writing instruction. These changes make up what is called an *emergent literacy curriculum.*

WHAT MUST CHILDREN KNOW BEFORE LEARNING TO READ AND WRITE?

Before children can learn to read and write, they must have a basic but strong grasp of spoken language and a rudimentary understanding of print as a symbol system. Table 4–1 details what children need to know and be able to do. As the table indicates, children must conceptualize the aspects of print, which is a massive task. However, without this understanding of the symbolic nature and purpose of words—the two-dimensional scribbles on paper—children will not be able to master the abstract complexities of reading and writing. These understandings often develop, at least in a naive way, before children actually know the meaning of terms like "letters" or "words," when their attempts at writing still appear as scribbles and they are still "playing" at reading.

In the best of situations, physical and neurological maturation, coupled with positive experiences with literacy and attention to environmental print, helps children gain the prerequisites for literacy acquisition. Their experiences in and out of the home have broadened their understandings of the world around them and have taught them language with which to discuss these experiences. Children's attention to environmental print, answers to their questions, and stories read to them have led them to understand that written communication symbolizes purposeful oral language. If children have been experimenting successfully with reading and writing, they think of themselves as literacy users and they are motivated to improve these skills. In essence, they have become ready to read and write, that is, to refine the knowledge they have gained from observations and experimentation and to strengthen their emerging competency.

What Is the Ideal Context for Learning About Literacy Prior to School?

Context is an important factor in early learning. Children must be surrounded by physical stimuli that prompt their curiosity about literacy and by emotional support for their efforts to figure out how literacy works. Holdaway (1979) has stated that the ideal context for learning about reading is in the *bedtime storybook cycle*: A parent and child select a book, share it warmly, and study it together for both its story (plot) and the way in which it tells its tale (style). Snuggled next to someone who shares his or her literacy skills, children have a view of the text as it is read and experience a sort of visual intimacy that conveys some of the feeling of reading. The same applies for writing; when children look over a writer's shoulder, they can combine their hypotheses about print with observations of actual text production. These experiences provide a truly individualized preliteracy "curriculum" that can build a strong foundation for subsequent development.

The School Context for Young Learners

Many children who lack these early positive experiences still become strong readers and writers because of a strong, supportive emergent literacy curriculum. Teachers can build on what these children do know, help them correct misunderstandings, and provide opportunities for them to learn to value reading and writing. Teachers in an emergent literacy program provide a malleable curriculum that is responsive to children's developmental levels, needs, and interests. They also recognize that acquiring literacy is a complex task that "places new demands on the child. He must use his old preschool ways of responding in novel situations and he must discover or invent new coordinations between oral and written language" (Clay, 1979, p. 11).

Experiences in class demonstrate to young learners that mastering literacy skills is worthwhile because these skills will allow them to communicate in new and diverse ways with their classmates, their teachers and other adults, and indeed with the authors of the books they encounter in and out of school. Depending on how teachers structure the classroom and plan instruction, they can optimize the support they provide to students.

The physical arrangement of the classroom is vital because children must have room to explore literacy privately and in small groups. A rich variety of materials, supplies, and books should be carefully stored but readily accessible to learners. Manipulative materials are a standard feature in early childhood classrooms. Literacy materials must be viewed with equal respect because manipulating the tools of literacy production is a valuable part of children's early learning. Figures 4–1a and 4–1b on pages 64 and 65 show sample room arrangements that balance public and private areas for literacy work. The physical arrangement of furniture and supplies shown in these plans can foster beginning literacy growth. Table 4–2 lists "bare essentials" supplies for an emergent literacy classroom.

Knowing the Students

Teachers in emergent literacy classrooms should want to know their students well. For them, nothing can act as a substitute for genuine knowledge of their students' prior knowledge, background experiences, attitudes, and interests. The first step in providing appropriate support for children's emerging literacy is ascertaining what they already know. Teachers accomplish this by talking to and observing children

Table 4–1
Understandings and Characteristics Prerequisite to Literacy Learning[1]

Language Mastery
- Basic fluency in a language, even if the language is not the one in which instruction will be offered. Children's normal development in a language, whether it is a mainstream language, a dialect, a vernacular/code switching combination of two languages, or a visual language such as American Sign Language, represents a cognitive organization of words and grammar that is essential for beginning literacy.
- Adequate basic vocabulary to understand what teachers and classmates say and what teachers read from storybooks _or_ an instructional environment that will encourage second-language growth
- Emerging sense of the "technical" vocabulary of instruction, including words like "book," "word," "sound," and "letter"

Awareness of Conventions of Print
- Recognition that words are composed of distinct letters that appear in specific order in text
- Recognition that letters are composed of a specific and limited number of circular and straight lines
- Understanding of directionality, that is, that the direction in which print goes across a page. This understanding is foundational to control of left-to-right organization.
- Ability to distinguish words as distinct units within a string of printed symbols. This understanding is foundational to being able to distinguish what the words actually say, that is, to being able to read them, because it indicates that children recognize this major difference between spoken and written language
- Ability to see that word units are composed of small units, that is, of letters, and that these are related to the sounds of spoken language

Awareness of the Nature and Use of Books
- Recognition that the graphic images on a book's pages carry the meaning of the book, that is, that the printed words are language and convey meaning

---

[1]Additional information can be gained from *The Early Detection of Reading Difficulties* and *Reading: The Patterning of Complex Behaviour* by M. M. Clay, 1979, Portsmouth, NH: Heinemann Educational Books; and from *Language Assessment in the Early Years* by C. Genishi and A. H. Dyson, 1984, Norwood, NJ: Ablex Publishing.

in both spontaneous and systematic ways; they make notes of incidental observations, and they structure interactions in which they can pose questions and assign tasks to determine children's understandings of emerging concepts and skills.

As mentioned in Chapter 3, data gathering is an arduous task. In schools that have adopted a portfolio approach to assessment, observations and work samples are collected from the time a child enters school; thus, a child's first teacher (in preschool or kindergarten) begins the process of documenting growth. The portfo-

Table 4–1
continued

- Recognition that books, as well as environmental print, convey meaning
- Understanding that the objective of listening to a story read by a parent or teacher and later of reading a story oneself is to gain meaning
- Basic awareness of the use of parts of books, that is, beginning at the front of the book, looking at the print on a page
- Basic awareness of how to gain meaning from books, that is, scanning the print, using pictures as aids, etc.
- Ability to develop some coherent story from a book by using pictures, even before word recognition skills have developed
- Understanding that there are many uses of print

Basic Neurological and Psychomotor Preparedness
- Hearing acuity to distinguish separate words and sounds within words
- Visual acuity to distinguish individual words, individual letters, and white space between them. However, children may still reverse letters in their reading and writing.
- Adequate psychomotor control to be able to swing eyes from the end of a line of print on the right of a page and then back to the beginning of the next line of print at the left
- Adequate psychomotor control to make a similar swing as one writes so that text production follows a directional pattern that initially may not be left to right
- Adequate psychomotor control (and visual acuity) to change gaze from near point (a page in a book or sheet of paper) to far point (the chalkboard or other display surface in the classroom)
- Neurological capabilities to take in information aurally and visually and to produce information orally and eventually in writing

Motivational and Affective Preparedness
- Confidence in one's ability to tackle initial literacy tasks
- Positive values about the benefits of acquiring literacy
- Emotional stamina to persevere in learning to read and write

lio collected for each child during the course of a year is analyzed at the end of the year; observations and trends are summarized; a few representative pieces of work are selected; and the condensed portfolio is passed on to the next year's teacher. The advantage of a portfolio over a cumulative record folder is that a portfolio includes actual work samples, more material, and more narrative explaining each child; the developing picture of each learner is richer and more useful to the child's next teacher. If no portfolio system is in place, teachers must begin their own observing and data gathering as soon as school starts. Suggestions for what teachers should seek to learn about their students are shown in Table 4–3.

An underlying premise of emergent literacy theory is the idea of *support*: teachers endeavor to provide verbal, intellectual, instructional, emotional, and

Figure 4–1a
Room Arrangement—Kinder-garten or First Grade

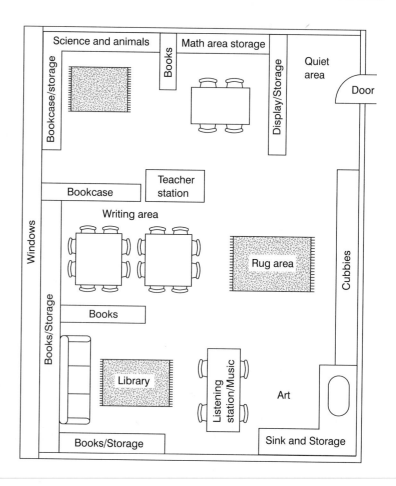

physical support for children's explorations of literacy. The Russian psychologist Lev Vygotsky (1962) used the term *zone of proximal development* for what he identified as the "discrepancy between a child's actual mental age and the level he reaches in solving problems with assistance" (pp. 103–104). Vygotsky asserted that adults must interact with children to support emerging learning because "what the child can do in cooperation today, he can do alone tomorrow. Therefore, the only good kind of instruction is that which must be aimed not so much at the ripe as at the ripening function." Beginning literacy, a truly ripening function, lends itself easily to such instruction, and teachers can readily provide the kinds of support that will approximate parent-child interaction in the storybook learning cycle.

Inherent in this conceptualization of literacy is the idea of a developmental continuum from preliterate behavior to literacy mastery. There is no real point at which a child suddenly, dramatically, begins to read or write. Instead, children approximate reading and writing behaviors in their attempts to piece together the puzzle of how these behaviors function. Important benchmarks tell teachers how children are progressing in their understanding of what readers and writers actu-

Figure 4–1b
Room Arrangement—Second Grade

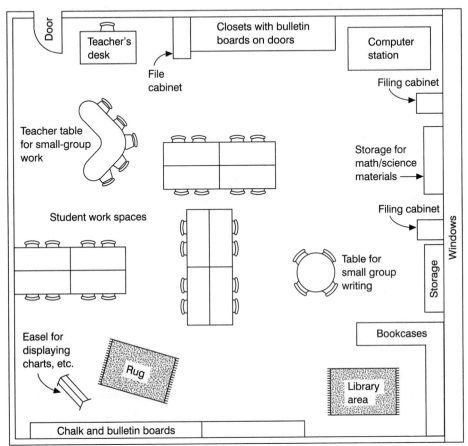

ally do. By attending to those benchmarks, teachers recognize when to nudge children forward, when to reinforce existing skills, and when to help children correct misunderstandings about reading or writing. Knowledge of children and knowledge of specific supportive strategies for instruction are the tools teachers use to enhance children's progress.

THE EMERGENT LITERACY CURRICULUM

There are three major components of an emergent literacy curriculum, each of which provides support for students' growth:

1. Shared literacy experiences and supportive reading groups

Table 4–2
Supplies for an Emergent Literacy Classroom

Furniture
Desks or tables and chairs for all children
Teacher space, either as a desk or table at which to work privately with children
Movable furniture to provide private and open spaces

Storage spaces
Storage space for supplies that are to be accessible to children
Storage space for supplies that are not to be accessible
Book storage space
- bookcases
- revolving book racks for paperbacks
- crates
Cubbies or other storage space for students' belongings
Storage space for students' work
- crates for file folders
- teacher file cabinet
- individual cubbies

Printed material
Books
Magazines
Reference sources
Other print material, such as catalogues and junk mail

Environmental print/display space
Calendar
Teacher- and student-produced charts

2. The language experience approach to literacy development
3. Extensive writing experiences

These components exist on a continuum also. The nature and shape of the experiences change as children gain knowledge about literacy, but the basic approaches—and their theoretical underpinnings—remain essentially the same.

Shared Literacy Experiences and Supportive Reading Groups

Student-teacher sharing of books is as important as intimate child-parent sharing for all children, especially for children who have not had these experiences at home. In preschool, kindergarten, and first grade (and in all grades thereafter), teachers should read to students daily. Good storybook reading is an active

Table 4–2
continued

Commercially produced charts
Signs and labels designating areas of the classroom
Notices to students and parents
Samples of students' work
Artwork with dictation or written comments
Letter charts and other graphic reference materials
Written explanations of tasks, rules, and so forth

Text production supplies

Various kinds of paper
Various kinds of writing tools
Staples, tape, and so forth for bookbinding
Computer (not absolutely essential)
Typewriter (a nice extra)
Letter stamps and stamp pads and other manipulative letters
Pocket charts and other devices that allow students to manipulate word cards and create sentences

Other Supplies

Interesting things to observe and write about
Materials for experimentation that can be written about
Art supplies
Globes, maps, and other social studies equipment
Science and math equipment
Easels to hold chart tablets
Bulletin boards to display charts, big books, notices, and student work
Tape recorders

process that includes talking about pictures and text, predicting what will happen, evaluating stories, and engaging in specific follow-up activities like drawing, manipulating puppets, or role playing. In addition to providing pleasure, story-book reading should teach children that reading makes sense, that print provides a comprehensible message, and that stories follow a specific pattern or "gram-mar." These concepts may seem obvious to adults, but they are keys to under-standing reading that many children simply do not possess as they start school. Children failing to gain this insight while they are still at the listening stage may encounter difficulties later when they themselves begin to read; they may learn to "call" out the words they see by identifying letter-sound correspondences and never realize that what they utter should have meaning.

The *shared book experience* translates Don Holdaway's concept of a bedtime story learning cycle into a workable classroom approach. Books that work best

Table 4–3
Important Questions About Young Learners

Some of these questions can be asked directly in conferences; some may be asked of parents; and some can be answered primarily through observation of students' behavior in instructional and freetime periods in the classroom context.

How much do children know about print production?
- Directionality of print
- Letter formation
- Letter discrimination and recognition

How much do they know about the conventions of writing?
- Capitalization
- Punctuation
- Story structure

Do children write on their own? Do they incorporate writing into freetime activities? How much writing do they do spontaneously?
- This may be difficult to determine because many young learners will not write in front of their teacher, yet they compose many notes for their friends, siblings, and parents, and frequently state their wishes and claim their territory with notices and signs.

For what variety of purposes do children write?
Are they aware that there are multiple purposes for writing even if they do not use them?

How willing are they to share their writing?

have relatively simple stories, related illustrations, large, clear print, and topics that are familiar enough to make sense but challenging enough intellectually to maintain children's interest. They provide a bridge between oral language and book language, and they are the first stage in children's learning to read independently. However, books with relatively small print and illustrations are not ideal for instruction with large groups of children. Teachers can compensate in two distinct ways:

1. Use enlarged print versions of favorite books, usually designated *big books*.
2. Make copies of books available to children for independent browsing and use in storybook reenactments or as source material for artwork, dramatizations, puppet plays, or similar activities.

Big books with enlarged print allow small groups of children sitting in a circle in front of the teacher to approximate the visual intimacy of parent-child book

Table 4–3
continued

> What do children know about reading?
> - Purposes for reading
> - Book-handling skills
>
> How much have children been read to at home?
> How much have they seen parents and siblings reading and writing?
> Have they been in preschool situations that offered a strong literacy program and a considerable amount of reading to the children?
>
> Can/will children engage in storybook reenactments?
> Can they read some words at sight?
> If they can read, what cues do they use?
> - Letter-sound correspondences
> - Picture clues
> - Context clues
>
> Do beginning readers seem to monitor their comprehension?
> Do they have multiple strategies for gaining meaning?
> Do readers have "fix-up" strategies when their comprehension falters?
> Do children seem to turn to reading or browsing through books as a freetime activity?
> Do they incorporate reading into their play, as in consulting a "cookbook" in the kitchen area, reading the "newspaper," and so forth?
>
> Do children seem frustrated by reading instruction?
> Do they have the basic vocabulary to understand instruction?
> Do they have the background information to make sense of books they encounter?
> Do children seem to have vision or hearing problems that are hindering their progress in reading and writing?

sharing. Big books are available commercially; teachers can also make big books themselves. Directions for teacher-made big books are outlined in Figure 4–2. Big books should be made from stories with proven appeal. They should be predictable books, caption books, books that invite audience participation by encouraging children to "read" along with the teacher, and even books that cover content areas simply to provide an early primary approach to "reading across the curriculum." A unit on weather, for example, might be accompanied by a big book discussing weather changes, thermometers, and clouds. Teachers can also compose their own stories for big books, and should provide small-sized versions of big books as well. A first grader wrote about a big book made by a university student: "I think it's fun haveing a big book and a litle book becas you can rede awt of the tine wune and see the pichrs in the big wune. Big books are easyer to rede" (Salinger, 1988, p. 211).

Working with children and big books enables teachers to observe children closely and determine who is progressing rapidly, who needs more challenging

Figure 4–2
Big Books for Beginning Reading[2]

Materials

Chart tablet or sheets of large, heavy paper
Magic markers with clear, strong colors
Children's art work and/or teacher's drawings
Laminating equipment (optional)
Chart stand or easel

Procedures

1. Decide on the contents of the big book; it may be an original book or duplication of a commercial book.

If using a commercial book:

2. At first, reproduce the pictures as closely as possible; using an overhead projection machine helps those whose art skills are weak.

3. Later, rough sketches or children's drawings can be used.

4. Duplicate the text in neat, clear handwriting; try to keep to the same number of words per line of text that children will see in the book so that children can make a one-to-one correspondence between the original and the new book.

If using an original idea:

5. Keep text and illustrations simple; make sure contents will be relevant to the children.

6. Write text horizontally, usually across the bottom of the page.

7. As children become familiar with big books, use their drawings to illustrate.

8. Use pictures cut from magazines or other illustrations for books, especially if they are to be laminated; or draw your own illustrations.

---

[2]Adapted from *Language Arts and Literacy for Young Children* (pp. 212–213) by T. Salinger, 1988, New York: Merrill/Macmillan. Copyright 1988 by Macmillan Publishing Company. Adapted by permission.

reading tasks, and who continues to need the close support and repetition of the big-book interaction. Logical groupings of children emerge from these observations—not reading groups in the traditional sense, but informal, fluid groupings of children who can be called together to work with the teacher on new reading tasks. The purpose of these groups is to tap mutual interests and shared energy; for beginners, reading should be a social activity during which children learn from each other. Together, children can cut through the "language of instruction" their teacher presents and help each other gain control of new concepts and skills. Instruction should remain low-keyed, although teachers should constantly assess children's emerging skills. The objective is to move from teacher-directed to independent student reading without sacrificing support that the teacher has provided. The transition should be smooth and natural; there should be no one point when

Figure 4–2
continued

Display/presentation for either kind of book:
9. If the book is in chart tablet form, display it on a chart stand or easel; punch holes in tops of pages made from large sheets of newsprint or tagboard, reinforce the holes, and use rings to hang them from chart tablet stand or easel. Leave chart stand in clear sight so children can reenact story.

10. If books are smaller than chart tablet size and cannot be hung, and will be handled by children, laminate pages for durability; punch holes, reinforce if necessary, and use rings, string, or yarn to bind together.

Use an easel or chalk tray as support. Leave these readily available for individual or small group browsing and reenactment.

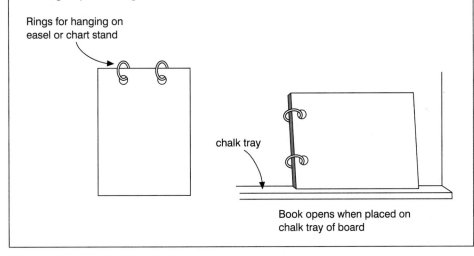

Rings for hanging on easel or chart stand

chalk tray

Book opens when placed on chalk tray of board

reading skills move from "play" to "real." Table 4–4 summarizes procedures for using big books within a group for supportive, shared reading experiences.

As children gain skills and confidence, teachers introduce new instructional strategies and new challenges. Enlarged print format lends itself to the use of sliders or masking devices, which are illustrated in Figure 4–3. Masking involves a strategy called *cloze*, which is based on the idea that readers search for meaning in print and can fill in missing words if they are reading with comprehension. Guided by sight words and letter-sound correspondences, children read as teachers unmask text, and they use knowledge of word meaning and sentence structure to predict the words or ideas that will come next in particular sentences. They learn to predict story lines, and teachers can stop at appropriate places to elicit guesses about what will happen next. This method of slowly unmasking text while modeling self-questioning and predicting comes close to externalizing the unseen, mental processes of reading, in that children must evaluate not only what they have seen but also what they have thought in order to make predictions and con-

Table 4–4
Supportive and Shared Reading Groups[3]

Materials

Multiple copies of children's literature or basal readers and an enlarged print (big book) version of what children will read

Procedures—Day 1

1. Teacher presents the enlarged print version of the material and reads it in a normal voice, pointing to each word and emphasizing words like POW! dramatically and with comments.

2. Children are invited to point out or guess words they think they know at sight.

3. Children look through regular-sized copies of the material for about five minutes; they should note and discuss pictures and any words they know. This gives them a chance to coordinate the teacher's oral reading with the regular text.

4. Teacher reads the text again as children follow along either on the enlarged print or in the regular books; children are encouraged to echo the teacher's reading as much as possible; teachers should note who does not seem able to track the print in the text or in the big book and who can echo read most of the text.

5. If the story is appropriate, the children may act it out or draw about it; these activities reinforce their understanding of the story and increase comprehension.

6. Copies of the material are available for browsing.

Procedures—Day 2

1. Steps 1–4 are repeated at a more rapid pace.

2. Echo reading behaviors should increase during this session. Children should be called upon to read words, phrases, or whole sentences from their books or

---

[3]From *Language Arts and Literacy for Young Children* (pp. 232–233) by T. Salinger, 1988, New York: Merrill/Macmillan. Copyright 1988 by Macmillan Publishing Company. Adapted by permission.

tinue reading. Teachers are in control of what children see; they demonstrate the predicting that children should do in independent reading so the experience is in no way intimidating. Teachers can respond to random, inaccurate guesses immediately to help children understand what they are supposed to be doing.

Language Experience Approach (LEA)

The language experience approach (LEA) is a venerable and dependable method of teaching initial reading; its role in supporting writing growth is equally important. The language experience approach is a method for encouraging literacy growth that, in its early stages, uses materials developed through the transcription of children's dictation. LEA involves all the language channels—speaking, listen-

Table 4–4
continued

---

from the enlarged print version; approximations of the correct text are accepted.

3. Teacher provides appropriate low-keyed instruction by pointing out words that have a specific sound or that represent a particular part of speech, grammatical principle, or other aspect of reading.

4. Teacher observes the extent to which children participate and determines who needs advanced work and who needs continued close support.

5. Copies of the material are available for browsing and rereading; peer interaction and story reenactment are encouraged.

Procedures—Day 3

1. A new book may be presented in the same fashion, or children may continue to work on the previous material.

2. From time to time, a familiar story is reviewed for fun and to reinforce past learning.

Alternative Procedures

1. A similar process can be used with dictated language experience approach (LEA) stories; teacher might reproduce copies of the LEA story for each child, but the basic procedure would remain the same.

2. Again with or without reproduced copies of the enlarged print material, supportive reading strategies can be used to introduce poems, informational charts, posters, bulletin boards, or song lyrics; children follow along as their teacher reads and read as much of the material as they can on their own.

3. Either of these activities can be used with small groups or with the whole class; the echo reading process allows even weaker or less confident readers to participate.

---

ing, reading, and writing—and it works because it is intrinsically motivating. Children like to see their ideas written down and are fascinated with the process of reading these words. LEA's major advantages include the following:

- It builds upon children's experiences in and out of school.
- It uses children's own ideas.
- It accommodates children's own vocabulary levels and idiosyncracies, even if children are not fully fluent in the language of instruction or if they speak a dialect.
- It provides clear models of reading and writing behaviors.
- It allows children to participate in the production of texts that are inherently their own.

Figure 4–3
Masking Strategies for Use With Big Books[4]

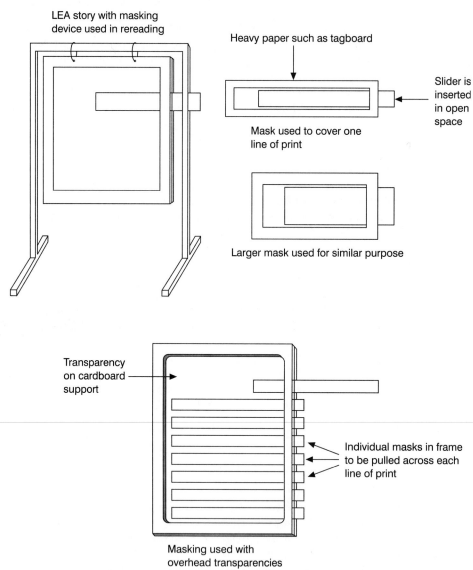

LEA story with masking
device used in rereading

Heavy paper such as tagboard

Slider is
inserted
in open
space

Mask used to cover one
line of print

Larger mask used for similar purpose

Transparency
on cardboard
support

Individual masks in frame
to be pulled across each
line of print

Masking used with
overhead transparencies

[4]Adapted from *Language Arts and Literacy for Young Children* (p. 234) by T. Salinger, 1988, New York: Merrill/Macmillan. Copyright 1988 by Macmillan Publishing Company. Adapted by permission.

The most common use of LEA is the chart story, which is often about a shared experience. The process is simple; children dictate and their teachers transcribe and guide learners in sharing or actually rereading their stories. Chart stories are appropriate instructional materials because they reflect children's vocabularies and levels of semantic and syntactic development. The wealth of language available for young learners to use is monumental, yet the average first-grade reading program limits the extent of vocabulary introduced in the stories children read. Syntactic variety may also be limited, although children are able to produce and understand relatively complex sentence patterns.

Language experience can also be used successfully with second language learners, in content areas, and as a means to develop highly personalized or "key" vocabularies. Suggestions for using LEA are presented in Table 4–5.

Other Benefits of Language Experience

In taking dictation, many teachers make the mistake of transcribing children's statements verbatim, often preceded by a monotonous "John said," "Rebecca said," and so forth, throughout the story. In doing so, teachers miss powerful opportunities to *shape* the text to illustrate specific aspects of language structure. Teachers might, for example, restate in more formal English those ideas that children have presented in vernacular or idiomatic language. If teachers make restatements without judgment or derision, children begin to realize that there are different "registers," or ways of speaking that are appropriate for different environments. This realization is essential if children are going to make sense out of the language of beginning readers and storybooks, which can be very different from their own speech.

Language experience provides many children with their first real introduction to the process of *authoring*. When teachers demonstrate that the material children dictate is a piece of text that can and should be reviewed, revised, and edited, as well as shared, children see how composition evolves. Even as children dictate, teachers can ask for "other ways of stating that" to stress the importance of adjectives in description; they can delay transcription to illustrate how several ideas can be combined; they can stress sequence and sequence words where appropriate; and they can insert and delete words and ideas while guiding children to reread their dictation. Moving the dictation-transcription interaction beyond a mechanical process of verbatim recording allows the teacher to become an *editor* who helps children shape their ideas and see real text unfold. Wrapped up in the process of shaping and expressing their ideas, children will not feel slighted if their initial statements are not transcribed exactly; instead they will feel more like participants in a composition session and are likely to remain attentive and involved.

Through group and individual work with LEA and word banks, children gain insight into literacy, skills in reading and composition, and confidence in their abilities to produce and understand text. They are supported and encouraged in their movement toward independent use of literacy skills.

BEGINNING EFFORTS AT COMPOSITION

Having discovered the basic principles of letter formation through observation, children begin to write. First efforts may appear as scribbles or pseudo-letters that approximate manuscript or cursive handwriting. Children's first efforts show the

Table 4–5
Steps in Using the Language Experience Approach (LEA)

SMALL OR LARGE GROUP SESSION

Step 1
Teacher and students share an experience, such as
- a trip
- a classroom visitor
- a classroom experience turned into a special event, such as observation of a pet or cooking a treat

Step 2
Teacher and students discuss the event, with the teacher modeling or extracting from students' key vocabulary and key concepts

Step 3
Students dictate their ideas for the teacher to transcribe. Teachers transcribe the stories on large chart tablets, using dark marker and clear, block printing. The teacher has two distinct styles of transcription to use:

- *Verbatim transcription.* The teacher writes down essentially everything the students say verbatim, stringing the statements together with children's names and verbs such as "said," "remarked," and so forth. The representation of children's ideas is accurate but uncreative.

The disadvantage of this approach is that artificial-sounding, boring texts result; the method is traditional *but not highly recommended*.

- *Editorial transcription.* The teacher elicits comments, listens to students carefully, and combines comments to form more well-developed statements. Some ideas may not be included in transcription immediately, but instead are woven into the story where they are appropriate. Teachers focus the text production by stressing sequence ("Tell me what came *first, next, last* . . . "), quality of description or expression ("Who can tell me *another* way of saying that?"), or other rhetorical or mechanical features. Children's names are not used, but their ideas are stated clearly enough and acknowledged so that they feel an appropriate sense of authorship.

The advantages of this *highly recommended* strategy are that the teacher is modeling the composition process for the children and the resulting text is more interesting and conducive to teaching.

Step 4
Teacher and students read the resulting story.

- *With nonreaders.* The teacher reads the text, pointing to each word and pausing to emphasize any words children might recognize or might find interesting to discuss. Children are invited to read whatever they can, whether it is their names, phrases, or, as their confidence increases, whole sentences.

Table 4–5
continued

- *With beginning readers*. The teacher may read the whole story first, but the students are quickly invited to read as much of the text as they can.

Step 5
Teacher uses the text for instruction, including work with word study, sentence construction, authoring, or reading subskills. Strategies can include the following:
- pointing out/asking students about the length, configuration, or composition of certain words, such as compound words
- pointing out/asking students about punctuation or capitalization
- eliciting words to replace words in the text, such as words that "describe better" than what was dictated
- asking students to combine two short sentences and suggest appropriate rewording

This approach works especially well when teachers have used the Editorial Transcription model.

Step 6
The LEA chart story, on an easel or other stand, is left for students to re-read, review, or illustrate.

VARIATIONS
Individual dictation. The teacher may take dictation from individual children and record their work in small books or in notebooks. Transcribing a caption for artwork falls into this category.

Sentence strips. The teacher records transcriptions on long strips of paper or on cards such as index cards and cuts the strips up into "word cards". Children use these word cards to create sentences on any flat surface or in pocket charts. Children are encouraged to copy their sentences into a notebook.

Word bank. Children request individual words from the teacher and keep them in a "bank" to study on their own, play with, swap with friends, and so forth. Periodically the teacher and students review the words and discard ones that students cannot read. This approach complements the sentence strip strategy.

Daily calendar. Each day, the teacher takes brief dictation about the day's happenings and records it on the classroom calendar (which may have to be specially made to allow enough space). This provides a model for children's own daily writing in journals.

Content area use. The teacher keeps records through LEA strategies of the work students do in content areas besides reading or language arts. Observations of experiments, social studies observations, or even math activities are amenable to this approach.

Figure 4–4 (pp. 78–87)
Stages of Writing Development in Emergent Literacy Classrooms with Samples[5]

As Part of Language Experience

1. **Drawing and Dictation: Labels and Captions**
   - Teacher response: transcribes and discusses; asks about the drawing; extends label to caption by restating in complete sentences; may ask questions to stimulate expansion
   - Child's behavior: continues to draw and label; engages in discussions

Sample 1b. Child labeled parts of his picture: "VOLCANO FIRED" and "VOLCANIC ACTION."

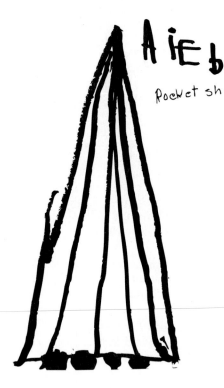

Sample 1a. Child wrote in deviant spelling and dictated label.

Sample 1c. Child wrote her own labels on pictures of her friends. She also wrote "SCHOOL IS OVER. I LIKE SCHOOL."

The beginning of writing is labeling. Children may request that teachers label parts of their drawings or may use deviant spelling to label parts themselves. Gradually, labels expand to captions.

[5]List adapted and samples taken from *Language Arts and Literacy for Young Children* (Chapter 8) by T. Salinger, 1988, New York: Merrill/Macmillan. Copyright 1988 by Macmillan Publishing Company. Adapted by permission.

As Part of Children's Independent Writing (with or without drawing)

2. **"I like" Stories**
   - Teacher response: transcribes if asked; may pose "Why" questions to encourage expansion
   - Child's behavior: may begin to use "love" instead of "like" and possibly indicate it with a heart

I LC Ployvv Mibe r ~~bies~~
~~WrTrots~~ WrTrots   *Marco*

Sample 2a. Child indicates what he likes to do, note correction of false start in spelling.

I li KW in J go to The ZUo - *Garett*
Ikcanran pasiy aiseo

Sample 2b. Child indicates what he likes to do and tells something about the activity; he is still uncertain about spacing between words.

Tik You mis Kidderfor being
Sow nis.
I Liked rideg.

Sample 2c. Child thanks her kindergarten teacher for being so nice and tells her that she like(s) reading; this child leaves ample space between her words; notice the emerging spelling skills.

I Loveyou my litte red wagin
becus it is pritty.!

Sample 2d. The child addresses her little red wagon and attempts to explain why she loves it; she changes number in the second part of her sentence but has clearly experimented with sentence construction; note two punctuation marks.

I Like My kite beekas   *Erin*
It has it A peeas s on
and it has white pritty
and My MoMMy Bot it for ME
and I Like it.

Sample 2e. This child also states why she likes a toy, and she goes on to describe the kite and tell where she got it; notice how she corrects false starts. This is a later effort of the child who wrote Sample 2d.

"I like" stories allow children to write about things and events of special interest and significance. The basic sentence "I like _____ " may be expanded with reasons and description. At times, teachers may prompt this expansion by requesting more information. These samples were collected as part of the regular writing period in a kindergarten class; transcriptions were done by the teacher.

Figure 4–4
continued

3. **"I" + action verb**
   - Teacher response: transcribes if asked; poses questions to stimulate discussion and encourage expansion.
   - Child's behavior: varies verb form, e.g., "I run," "I am running," etc.

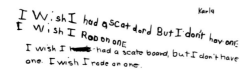

Karlq

I wish I had a scate board, but I don't have one. I wish I rode on one.

When I climbed up a mountain, I fell down.

Sample 3a. Child indicates that he wishes he had a skateboard. Note use of negative construction and embedded clauses.

Sample 3b. Child writes of climbing a mountain and falling down; note use of introductory clause; the simple line drawing contributes to the story because a mountain near the child's home has a cross and shrine on top; his drawing tells which mountain he climbed.

Sample 3c. Child expresses wishful thinking: "If I was a passenger on a shuttle, I would float down in the space shuttle."

"I + action verb" stories tell about what children have done or want to do; they may also express wishes or ambitions. They are easy for children to think of and write because they are so personal.

4. **Use of multiple first-person subject**
   - Teacher response: transcribes if asked; poses questions and seeks clarification; provides spelling as requested
   - Child's behavior: often expands story in response to discussion

Sample 4. The child gives lots of information about a family outing; her drawing gives additional information. Child adapts basic format to include multiple subjects.

5. **Use of third-person subject**
   - Teacher response: continues to transcribe if requested; discusses story as story to encourage more writing
   - Child's behavior: moves out of personalized writing and begins to create "stories" rather than comments on his or her own life

Sample 5. This is a much simpler story, written with less control of spelling; it reads: "When Donald Duck did throw a tray on the people, the people screamed." What is unique about the story is the characterization of Donald Duck, unless the child was reporting on something he had seen on television.

Figure 4–4
continued

6. **Writing with No Drawing**
    - Teacher response: seeks clarification; helps with mechanics as needed
    - Child's behavior: continues to show confidence in story-making abilities by creating extended pices of prose

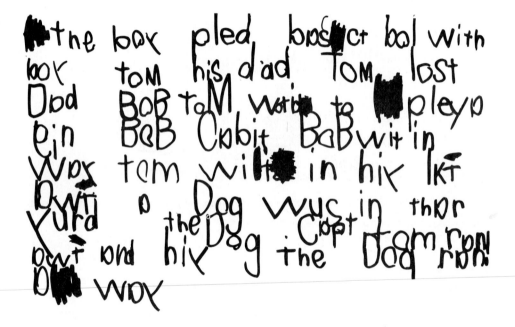

Sample 6. The left-hand side of this story lists a cast of characters. The story itself is not unique, except for the inclusion of one word. As the child read the story to his teacher, he paused and seemed to gauge whether or not to dictate what he had written; his teacher, the writer of Report No. 2, did not even flinch. The story reads: "The boy played basketball with his dad. Tom lost. Tom wanted to play again. Bob couldn't. Bob went in. When Tom went in, he looked. A dog was in their yard. The dog crapped. Tom ran out and the dog ran away." Note that the writer of this story was named neither Tom, nor Bob.

7. Exploration of Ideas, Format, Mode, etc.

- Teacher response: offers encouragement and help with story structure, mechanics, etc., as needed
- Child's behavior: demonstrates awareness of story and of audience; pieces often have a clear narrative style; child may attempt to "gross out" audience

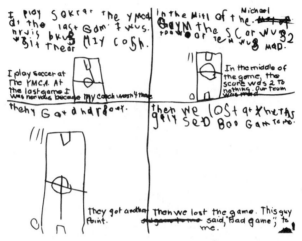

Sample 7a. The child wrote and drew about a real event; having four spaces to fill rather than a whole sheet of paper made his task more manageable. Note that the drawing shows the layout of the soccer field rather than children playing the game.

Sample 7b. This child drew individual "events" in his story in boxes like a comic strip; his writing was separated by dots rather than spaces; his story described the entire set of pictures; "A long time ago an old Model T just went putt, putt, putt along the road. All of a sudden a cat ran out in the road and splat the cat was gone." The child obviously enjoyed the gruesomeness of his story. Notice the "HaHaHa" in several boxes.

Figure 4–4
continued

Sample 7c. This child wrote about a dream: "When I went to sleep I was dreaming about the dog in space. The dog was drawing himself flying after a cat in space. And the dog got scared and turned back and now the cat was after the dog and the cat scared the dog away." His dreams include made-up characters and considerable action. Notice the arrows to indicate which drawing is which character.

Sample 7d. This child began on the back of his sheet of paper by writing a list of characters: "Sheep, wolf, farmer (named Larry), Frank, and Bob." His dictation read: "There was a sheep. When he went to eat he would always find a wolf. The sheep ran away. And the wolf would get lost because the sheep was clever. Then he went back to eat, and another wolf found him again. Then the farmer came out and chased the wolf away." The list of characters gives information that is not included in the story, and the story itself may be a take-off on something the child has heard or read.

"aoog WasomqhaFTOGOiNFor olFthe Wasenxwa"

oda vod

Sample 7e. The drawing conveys the action in this story; it is full of red and black and unhappy faces. The child's text (which he read tentatively to his teacher in case she might disapprove) was: "A Dog was dumb enough to go in front of the racing track."

One Doy aaoy wos PLaeg Sokr. weth hs Fnsand ThegoY hoo vyneg ol aVasonnThe Doy Fol hefo lagn andogn andagn he kak̄D hos hϕopen he bob   The end

Sample 7f. This child also tested his teacher's tolerance for gruesome subjects; his story, written without drawings, reads: "One day a boy was playing soccer with his friends and the boy was winning. All of a sudden, the boy fell. He fell again and again and again. He cracked his head open. He died. The end." The child might have been trying to imitate a sportscaster or merely shock his teacher. The writing (done without spaces between words) has a definite book-like tone that would not have been present if the child had been reporting on a real incident.

Figure 4–4
continued

8. **Editorial Changes/Revision**
   - Teacher response: discusses reasons for changes; makes suggestions for and help with revisions
   - Child's behavior: while child may have made changes in work previously, this stage represents a real attempt to rethink pieces from the perspective of an audience with whom to share the work

Sample 8a. This child merely crosses out words she wants to change; the story reads: "The elephant is going to the zoo. He is the man's helper."

Sample 8b. This story has no drawing; the child had learned (through language experience) that he could add words by using arrows. His text reads: "The man is cleaning the back yard and the man is playing soccer."

Sample 8c. This child makes corrections by writing needed letters over the letters he has already written (as in "frog") or by crossing out.

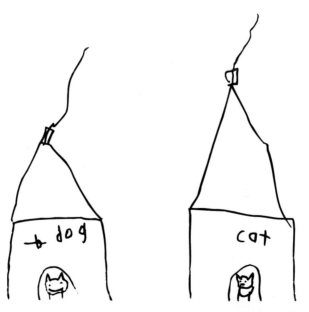

Sample 8d. This story is interesting because the child corrected the text and his drawing so that they would go together; he began with "The dog is in the box," changed the square box he had drawn to a house, and changed the word he used to describe the dog's location; then he changed the second part of the story as well.

deviant stage of invented spelling, with no letter-sound correspondences. Some beginning writers claim that they do not know what they have written and others read their messages confidently. The length and shape of the first efforts differ widely (see Appendix A for books that offer more detailed discussions of the development of writing).

Writing skills will progress as children see models of composition (for example, LEA) and are allowed to draw, encouraged to write, and reassured that invented spelling and experimentation are fine. The stages of development move from initial labels to exaggerated and wonderful experimentation, as suggested by the examples in Figure 4–4. Other language arts activities in the emergent literacy classroom prove to be mutually supportive and purposeful: learning standard spelling and legible handwriting is viewed as a means to communicate more efficiently in writing; reading is valued because it represents sharing ideas with other authors; practice in all language skills reinforces mastery of the others.

Invented Spelling

Invented spelling is a powerful tool for beginning writers. Children begin, quite confidently, to write random strings of letters and pseudo-letters (e.g., m, E) to express their ideas. As they gain more insight into letter-sound correspondences, their approximations of words become more and more recognizable. Table 4–6 presents the stages of invented spelling, and Figure 4–5 shows one child's invented and conventional spelling for the names of "all the states that she knows."

Drawing

Drawing serves as a warm-up or prewriting activity during which children generate and organize ideas; it can also help children remember what they want to write about. As they draw, they think about the pictorial and verbal representations of their story. Because the process of invented spelling can take a long time, children may forget what they want to convey in print. Pictorial representations jog memories about content and help children stay on task. In similar fashion, drawing may sometimes replace writing, as when children convey the emotions of characters in a story by giving them all smiling faces. Drawing can also help children organize the format or conventions of writing. Small pieces of paper for small drawings invite relatively short stories, and are perceived as manageable tasks for beginning authors. Several sheets of small paper can be stapled together to form a short book composed of separate drawings and individual, related sentences. Large pieces of paper may be more intimidating in terms of drawing and writing requirements, but divided into sections, they offer a handy format for telling a sequential story with each section approximating a page.

Because drawing is important, teachers should provide ample paper and a variety of writing and drawing tools. Early childhood penmanship paper with wide lines and space at the top for a picture can work well in some cases but will not accommodate work with markers or implements with other ink. The backs of used computer papers are convenient and economical.

Figure 4–5
Invented Spelling on Spontaneous Writing Sample "All the States That I Know"

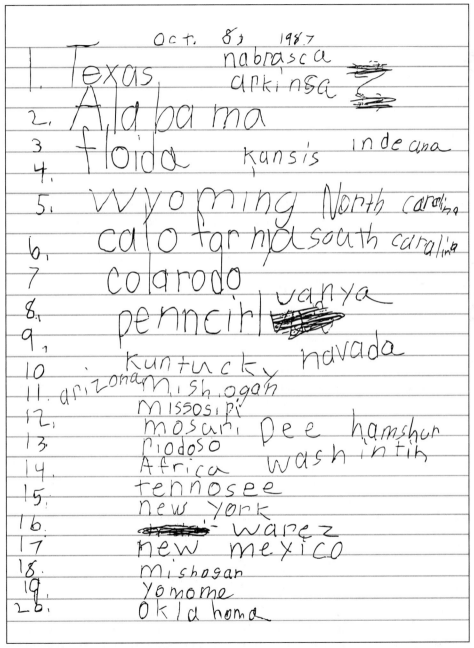

Oct. 8, 1987

1. Texas,   nabrasca   arkinsa
2. Alabama
3. floida   kunsis   indeana
4.
5. Wyoming North carolina
6. calo farnia south caralina
7. colorodo
8. penncirl   vanya
9.
10. kuntucky   navada
11. arizona mish ogan
12. missosipi
13. mosuri, Dee hamshur
14. riodoso   washintin
15. Africa
16. tennosee
17. new york
18. warez
19. new mexico
20. mishogan
    Yomome
    Oklahoma

This work sample shows a first grader's attempt to "write the names of all the states that I know."
Note that the sample was collected in a school in El Paso, Texas, hence the abundance of names of
southwestern states. Note also entry number 16, a phonetic spelling *Juarez*, the Mexican city directly across the Rio Grande River from El Paso.

Table 4–6
Stages of Invented Spelling

Stage	Characteristic	Examples
Deviant	No letter-sound match; random or pseudo-letters	"mplzt" for cat
Prephonetic/ early phonetic	One-, two-, or three-letter strings with primitive letter/sound awareness	"d" for dog
Letter-name	Good match between letters	"mstr" for monster "ylo" for yellow "wos" for was
Transitional	Many words correctly spelled; "understandable" misspellings because of irregular spelling patterns in English	"thay" for they "onse" for once "empte" for empty

Invented Spelling and Experimentation

Writing can be perceived as risk-taking, from making oneself vulnerable to criticism and judgment, to being called *wrong*. Yet, to advance literacy, writers must take risks. Harste, Woodward, and Burke (1983) commented: "Counter to current instructional folklore . . . it is only when language users get themselves in trouble within what was perceived to be a moderately predictable setting that growth occurs. . . . [Children's] latest language discoveries are always more fun to think about than those which [they] already think [they] have sorted out" (pp. 136, 192).

Teachers need to work toward creating a warm and accepting climate in the classroom so that even cautious children will be willing to take the risks that writing demands. Encouraging the use of invented spelling is part of this effort. Invented spelling progresses through distinct stages as children figure out more and more about letter-sound correspondences and the irregularities of English. After stressing that invented spelling will be accepted, teachers must then be willing to accept what is presented, not judge it, and use it diagnostically as a means of evaluating progress and fine-tuning instruction. Fortunately, teachers who encourage writing in their young students quickly learn to read invented spelling and can easily engage in dialogue with the children about the content of their work (see Figure 4–4 and Figure 4-5).

Children learn about the conventions of writing from the environment, LEA sessions, storytime, and their own reading. It seems natural to them to try these devices on their own, and as they experiment, they show confidence in their skills and show interest in language itself. Children will experiment with capitalization, sentence structure, figures of speech, stilted "book language," and other conventions of writing, such as embedded clauses. Realizing that printed material contains punctuation, children may sprinkle periods, question marks, and exclamation points throughout their stories. They may also attempt to vary sentences by posing and then answering questions. Young children also may play with ideas, venture into fantasy, express outrageous wishes, write about supposedly taboo subjects, or attempt to shock, surprise, or even "gross out" their readers. Some of the best examples of young children's writing result from their attempts to master the more complex conventions of sophisticated text (Figure 4–4, Figure 4–5).

As they experiment with writing, children also show that they have understood certain conventions of book format. They may refer to themselves as authors and illustrators and may use elaborate formatting devices, such as writing "The End" with ruffles and flourishes. Children also demonstrate that they have noticed specific aspects of print production and try to use them in their own writing. Breaking books into chapters, designating themselves as illustrators, providing brief dedications, and using other devices reflect children's awareness of "grown-up" books and show their enthusiasm for their own efforts as authors.

Experimentation with writing indicates several things about these young writers. First, it shows emerging confidence and enthusiasm; children are willing to take risks and try out what they have observed in others' printed works. Experimentation also shows that children are trying to find a "voice"—a personal expressive voice of their own—with which to speak to their readers. Finally, these attempts to vary writing indicate that children have realized that writing *sounds* different from spoken discourse, that there is both "book" and spoken language.

After young writers have produced a piece of writing, they should then be encouraged to revise their own work, to discuss it with others and with their teacher, and to make changes that improve their ability to communicate their ideas. But often, children in early childhood classes are impatient to get a piece finished or simply are not inclined to spend the time revision requires. In addition, they often really do not see any need for improvement in what they write. Teachers must themselves be patient, suggesting changes, encouraging revision, but not demanding drastic overhauls of pieces. It is essential that the desire to revise stems from children's own sense of writing and that "revision" not be construed as merely copying over. Felt-tipped pens and markers actually help children learn to revise. First of all, they are motivational and children like to write with them. And, because the ink cannot be erased, children realize that they *must* cross out errors and false starts and recognize that they, as authors, must take their work through several drafts. Samples in Figure 4–4 show different purposes and styles of revision.

How Much Can Teachers Expect?

Many teachers who enthusiastically begin a writing program in their emergent literacy classrooms become disappointed by their students' output and progress. The development of writing skills takes time and energy, and progress is rarely made overnight. Teachers must be patient and supportive but also insistent that children do write as part of their regular classroom work. As children mature in spontaneous writing, teachers should help them refine their skills and reach for more sophistication. A balance of spontaneous writing, structured assignments, language experience, and direct instruction characterizes those classrooms in which children make progress in composition. In addition, children should keep logs or journals and, if using language experience, a word bank as a personal dictionary. The actual writing output of any one class during any one year will be influenced by many factors, including the amount of writing children have done previously and what kind of expectations and opportunities the teacher places before the class. When teachers state emphatically, "Children in my class write" and follow up on the statement, children will progress.

THE READING-WRITING CONNECTION

An emergent literacy classroom, in allowing students to experiment with reading and writing and encouraging them to integrate what they learn, provides them with useful strategies for solving diverse literary puzzles. Emphasis is on integration rather than instruction of discrete subskills because teachers in these classrooms believe that learning literacy consists of unified, mutually reinforcing reading and writing behaviors.

Children in emergent reading classes read extensively as part of daily routines and as independent activities. They also write, and read their own and their classmates' compositions. As long as there is a good selection of books in the class, Sustained Silent Reading (SSR) can be initiated even with beginning readers. In this process, everyone in the class, even the teacher, reads silently in a self-selected book for a specified amount of time. Of course, beginners will not read silently; but the transition from mumbled to whispered to silent reading does occur over time. Children must realize that silent reading is a time for enjoyment of books, for reading for fun.

Still, questions are often raised. Do teachers take care of "basic skills" in an emergent literacy classroom? Do students learn "enough" about phonics and mechanical aspects of composition to support further learning? Will students be able to "emerge" from beginning levels of mastery to become competent literacy users? The answers to these questions are emphatically "yes, yes, and yes."

Students master reading and writing most readily when they practice literacy in real reading and writing tasks, rather than on worksheets, in workbooks, or on computer drill-and-practice software. By practicing skills in context, children integrate what they know and what they are learning. As summarized in Table 4–7, an emergent literacy program provides opportunities for such practice as part of daily classroom routines. Children hone their skills through activities that are purposeful and that emphasize functional and recreational uses for literacy. The next chapter discusses how the momentum children develop in an emergent literacy classroom can be maintained as they progress through elementary school.

Table 4–7
Authentic Reading and Writing Activities for Emergent Literacy Classrooms

Logs and Journals

The major purposes of logs and journals are:

- to give students frequent, if not daily, opportunities to produce writing that will not be graded
- to allow teachers to evaluate students' emerging understanding of the processes of writing and the content areas they are learning

Possible uses include:

- daily entries about whatever the children wish to write about
- dialogue journals that require daily responses from teachers
- literature logs with entries about what children are reading
- learning logs about content area work that record the stages of developing understandings

Sustained Reading and Writing

Sustained silent reading and writing (SSR and SSW) activities are periods during which both students and teacher read or write in silence. Children select the books they will read and write on topics of their own choice. Teachers must engage in silent reading and writing as well. The time periods for SSR or SSW are determined by children's age, skills, attention span, and motivation. Used daily or as a routine practice several times a week, these activities have the following advantages:

- students develop appropriate habits for focusing their reading and writing behaviors
- students see their teacher reading and writing
- students become more independent
- students realize that not all in-school reading has to consist of assigned work

Reading and Writing as Part of On-Going Content Area Work

Reading and writing activities in early childhood classes are often fragmented so that students do not see that literacy skills are tools to be used in all learning. By integrating reading and writing into all content areas, teachers help students make the important realization that literacy extends beyond practicing simple reading and writing skills to encompass ways of:

- communicating with others, including experts of various sorts and the authors of books they read
- learning more about the world around them
- enhancing their own learning in other areas

Possible activities include:

- reading as part of project work in content areas
- writing, even dictation to teachers, as part of project work

Table 4–7
continued

- writing letters to authors of books that have been read or to solicit information related to other learning, as long as letters are directed toward real audiences and are actually sent
- writing as demonstrations of comprehension in reading work
- writing notes and process reports of independent work or small-group work to keep track of what they are doing and learning; this includes individual log entries

Assigned Writing for Young Learners

Children in emergent literacy classes benefit from freewriting and from more structured writing activities. Teachers must attend to developmental and motivational differences in assigned writing tasks and must be aware that some students may not readily draw on background experiences as sources of topics and ideas for their work. Assigning specific writing activities encourages students to practice their skills but also establishes habits and discipline for ongoing development. Possible writing activities include:

- daily or regular writing in logs or journals, as discussed above
- sustained silent writing, as discussed above
- periodic assignments to write a story or write a letter, as long as the assignments are clearly stated and within the grasp of the students
- regular "assignments" in writing in preparation for peer or teacher conferences or "author's chair" sessions (see Chapter 9)
- writing with a friend

Assigned Reading for Young Learners

Children should read extensively both books of their own choice and books that the teacher selects. Instruction in supportive reading groups provides skills for independent reading and gives children confidence to read on their own. Appropriate tasks require reading in real texts, that is, in books or magazines, not in workbooks or on worksheets. Possible reading activities include:

- sustained silent reading, as discussed above
- browsing through a book shared in big-book format
- sharing a big book in small groups, often "playing school"
- doing "research" for small-group or class projects
- reading in preparation for a conference with a teacher
- reading with a friend, for recreation, or to complete an assignment
- reading with a student from a higher grade
- reading in preparation for small-group work with the teacher
- reading to complete independent comprehension assignments

SUMMARY

Bombarded by print in their environments, young children are curious about how reading and writing work and what role these skills can serve in their young lives. This curiosity leads to initial experimentation and hypothesizing and eventually to rudimentary but often accurate assumptions about literacy behaviors. The literacy curriculum offered to young learners must support and extend this curiosity; it must build on what children have figured out for themselves and help them refine their basic conceptualizations. For this to happen, classrooms must be lively places, full of opportunities for children to experiment with literacy, make mistakes, and fix up their emerging skills. No actual curriculum can be outlined, but experiences, activities, and attitudes of support and encouragement should prevail. Guided by their knowledge of how children learn, sensitive to what children bring with them to school, and aware of the basic elements of reading and writing that children must master, teachers in emerging literacy classrooms guide, prod, nudge, celebrate, and extol children's growth in skills and understandings.

QUESTIONS AND TASKS

1. Be sure that you understand these terms:
   a. bedtime storybook learning cycle
   b. big books
   c. emergent literacy
   d. environmental print
   e. language experience approach (LEA)
   f. supportive reading groups
   g. zone of proximal development

2. Arrange to observe an early childhood classroom (kindergarten to grade two). Make notes about the environment, the classroom climate, and the activities in which students engage. Your observations summary should be as objective as possible. Compare your experience with those of others in your class, and in your discussion, bring in your personal responses to the classroom you observed.

3. Brainstorm to come up with ideas for opportunities to model a love of reading and writing in emergent literacy classes. Think of as many opportunities as you can. Also brainstorm opportunities to model the functional uses of reading and writing. Compare the lists to see how they overlap.

4. In pairs, role-play teacher and parent. The situation is a parent conference. The parent is asking for clarification about how much "play" is going on, how little work children seem to be doing, and all the "misspellings"

that appear on the work displayed around the room and the work brought home by the parent's child. The teacher's task is to explain and reassure the parent. Together, critique the interaction and decide how it could have been handled differently.

Development of Literacy Skills

T his chapter discusses how students grow as literacy users. We can think of this progression as movement from emergent to early and finally to fluent reading. This refinement happens as students practice their skills through activities that make sense to them and that challenge them. In most cases, language learners "learn by really using language, not by going through exercises in artificial language-like activities. Just as babies learn to talk by really talking, by really asking for more water (not practicing so they can then ask for more when they're older), children learn to read by really reading . . . and to write by really writing. . . . They don't learn by 'practicing' reading and writing. Nor do they have to wait to use written language until they have 'mastered' the skills" (Edelsky, Altwerger, & Flores, 1991, p. 16).

Literacy growth during the elementary school years involves many complex interactions between teachers, students, and texts. Essentially, students learn from two sources. The first is their own, self-motivated, ongoing discoveries of literacy principles and of the purposes, functions, and mechanics of reading and writing. The second source of students' information about literacy is their meaningful interactions with thoughtful, knowledgeable literacy users, both in and out of school. Often the most significant literacy user in learners' lives is their teacher.

The task before teachers in both primary and later grades is to maintain a balance between support and challenge that facilitates students' optimal growth. Students need to learn to work independently and to use reading and writing to learn. Aspects of the emergent literacy classroom should carry over to classes for older students. Teachers continue to model, discuss, and verbalize literacy procedures; they also continue to let kids mess up and are there to help them learn how to fix up their messes or to provide the direct instruction that will help students progress.

Undergirding teachers' decision making and instructional planning is a strong awareness that literacy learning occurs in a social context. Students must be initiated into a learning community in which they feel a comfortable accord with their teacher and peers. Frank Smith (1988) refers to this as "joining the literacy club." Smith (1992) wrote: "Children must learn [to read] from people: from the teachers (formal and informal) who initiate them into the readers' club and from the authors whose writing they read. It is the *relationships* that exist within the classroom that matter: students' relationships with teachers and with each other and their relationships with what they are supposed to be learning—with reading and writing" (p. 440).

Instruction is essential if learners are to grow and mature as literacy users. Durkin (1990) proposed a cogent description of what is needed: "Instruction refers to what someone or something does or says that has the potential to teach one or more individuals what they do not know, do not understand, or cannot do. . . . [S]uccessful instruction is a realization of the potential achieved by such means as imparting information, citing examples and nonexamples, making comparisons, raising questions, modeling, and so forth" (p. 472). Durkin's comment echoes Vygotsky's (1962) construct of a zone of proximal development, the critical time span in a learner's mastery of new concepts, strategies, and skills during which collaboration with someone more expert is essential for ongoing learning. That expert, often a teacher, asks the right questions, provides necessary information, or challenges the learner just enough to move him or her forward smoothly and independently.

As they think about literacy instruction, teachers need to remember what may at first seem a contradiction. Lessons should function holistically, but they should also consist of three distinct parts. To ensure that lessons function holistically, an instructional interchange between teachers and students must be meaningful, unified, and coherent; students must feel that they are engaged in a meaningful experience that will serve some purpose in advancing their learning. In other words, teachers must offer instruction that flows smoothly and does not appear fragmented.

Instruction should also be divided into three parts to reflect the actual phases of many literacy activities. For reading, the components are prereading, during-reading, and post-reading instruction. Each phase helps students learn how they should tackle reading tasks in general by guiding them through specific pieces of text. Students perform particular behaviors at each juncture of their reading and gain feedback on their performance. For writing, instruction is usually offered in the prewriting phase, to be followed by independent or collaborative work during the actual writing phase (see Chapter 9). Additional instruction is often provided during the post-writing phase. Table 5–1 provides more information about the three phases of literacy instruction.

In addition to conceptualizing instruction as a three-part but holistic interchange between students and teachers, teachers must incorporate into their instruction certain assumptions about learning to read and write. Among these assumptions is the idea that students need more than isolated skills if they are to be competent literacy users. Skills, in this sense, are learned procedures for solving specific reading and writing puzzles; they have usually been introduced, explained, and practiced separately. It is also essential that students master many strategies that they can use during reading and writing. Essentially, individual skills become automatic with time and are combined into clusters of strategies that literacy users can flexibly and purposefully activate, adjust, and modify as needed to meet challenges presented by reading and writing tasks. Faced with a challenge, literacy users "run through" a series of strategic behaviors to find the one that will help them accomplish their tasks. This process represents the self-directed and self-regulatory nature of competent literacy use; it also represents a goal toward which children should be encouraged to strive. Achieving this goal takes time and effort (and attention to instruction); it is part of the overall developmental pattern of reading and writing growth. Other assumptions about literacy are listed in Table 5–2.

WHAT STUDENTS MUST LEARN TO DO

The continuing momentum of learning from emergent literacy classrooms propels most children to gain competency in many areas. In a continually supportive classroom, they learn when and how to use various strategies to make sense from and with print.

Vocabulary and Word Recognition

The danger in discussing instruction in vocabulary and word recognition strategies is the risk of oversimplifying what reading and writing actually are. Reading involves much more than recognizing words; writing entails more than putting down any word that will make sense in a particular context. But having a deep and broad vocabulary and knowing many strategies to identify unfamiliar words are essential for literacy growth.

For the purpose of this chapter, "vocabulary" is defined globally as the storehouse of words an individual can use correctly in speaking and writing and can

Table 5–1
Three Stages of Literacy Activities

Pre-Reading Behaviors
- Using clues from text (e.g., pictures, title) to determine what aspects of background knowledge to activate
- Using clues from text to make predictions about content and/or story line
- Using knowledge of the structure of expository or narrative text to form a preliminary set of expectations about how material will be presented
- Setting a purpose for reading, either because of own interests or instincts or in response to an assignment
- Determining an appropriate reading rate to accommodate the nature of the material, the context in which reading will take place, and one's purpose for reading

During-Reading Behaviors
- Confirming the accuracy of one's predictions
- Modifying predictions or making new ones
- Using context as much as possible to determine unfamiliar words
- Monitoring one's comprehension (see Chapters 8 and 9)
- Adjusting reading rate as needed
- Making notes, graphic organizers, or other records of what one is reading, as required by individual purpose for reading

Post-Reading Behaviors
- Confirming predictions
- Adjusting preconceived ideas on basis of what has been read
- Summarizing
- Recognizing bias, author's purpose, tone, etc.; rejecting ideas as appropriate
- Assimilating new information into existing knowledge
- Rereading as needed to clarify comprehension
- Following up on reading by writing or talking about what has been read

recognize in print and in speech. This includes both denotative meanings—those found in the dictionary—and connotative meanings—the specialized, technical, implied or personal meanings that words often come to have. Knowing words—being able to recognize and produce their graphic representation—is crucial for literacy; but more important is the understanding that words convey their meaning through context.[1] "Learning a word means learning the meaning *potential* for

---

[1]This is no less true for students learning English as a second language. They should be supported in their efforts to build upon existing communicative skills in their first language as they expand their competence in English. Young ESL students may be learning "instructional vocabulary" in English for the first time; older students will probably know much of this kind of communication in their first language and will need to make bridges between what they know and the new terminology they are seeking to master. Instruction to enhance ESL students' vocabularies in general can be very beneficial as long as the context for word use is clearly indicated and students are not being asked to learn words in isolation.

Table 5–1
continued

Pre-Writing Behaviors

- Generating ideas
- Brainstorming with others
- Making notes, graphic organizers, or other aids
- Engaging in writing-to-learn activities (see Chapter 9)
- Making preliminary rough drafts
- Making initial decisions about intended audience, tone, style, etc.
- Setting a purpose for writing

During-Writing Behaviors

- Working independently
- Conferencing with others (see Chapter 9)
- Working through initial ideas, adjusting and modifying as needed
- Organizing and reorganizing ideas
- Monitoring the development of the piece by reading and rereading
- Adding new ideas as needed to convey meaning

Post-Writing Behaviors

- Editing, revising, reading, and rereading
- Sharing works-in-progress and nearly-finished pieces with others
- Making sense of peers' and teacher's critiques
- Adjusting piece to convey meaning more effectively
- Correcting grammatical and spelling errors
- "Going public" with finished pieces of writing

While these behaviors may seem second nature to skilled literacy users, students need help developing proficiency at each stage of their reading and writing processes. The three-part model of literacy behavior should be reflected in instructional planning.

---

that word—the possible meanings connected with various social settings. . . . Knowing the word 'table' means knowing its meaning in context: for example, 'table the discussion,' 'check the water table,' 'table and chairs'. . . . There are no context-free, static meanings of words when language is actually *used*" (Edelsky, Altwerger, & Flores, 1991, pp. 32–33).

The most effective way for students to enhance their vocabulary is through reading, but they must often have guidance to do this successfully (Nagy, 1988). Traditionally, teachers introduced "new" words before conducting reading lessons, regardless of whether the words were actually familiar to students. Students essentially were to learn the words in isolation from context. There are three far more appropriate ways to help students increase their vocabularies.

The first way involves teachers' letting students try to figure out words themselves as they read, while at the same time staying alert to help students overcome

Table 5–2
Assumptions About Literacy Acquisition

1. Learning to read and write does not involve learning a series of discrete, isolated skills. Instead, students learn to build meaning from and with print, and they learn strategies to help in this process as they grow in competence.

2. Students learn to read and write from contact with more mature literacy users, from instruction, and from their own explorations of literacy.

3. Without sacrificing instruction, students should be encouraged to develop literacy strategies on their own. For example, "new" words do not have to be presented in a lockstep fashion before students read an unfamiliar piece of text; instead, students should try to figure out words on their own.

4. Reading and writing are related and should be learned together. Students do not have to be fully proficient as readers before they can write successfully.

5. Students must learn to draw upon graphophonemic (letter-sound), semantic (word meaning), and syntactic (grammatical) cues as they read. As they write, they orchestrate these cues to express meaning.

6. Reading competency increases as students encounter a wide range of authentic reading materials. Writing improves through engagement in varied, authentic writing tasks.

7. As students read and write, they must draw extensively on their background knowledge to help them construct meaning.

8. Students learn most successfully when their tasks are authentic. They should read in real literature and be asked to write to real audiences and for real purposes.

frustration about those words they cannot decode independently. For this procedure to be successful, students must know about context clues, which are discussed in the next section. The process is really simple. Prior to a reading lesson, the teacher tries to identify words that will be difficult, words that have unusual meanings, or words that are interesting. During reading group, students read orally or silently *as much of the text as they can.* The teacher helps students during the reading and later helps them hone in on words that merit attention. Instruction and discussion about vocabulary are interwoven in the reading itself, where definitions and word identification skills can be seen as most meaningful.

The second way to help students gain large, useful vocabularies is to encourage them to read broadly (Nagy, 1988). As they read material that interests and challenges them, they figure out words on their own, truly make them a part of their reading, writing, and often speaking vocabularies, and gain confidence in their strategies for figuring out words independently.

The third way is through focused activities such as semantic (or concept) mapping (Heimlich & Pittleman, 1986). In this procedure, a topic or theme is written in the center of what will be the map; students then brainstorm as many ideas as they can that relate to the topic or theme in the form of descriptive phrases or individual words. Initial ideas are written on spokes radiating from the center, with finer details added as relationships emerge. This kind of an activity can be used by itself or during the prereading phase of instruction. It works equally well for story themes (e.g., friendship, loneliness) and topics of content area work. It can also help students generate ideas as a pre-writing activity. This procedure increases students' listening, speaking, reading, and writing vocabularies and also enhances their abilities to think widely about how concepts are related. A sample is presented in Figure 5–1, and more information about graphic organizers in general is presented in Chapter 9.

Figure 5–1
Example of Mapping as a Way to Increase Vocabulary

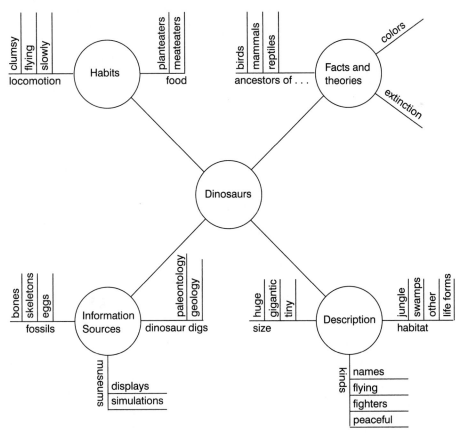

Students brainstorm ideas about the central concept, term, or idea. The teacher or a designated recorder writes the ideas on spokes of the map. As ideas are shared and recorded, students see the many aspects related to the central idea. As a result, their abilites to conceptualize, generate ideas, see interrelations, and use precise vocabulary all expand.

Word Analysis Strategies

Students need to master skills for analyzing words that they cannot recognize at sight or spell immediately, and they need to develop to the point where they use these skills automatically as part of their strategic literacy behaviors. There are two main categories of clues that can be used to mediate word recognition: the *phonetic and structural cues* that words present and the *context* in which words appear in text.

Phonics instruction traditionally has focused on teaching students to match letters and sounds as much as possible and to accommodate words with irregular features such as silent letters. Instruction on structural analysis (syllabication, word parts, root words, affixes, and so forth) has also been narrow in its focus. Because both forms of instruction have often stressed "skills" in isolation from continuous, meaningful prose, students learning under such instruction may miss some key concepts in word analysis strategies. First, they may not recognize fully that the words they are "studying" are in fact words that are part of their speaking vocabularies. Second, students may not make the connection between information about letter-sound correspondences and word parts as used in reading and the role this information can play in their writing. Finally, students may fail to see the very real importance of knowing letter-sound correspondences and structural analysis as part of their total set of literacy behaviors. This importance ought not to be underrated (Newman & Church, 1990; Adams, 1990).

The major failing of much direct instruction in word analysis strategies is lack of responsiveness to what students know and need. Some students will benefit from carefully paced, scaffolded instruction in a variety of strategies, while others may thrive with only support as they figure out a set of strategies largely on their own. Teachers who observe students as they read and write and who conduct conferences on a regular basis will be able to identify students' needs and offer instruction directed to keep them moving forward in their literacy growth.

When teachers realize that they cannot depend fully on commercial materials to teach phonic and structural analysis, they face the question of how to offer the best possible instruction. The answer goes back to the role of teachers as observers of children and decision makers within their own classrooms. By determining aspects of phonics and structural analysis that students will probably be able to figure out on their own from their ongoing reading and those that lend themselves to whole-class instruction, teachers can provide focused, meaningful instruction. Teachers also need to identify individual problem areas that can be addressed in focused small-group or one-on-one instruction. Variables such as students' dominant language (if other than English), regional or nonstandard dialects, and previous instruction influence how teachers plan for each class.

If instruction in phonetic and structural analysis is to be helpful, students must see their value. Instruction must make sense, practice activities must be meaningful and be embedded in pieces of real text, and mastery of the skills, strategies, and concepts presented must be viewed as worthwhile. Without underestimating the extent to which students can in fact figure out the "mechanics" of reading and writing on their own, teachers must plan mini-lesson and small-group instruction for aspects of phonics and structural analysis that are not easy to generalize from extensive reading and writing. Rules of syllabication, many silent letters, irregular vowel constructions, or the use of suffixes and prefixes are examples.

Instructional sessions, which should be kept relatively short, should provide many examples and engage students in interactive practice with real words presented in sentences and paragraphs. Teachers might use a "think aloud" process to demonstrate how specific strategies can be applied to figure out words so that students understand the nature and purpose of what they are teaching (see Chapter 9). Doing so demystifies the process students need to master. As students listen to the think aloud, they gain strategies for self-questioning to monitor their own progress. They not only see that talking one's way through reading and writing is appropriate behavior but also learn to determine points at which this self-talk can be most valuable.

Teachers also use prompting as students struggle to learn new skills. A prompt is a helpful comment or question that gives students the information they need at the time they need it to continue with a task. A teacher might supply a word that has baffled a student or direct the student to read to the end of the line to take advantage of context clues. Prompting helps shape students' self-regulatory and monitoring processes because, like think alouds, they convey to students that it is really all right not to know a word immediately and to have to reread or edit one's writing, and that there are many ways to solve puzzling aspects of reading and writing.

To be beneficial, instruction should balance what students know, what they need to know, and what they are ready to understand. For example, a teacher might decide to offer direct instruction of homophones during a mini-lesson. The decision to do so might stem from either of two sources: first, awareness that students are misspelling such words in their writing and need to have some clarification about the words, or, second, from the teacher's perception that the students are *ready* to make sense of this instruction. In either case, presenting the new information should provide students with necessary tools to use in both reading and writing work. Homophones may also be taught during a small group lesson to students who are ready to learn about them or to an individual child who consistently confuses *their*, *they're*, and *there*.

Appendix B provides reference material about letter-sound correspondences, aspects of word structure, and other components of word analysis that will be helpful to teachers planning instruction and observing students' progress. It also provides a sequence of questions students should ask themselves as they attempt to apply word analysis strategies.

Using Context Clues

Learning to use context to figure out unfamiliar words is an important step toward reading independence. When readers use context clues, they look at the words surrounding an unfamiliar word and try to arrive at a possible meaning for the word. The meaning is "possible" rather than definite because readers must compare their guess against the rest of the text to see if it makes sense. If it does not make sense, they know that they have determined the meaning inappropriately or have misunderstood what they have been reading. But even if the word seems to make sense, there is no guarantee that the context clues have yielded a correct meaning. Only continued reading and monitoring of comprehension will really confirm the reader's guess.

While learning to use context clues is important, there are certain limitations to their use. First, when the target word is relatively technical or specialized, the context in which it appears may not help readers determine a meaning simply because the meaning of the word is the focal point of the sentence in which it appears. The use of context clues is also limited when the target word is a low frequency word or the particular definition required in the sentence is infrequently used. Table 5–3 summarizes the kinds of context clues readers can often find in text.

Text Structure

Proficient readers are aware of the various ways in which ideas can be arranged in texts and of the nature of the relationships among those ideas. These aspects of text can be referred to as *text structure*. They include the actual ways in which ideas are organized in various kinds of text and the many aspects of text listed in Table 5–4.

As students learn about text structure and learn to apply what they have learned, they must distinguish between narrative and expository texts. Narrative texts—most often in the form of stories—comprise much of the literature to which children are initially exposed. If children know about the parts of stories and the usual sequence in which events are arranged, they are better able to anticipate and comprehend the cumulative information presented in the narrative texts they either hear or read themselves. They are also better able to focus on parts of the stories they encounter because they have confidence in how the parts will be arranged and developed.

Teachers can help students understand narratives by reading to them and talking about the stories, by discussing stories students read independently, by assisting students in writing their own narrative pieces, and by presenting story maps and other appropriate graphic organizers (discussed in Chapter 9). As teachers talk about stories and lead students in discussing what they have read and written, they should use appropriate story-related language. Mastery of the vocabulary and concepts related to narratives helps students be more precise in their discussions and more thorough in their comprehension. Terminology provides "hooks" on which to "hang" an emerging sense of story. As students use these terms and gain greater understanding of their meaning, they gain insight into the overarching central organizational patterns of stories and novels. As will be discussed in later chapters, they can use this insight to better understand and recall concepts about narratives and to extend their comprehension through critical analysis and evaluation of what they have read. Their growing understanding of

Table 5–3
Using Context Clues

Kinds of Context Clues

Definitions. In sentences that contain forms of the verb *to be* or the word *called* or similar constructions, they provide definitions of words.

Example: A context clue is a means by which readers can often figure out the meaning of unfamiliar words.

Adjectives or other modifiers. In sentences that contain single words, phrases, or clauses that modify unfamiliar words, they provide clues to meaning. Predicate adjectives and relative clauses are especially useful.

Example: Using context clues, which are parts of sentences that help readers figure out unfamiliar words, is a beneficial reading strategy.

Examples. In sentences that contain terms such as *for example*, *such as*, *like*, and similar expressions, they suggest meanings.

Example: The meaning of unfamiliar words can sometimes be determined by using context clues; for example, a relative clause modifying the unfamiliar word will often suggest a definition.

Restatement, Conjunctives, and Appositives. In sentences that contain appositives, direct restatements, terms such as *in other words* or *that is*, or constructions with parentheses or dashes, can provide clues to meaning.

Example: Appositives, a restatement set off by commas from the word or term held in apposition, are often good sources of context clues.

Example: Appositives, that is, restatements set off by commas from the word or term held in apposition, are often good sources of context clues.

Meaning by Generalization or Application of Knowledge about Text Structure. Often, the entire sentence or paragraph, rather than a particular grammatical construction, will suggest a meaning for an unfamiliar word. Readers should look for parallel sentences that supplement each other, repetition of key words that cumulatively provide a meaning of an unfamiliar word, or implied connectives expressed in compound or complex sentences.

Example: Although context clues can be very useful, they are only one of the strategies readers have to figure out the meanings of unfamiliar words.

---

how authors structure narratives then enhances their own writing. Meek (1982) maintained that knowledge of various aspects of narrative ". . . are exclusive literary skills that come from a literary culture. They are exclusive in that inexperienced readers do not share them and are puzzled by them. They are not taught in exercises or practice. They are part of the author's way of telling his story and sometimes a teacher draws attention to them if she thinks the [students] have not understood what is happening" (pp. 155-156). Table 5–4 presents the basic story structure.

Table 5–4
Information About Text Structure

Basic Components of Narratives

Stories usually consist of the following components:

- *Theme* is what the story is about in terms of the main ideas (concrete level), and the abstract theme that transcends the story itself (e.g., friendship, revenge).
- *Setting* is where the story takes place.
- *Characters* are who is in the story.
- *Problems/Goals* are what the characters are trying to do, or must confront: challenges and obstacles to be overcome, mysteries to be solved, and so forth. The story will be focused around this component.
- *Major events* are what happen as characters seek to solve their problems or achieve their goals.
- *Resolution* is how the problem is finally solved.
- *Conclusion* is how everything turns out at the end.

Stories usually consist of (but are not limited to) the following kinds of paragraphs:

- *Descriptive paragraphs* provide description and details and do not advance the story line.
- *Transitional paragraphs* indicate a change in ideas, characters, or setting. Sometimes they indicate that time has elapsed. They often include signals, such as "And then who should come along but . . .?" or "Later that month, . . ."
- *Concluding paragraphs* bring the piece to an end, often by telling what has happened to the main characters.

Basic Structural Patterns for Expository Text

Expository material, which serves to provide information or discuss ideas, usually consists of the following kinds of paragraphs:

- *Introductory paragraphs* begin a whole section or introduce new ideas within a section of a text.
- *Explanatory paragraphs* provide information, tell about, explain, inform, or provide support for an author's premise. They may be full of details or facts.
- *Descriptive paragraphs* provide description and details.
- *Definitional paragraphs* usually do not add new information but help readers understand the terms or concepts that an author is presenting.
- *Transitional paragraphs* indicate a change in ideas or sometimes introduce a

---

Because so much early childhood literature consists of stories, students in elementary school are often unfamiliar with expository text structure (Winograd & Bridge, 1986). As a result, they often have difficulty with nonfiction trade books, reference books, materials such as pamphlets and newspaper articles, and content area textbooks. The organizational patterns or structure of expository texts will vary depending on the content area, but as children broaden their reading range both in independent and study reading, they need to learn to gather information

Table 5–4
continued

new idea. They often include signals, such as "in other words" or "another way to look at this point is. . . ."
- *Concluding paragraphs* bring the piece to an end, often by summarizing the author's points.

Expository material is most often presented in one of these organizational patterns:
- *Generalization*: a broad statement presented and supported in subsequent sentences and paragraphs through examples, details, explanations, or reasons. This is very close to the traditional main idea kind of presentation of information.
- *Enumeration* involves the use of a topic statement that is presented in the first paragraph and is then followed by several subordinate statements or paragraphs that elaborate and provide additional information. Signal words include "another," "also," "additionally," and so forth.
- *Sequence* is an organizational pattern that presents ideas, procedures, events, etc., in a specific order. Sequence may be confused with enumeration, but the order of presentation is essential for accurate comprehension.
- *Comparison/Contrast* shows how an idea or ideas are compared (how they are similar) and/or contrasted (how they are different). Signal words such as "but," "although," or "yet" are sometimes used.
- *Cause/Effect* shows one idea, event, or procedure in relationship to another, often in a specific sequence. The effect is usually subordinate to or dependent upon the cause. Separate paragraphs may be used to present causes and effects, requiring readers to infer relationships. Signal words include "If . . . then."
- *Pro/Con* shows relationships. Two opposing points of view, reasons, attitudes, or opinions are presented. Signal words set up the contrast, e.g., "another view . . . ," "then again, . . ." and so forth.
- *Question/Answer* involves posing a question directly or indirectly and then answering it. Answers may be simple or elaborate and may present different interpretations of the questions. Signal words often introduce embedded clauses, such as "why," "how," "when," or "what."

Awareness of different patterns of text structure helps students become stronger readers. This awareness also enriches their writing, for they are able to write in more varied, creative, and precise ways.

from expository materials and to perceive the underlying logical arrangements of diverse forms of text. The most common organizational patterns are described in Table 5–4, which also includes the basic understandings that students must gain about expository texts.

Helping students understand expository text structure involves close inspection of the various organizational patterns encountered in the material students read. For example, teachers might present a lesson on the organizational aids included in a chapter—headings, subheadings, marginal notes, highlighting, and so forth. Additional instructional sessions could address each of the various organization patterns described in Table 5–4, with follow-up readings to reinforce students' understanding. Students might also use information from texts to fill out graphic organizers, which are discussed fully and illustrated in Chapter 9. These will give them a clear outline of the relationships presented in texts and help them better perceive the structure underlying the words they actually read.

Students should be encouraged to write expository material as well as stories. They may begin simply by describing experiences or objects in factual, straightforward ways. They can move toward more extensive writing projects and even master skills for developing research projects. Chapter 9 elaborates on this kind of writing.

HELPING STUDENTS BECOME MATURE READERS AND WRITERS

There are many skills that students can learn as early as elementary school that will help them to become mature readers and writers. These include study reading strategies, research and reference skills, and library skills.

Learning Study Reading Strategies

In an elementary school context, the term *study reading* refers to behaviors that students can use consciously to help them perform their literacy tasks efficiently and effectively. These behaviors become increasingly important as students are expected to read longer content area material on their own. As they learn strategies for negotiating their way through reading and writing, many students develop study reading strategies on their own; however, direct instruction can help students apply their various strategies independently.

The study reading strategies that are appropriate for elementary school students will help them do three things:

1. Prepare themselves for reading tasks.
2. Keep track of what they are reading.
3. Review their reading work.

As part of their pre-reading behaviors, students prepare themselves for reading by setting a purpose for their reading, determining the reading rate they will use to gain the most from the text, activating background knowledge about what they will read, and formulating questions to guide their study. Teachers should not assume that students know how to vary their purposes for reading and reading modes; students have to be taught these skills. Typically, when students read in school, their purpose is immediate: enjoyment, information, answers to a set of questions, and so forth. Study reading requires students to synthesize new information and assimilate it into what they already know about a topic. Students must set a more complex purpose for reading if their goal is to learn and remember over time.

Activating prior knowledge is an important part of successful reading. Students must learn to "quiz" themselves about what they know about the topic they will study so that they bring prior learning from long-term memory. Thus, new learning will enrich what students already know.

To be successful study readers, students may need to read more slowly and methodically than when they are reading for pleasure. This idea may seem very strange to elementary school students who are only just beginning to perceive their reading abilities as a unified set of behaviors over which they have some control.

Students also need to learn to formulate questions to guide their reading. Instruction may begin with a set of generic questions that students can ask about almost any piece of text:

1. What do I expect to find out?
2. How will this material be different from other pieces I have read?
3. What will happen or what will I learn?

Teachers help students develop more focused questions by directing attention to the title and illustrations of the material they will read. Students learn to make predictions about what they will encounter and to pose questions that they want to answer. Such questions guide their progress through their texts. Teachers might use the following instructional sequence: teachers present a series of model questions, students read silently, and then teachers and students discuss the reading selection in terms of the questions posed at the beginning and the components of text that provided answers. At the next session, teachers might pose some questions and elicit others from the students; again silent reading is followed by discussion and reference back to the text. Throughout, teachers emphasize integration of previously learned and new content or ideas. Eventually, teachers guide students in generating their own questions based on what they know about the text they will read and on graphic clues such as headings, charts, or other textual aids. As students get the "feel" of what they are supposed to do in different reading situations, they more readily practice these behaviors independently.

The most effective ways to help students understand the procedures for efficient reading are by teacher modeling and discussion. Initially, teachers can use scaffolding to help students understand what they must do; they then gradually introduce guided and independent practice with carefully selected, authentic pieces of different kinds of text that reflect the kinds of reading in which students will actually use the strategies that teachers are showing. Teachers might, for example, make overhead transparencies of a chapter from a social studies book and use them to model study reading procedures within the context of material students will actually have to read. The teacher would stop at appropriate places, review what had been read, monitor comprehension, formulate questions for further reading, and continue with the text—just as students should do independently.

The best ways for students to keep track of what they have read during reading is by recording entries in learning logs or journals and making graphic organizers. The more traditional approaches of taking notes and making detailed outlines tend to encourage students simply to copy what they have read almost in its entirety. In helping students learn to keep track of what they read, teachers need to emphasize how to summarize and synthesize what has just been read and what has been read over time. Learning logs or journals provide means for students to write summaries and make connections across their learning in a prose or list format. Graphic organizers help them visualize the relationships and patterns in what they read in more skeletal ways. Students might begin a graphic organizer at the start of a unit of study and refine it after each reading assignment.

Teachers can keep track of students' reading by analyzing learning logs or graphic organizers. Even in these relatively sketchy formats, teachers can see miscomprehension, faulty concept formation, or missed connections and can offer assistance to keep students on track.

Students can also keep track of their reading by self-questioning. Again, a generic list of questions can help them gain facility with this strategy:

1. What was the concept or theme or main idea in the selection just read?
2. How does it relate to other texts I have read?
3. How is it different from other texts?
4. What have I learned and what must I remember from the text I have read?
5. How does the selection just read relate to other material about the subject?
6. How has the author conveyed information about the subject?

If students learn to keep track of their reading efficiently, *reviewing* during the post-reading phase should be easy. Large- and small-group discussion is also helpful, especially if students are encouraged to refer back to their books, graphic organizers, or learning logs to check on terminology, understandings, concepts, or facts. As teachers observe and participate in review discussions, they can conduct informal assessments of students' grasp of what they have read. Teachers can then determine who might need more study, instruction, and review before taking a more formal assessment such as a test or quiz or before moving on to more difficult levels of study. These processes also help students learn to monitor their own progress realistically so that they can determine when they need to review more carefully or gain additional information before moving on.

Learning About the Library

As stressed throughout this book, the classroom library should offer many different kinds of books. Letting children help in arranging the library and keeping it orderly teaches them basic library skills, but visits to the school and public library are necessary as well.

Classroom teachers and the school librarian often can work together to develop appropriate programs for each grade level. The librarian can then introduce students, independently or in small groups, to the routines for using the library during a specially designated library period. Students should learn to use the card catalogue or any computer retrieval system and the library's methods for shelving books (Dewey Decimal or other system). They should also learn how to request help or reserve books they want to read.

The school librarian can also supplement the classroom teachers' efforts to expand students' interests in books. Reading new and unusual books to students, engaging in "book talks" about specific books, presenting arrangements of books thematically, or simply recommending certain books can all stimulate students' interest in books they have not previously encountered.

If a public library has a strong children's room, a visit there makes an excellent field trip, especially for students who need library cards. Children's librarians often have a prepared talk to orient visitors to the features of the library and will give students time to select books and check them out. As a result, students feel more comfortable and willing to return to the library on their own.

In the school or public library, students should be directed to many different kinds of books. The sooner students become accustomed to using reference materials such as encyclopedias and atlases, the more readily they will turn to them as sources of information. Collections of pictures and brochures and multimedia materials such as filmstrips or videotapes can be useful. Making students aware of the vast number of sources beyond their own immediate libraries and their textbooks helps them see the possibilities for independent reading and writing.

Learning Research and Reference Skills

Research and reference skills can be taught as part of the instruction that acclimates students to the library, as part of a separate unit, or as aspects of a long-term project. These skills are essential if students are to engage in the kind of extended research project detailed in Chapter 9. Students should become familiar with book parts: table of contents, glossary, index, and other informational sections. They should learn to use dictionaries, thesauri, atlases, yearbooks, encyclopedias, and other reference materials. Student versions of these reference materials are readily available, although teachers must be wary of student editions that present so little information and challenge that students fail to see their inherent value.

Helping students find answers to specific questions by using varied reference materials can be challenging and fun. Students see that information is contained in many different kinds of sources, and they may even realize that sources can contradict each other. As students search for facts, they begin to see more global relationships among ideas, concepts, topics, and subject areas.

Using reference materials also helps students learn new sets of reading strategies and new reading rates. Teachers should help students understand skimming and scanning skills. *Skimming* involves reading the first and last sentence of each paragraph and looking quickly at intervening lines of text; *scanning* involves quick but highly focused reading when one is looking for a specific piece of information.

But What If Students Do Not Read and Write Well?

There are no easy solutions for students who have difficulty mastering literacy skills, and methods for long-term remedial attention to these students are beyond the scope of this book. Teachers in regular classrooms, however, often must contend with students whose skills seem marginal, students who should be reading and writing better than they actually are.

One of the first issues teachers must face as they work with such students is simply knowing how to refer to them. This may seem like a minor dilemma but, in an almost philosophical sense, it is a serious concern. Students within this particular elementary school subpopulation are frequently referred to as remedial or reluctant readers, and recently are termed "at risk" for learning (Flores, Cousin, & Diaz, 1991; Pellegrini, 1991; Allington & McGill-Franzen, 1989). Categorization of students into particular groups, even for the purpose of convenient grouping and instruction within the classroom context, can quickly evolve into labeling that sticks—like the toughest glue—to students throughout their school career. This kind of categorization can also imply that someone or something is responsible for the students' situation—the students' cultural or linguistic background, their families, or perhaps the school system or teachers' interaction styles (Pellegrini, 1991). Assigning responsibility does not lead to the understanding of ways to assist children any more than labeling leads to sensitive instruction.

This book proposes an alternate descriptor in the hopes of reflecting the dynamic nature of students' acquisition of reading and writing. The term is "inexperienced." Discussing students labeled "reluctant readers," Meek (1982) wrote: "Children are never reluctant to do something they have mastered and enjoy. Usually they have not yet discovered what's in it for them, either because they don't read well enough or because they have had the wrong kind of books, or too restricted a choice. Inexperienced [literacy users] need more experience" (p. 165). Thinking of students in this way gives teachers a clear direction: to enable students to practice reading and writing in purposeful ways.

Even with a less pejorative term for students in their class, teachers may still puzzle over the origin of their difficulties. For many of these students, reading and writing simply serve no purpose. Students do not view writing as a way to communicate with the world and they do not realize that reading should be an interactive process of questioning what appears in print, finding out new information, and building increasingly sophisticated knowledge structures. This lack of appreciation of the value and purpose of literacy can result in a devastating cycle. Students who do not see value in literacy will not read and write nearly enough to gain the competence and confidence that will ensure future growth. Thus, skills may stay at a relatively unsophisticated level, and students are left farther and farther behind their peers.

A second possible cause of students' lag in literacy development may be instructional; they may simply not have had enough or appropriate instruction to help them integrate rudimentary skills into a cohesive set of behaviors for tackling increasingly difficult literacy tasks. This contention does not suggest that students need instruction in what are often loosely called the "basic skills" of phonic analysis, writing mechanics, and other subskills of literate behaviors. To go back "to basics" with these students may mean forcing them to repeat instruction that did not make sense the first time and does not make any more sense after they have had the adverse experience of not doing well as a reader or writer. A better approach is for teachers to ascertain students' strengths and weaknesses through what are often called "interactive" (Brozo, 1990) or "dynamic" (Kletzien & Bedner, 1990) assessment methods that seek to find out what students actually do know. These kinds of methods, which are discussed in detail in Chapter 3, give teachers an efficient way to gain a full picture of what students can do, what aspects of literacy are confusing to them, and what they need to learn. By knowing more than single test scores, teachers can group students effectively, provide efficient one-on-one instruction, direct students toward appropriate reading material, and make reading and writing assignments that will minimize frustration and enhance learning.

Knowing what to do to meet the needs of inexperienced literacy users is often a puzzle for teachers. As a general rule, teachers need to offer scaffolds and safety nets. Teachers must verbalize what students are to do and what is expected of them; they must help students see through the instructional language of the classroom to take ownership of a set of strategies for reading and writing. As in all good classroom settings, teachers must create an atmosphere that allows inexperienced literacy users to take risks and make mistakes, but teachers also need to be quick to teach "fix-up" strategies to help students free themselves of frustration and confusion.

This short discussion is not meant to minimize the importance of paying close attention to those students who appear to be having difficulty learning to use literacy skills productively. Teachers must work conscientiously with these students to accomplish two goals. The first goal is, of course, to help students gain needed strategies to handle literacy tasks in and out of school. Application of instructional methods discussed throughout this book can help in this goal, especially if accompanied by thorough, clear discussion of the whys and hows of each approach.

The second goal is affective and managerial: Teachers must work hard to be sure that students do not feel separated from the main literacy activities the rest of the students participate in. Inexperienced literacy users can easily "turn off" to what other students are doing and sink into a self-fulfilling cycle of failure. Their initial difficulties can magnify and become increasingly complex as they fall farther and farther behind. The workshop approach to instruction provides mechanisms for including students in as many literacy activities as possible and for offering focused small-group and one-on-one instruction. Unfortunately, a workshop environment can also allow some students to get lost until small literacy problems become large ones; teachers must guard against this phenomenon.

SUMMARY

Teachers help students become proficient literacy users when they balance support and challenge. Teacher support enables students to take the risks needed to grow, and the challenge of interesting reading and writing tasks motivates them. The most productive climate for growth is one in which students encounter authentic materials and real tasks to perform. They should read real literature and be asked to write to real audiences and for real purposes.

Teachers can help students who do not progress at expected rates by applying some of the tenets of an emergent literacy classroom. These students will benefit from forthright, supportive instruction that demystifies what they are supposed to be learning. Teachers can use scaffolds and think alouds to help students make sense of instruction and then can provide these learners with meaningful, challenging tasks appropriate for their levels.

QUESTIONS AND TASKS

1. Be sure that you understand the meaning of the following terms:
   a. context clues
   b. study reading strategies
   c. text structure (and all the terms listed in Table 5–4)
   d. three-phase instructional plan
   e. word analysis strategies

2. Find a children's short story and analyze it for its structural components. Think about the ways that the story could be used to help students understand text structure.

3. Analyze several examples of science or social studies textbooks or children's books (trade books). What structural patterns are obvious? Do any of the books seem to use a narrative pattern to present factual information? Analyze the texts for examples of signal words and specific instances where students could use context clues to assist them in their reading.

4. Try out the mapping procedure. Think about the ideas presented in this and the previous chapter and draw a map whose central idea is "The Growth of Literacy Skills." Do this activity alone and share it with someone or do it collaboratively and discuss your ideas as you develop the map.

5. If you are working in an elementary school classroom or have access to individual students, interview and spend some time with an "inexperienced" literacy user. Find out what he or she thinks reading and writing are all about. Read with the student and collect some writing samples, ideally over an extended period of time. Keep a log of your experiences to share with the student's teacher and with others in your class.

Introduction to Children's Literature

As approaches to literacy instruction change, teachers need more than
ever to be knowledgeable about children's literature. As Judith Langer
(1990b) wrote, "The teaching of literature is often misunderstood. Too
often it is considered a way to indoctrinate students into the cultural knowledge, good taste, and elitist traditions of our society, neglecting the role of literature in the development of the sharp and critical mind" (p. 812). Even if they do
not develop a full-scale literature program such as the one discussed in Chapter
7, teachers should feel comfortable introducing a wide range of literature into
their instruction. The benefits of using literature are listed and briefly discussed
in Table 6–1.

This chapter provides several perspectives on children's literature.[1] In the first section, literature is defined in terms of its basic characteristics, purposes, and function: what literature is, what it does, and why it is important. The second section presents a brief, practical overview of children's literature; references for more elaborate compendia about children's literature are provided in Appendix A. This chapter serves as background for the next chapter, which describes methods for using literature as the primary basis of reading and writing instruction.

WHAT IS LITERATURE?

A former student wrote beautifully of the importance of books in children's lives:

> I have not always been myself. Throughout my life I have been many persons. For a time, when I was very young, I was Little Red Riding Hood and I was smart enough to fool any wolf that might want to mess with me. Later in my life I was Laura Ingalls and I was very busy playing in the fields of the prairie. Growing weary of pioneer life, I moved to the city where I became Nancy Drew. I was very popular, drove my own car and even had a boyfriend who did not mind the fact that I was smarter than he. I enjoyed being all of these people and sharing in their many adventures. I was able to leave my own world and experience things which I would never see or do because of teachers and reading programs which motivated me to become involved in the wonderful world of children's literature.

Helping all learners develop an appreciation of literature is an important goal of the elementary literacy curriculum. To attain this goal, teachers must first understand what literature is. Although literature as a concept is very broad, it also has distinct parameters.

> Literature is more than a collection of unrelated poems and stories; the more we read the more obvious this becomes. Hercules and Superman were created centuries apart but they are recognizable as the same character type: the hero with magical powers. We find images like gardens and wastelands in the Old Testament and in the songs of Bob Dylan and Pete Seeger. That love is more powerful than any evil or even death itself is a theme found in stories as different as "Beauty and the Beast" and *Charlotte's Web*. We recognize the shape of the romance story in ancient epics and in today's westerns. The "good" cowboy, remarkably like the knightly hero of old, goes forth with faithful horse and trusty weapon on a quest to rid the world of evil. (Sloan, 1975, p. 17)

This quotation alludes to *attributes* or *patterns* that are common in literature from its very beginnings through today. Passed from culture to culture over time, these attributes and patterns are easily recognized in their various guises in contemporary and traditional literature. As stated in Chapter 5, specific patterns and attributes can be found in expository/nonfiction literature as well. Readers also

---

[1] The term *trade books* is often used interchangeably with *children's literature*. This term is a generic term for books other than textbooks.

Table 6–1
Advantages of Using Children's Literature

1. Literature is a pleasurable way to provide a foundation for reading instruction and growth.

2. Literature gives students experiences that they might not otherwise have. Depending on the selections they read, they can gain:
   - heightened sensitivity to people other than their neighbors, family, and immediate circle of friends
   - intellectual and aesthetic growth
   - awareness of human experiences recorded over time and an accompanying sense of the human condition, regardless of time period, locale, cultural group, and so forth

3. Literature provides both intellectual and emotional vicarious experiences.

4. Nonfiction, informational literature can expand students' knowledge base, increase their understanding of diverse areas, introduce them to new topics and ideas, and generally enhance their learning in content area subjects.

5. Literature can serve as a bridge from one content area to another. For example, students may become interested in art from the study of illustrations in picture books or may want to learn more about specific individuals from the study of biographical literature.

6. Literature about ethical issues (e.g., world peace, pollution) can foster awareness of society and promote the development of responsibility and ethics when students think critically about what they read.

7. Literature invites independent reading and group reading; it encourages students to share ideas about what they have read and to discuss connections between literature and their own lives.

8. Literature provides models of writing and thinking; it broadens students' vocabularies and awareness of language.

come to recognize specific *conventions* that authors use to manipulate attributes to achieve a specific effect or purpose. These conventions contribute to both literary unity and literary diversity; although they often vary according to *genre,* or broad category of literature, the basic conventions within each genre are essentially the same. For example, in the mystery genre, conventions usually include the commission of a crime and the discovery of clues. In a tall tale, a standard convention is a larger-than-life main character who accomplishes superhuman feats. A somber, dank, and dreary locale is a convention in a horror story. And, the use of charts, graphs, and figures in certain kinds of nonfiction is also a convention.

Children who have stories read to them gain a sense of these basic patterns of literature. Indeed, even very young children have naive generalizations about how stories work; this "story sense" becomes increasingly sophisticated as they gain experience with different genres (Applebee, 1978). Children's retelling of stories and beginning writing illustrate their awareness of story structure (Purcell-Gates,

1988). If children have not been read to, they have gained some sense of these patterns, structures, and conventions through exposure to oral story telling or even television. By the time they enter school, children are ready for literature to be part of their school experience.

An understanding of these aspects of literature, at even the lowest level, is a tangible means by which readers can increase their literary appreciation and reading comprehension. Intuitively, children anticipate a particular kind of structure in what they hear and read, much like benchmarks that guide comprehension. Knowing more or less what the structure of discourse will be, children concentrate on the act of constructing meaning, that is, comprehending text. This process makes sense to them, becomes easier with practice, and reinforces a sense of competency as they listen more intently, read more enthusiastically, and eventually use these structures in their own writing. Thus, reading widely can be considered the best method to strengthen reading skills because the more students read, the more they appreciate the common elements of all literature and the more they perceive themselves as capable of in-depth comprehension.

As mentioned in Chapter 5, much of the awareness that children bring to their initial experiences with literature stems from exposure to stories. Some critics and theorists cite the story, or narrative, as a fundamental part of young children's acclimation to their world. However, the pre-eminence of stories causes a certain tension because children steeped in narratives may have difficulty adjusting to reading tasks in other kinds of literature (Winograd & Bridge, 1986). This speaks to the need to introduce students, as part of their early experiences with literature, to a broad range of expository text using nonfiction books. Exposure to nonfiction books can help students perceive the structural characteristics specific to nonfiction books, so that they can comprehend a full range of literature. However, some nonfictional, informational books for children are written in a distinctly narrative style (Rosenblatt, 1991).

Finding and Evaluating Literature for Children

Several criteria for evaluating children's literature cut across all age levels and genre; other criteria pertain to specific kinds of books and stories, purposes for use, and children's developmental levels. Adults selecting books and stories to present to or share with children should consider the questions presented in Table 6–2.

Information about children's literature is available from many sources. There are several excellent compendia that are updated frequently (Huck, Hepler, & Hickman, 1987; Norton, 1991; Stewig, 1988). Journals such as *The Reading Teacher, The Journal of Reading,* and *The New Advocate* offer reviews of current books, as does the *New York Times Book Review.* The International Reading Association and The Children's Book Council provide yearly summaries of recent books, and several excellent bibliographies are readily available (see Appendix A).

Even software is available to help students and teachers select books. *Bookwiz*™ (Educational Testing Service, 1990) asks children a series of questions to determine

Table 6–2
General Criteria for Evaluating Children's Literature

1. Is the work developmentally and conceptually appropriate for its intended purpose and audience? Are concepts, vocabulary, or language patterns too difficult? Does the work seem to assume more background knowledge than the students probably possess?

2. Is the work well-illustrated? Do illustrations contribute to the effectiveness? Are illustrations consistent with the work?

3. Is the book sturdy and attractive? Will it withstand handling by many students?

4. Does the work compare favorably to others that concern the same topic or are of the same sort? How has the work been reviewed—by professional reviewers, by other teachers, and by students?

5. Are all characters and situations presented fairly and without stereotyping?

6. Is the work *good*? Is it accurate, current, objective, honest, nonsexist, and nonracist? Is it well-written? Is the point of view appropriate to the purpose of the book?

reading preferences. It then draws on a database of more than 1,000 books spread over three different levels to suggest titles and provide brief summaries of books that might interest students. Teachers and students can add books and comments to the database. A sample screen from *Bookwiz*™ is presented in Figure 6–1.

OVERVIEW OF CHILDREN'S LITERATURE

The categories of children's literature discussed in this section have been selected to orient teachers to using literature in their classrooms. Because of sources such as *Bookwiz*™ and references included in Appendix A, this chapter offers only a brief overview of this extensive topic.

Picture Books

The first books that most children encounter, including squeezable bath and toy books, can be categorized as *picture books*. Picture books may be of many sorts: Mother Goose and nursery rhyme books, number books, alphabet books, concept development books, wordless books, and simple story or informational books. Illustrations in these books complement and enhance the short text and carry much of the message, instruction, or story line. Text is more prominent in *picture storybooks*, in which text and illustrations are integrated, but the story itself cannot be garnered through the pictures alone. Table 6–3 lists the kinds of books that can be categorized as picture books and cites criteria for evaluating this genre.

Although the overarching purposes of picture books are to provide pleasure and to introduce children to literature, their usefulness extends much further

Figure 6–1
Sample Screen from *Bookwiz*™

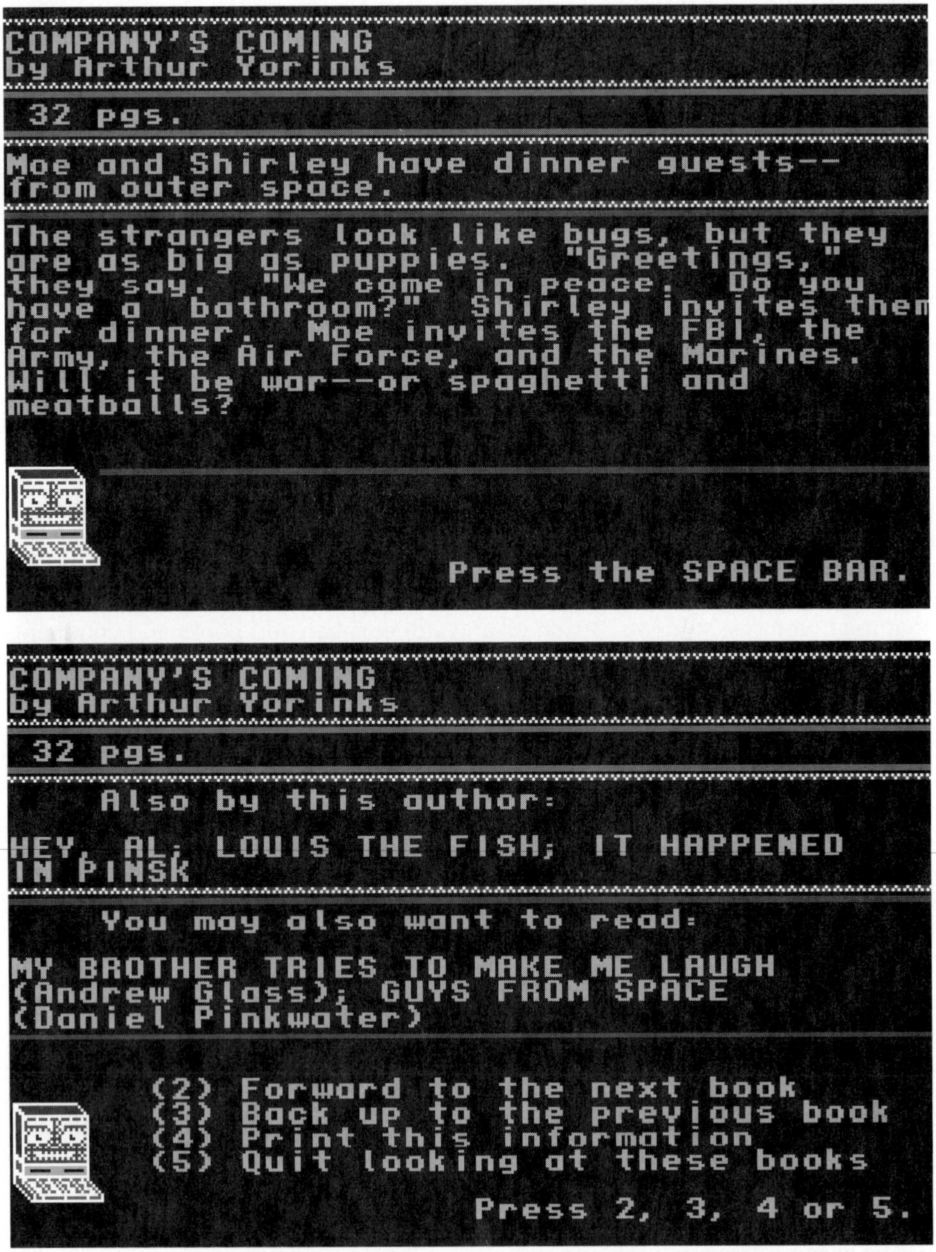

```
COMPANY'S COMING
by Arthur Yorinks

  32 pgs.

Moe and Shirley have dinner guests--
from outer space.

The strangers look like bugs, but they
are as big as puppies.  "Greetings,"
they say.  "We come in peace.  Do you
have a  bathroom?"  Shirley invites them
for dinner.  Moe invites the FBI, the
Army, the Air Force, and the Marines.
Will it be war--or spaghetti and
meatballs?



                        Press the SPACE BAR.
```

```
COMPANY'S COMING
by Arthur Yorinks

  32 pgs.

    Also by this author:

HEY, AL; LOUIS THE FISH; IT HAPPENED
IN PINSK

    You may also want to read:

MY BROTHER TRIES TO MAKE ME LAUGH
(Andrew Glass); GUYS FROM SPACE
(Daniel Pinkwater)

         (2) Forward to the next book
         (3) Back up to the previous book
         (4) Print this information
         (5) Quit looking at these books
                   Press 2, 3, 4 or 5.
```

From Bookwiz™ software. Copyright 1991 by Educational Testing Service, Princeton, NJ. Used with permission.

Table 6–3
Evaluating Picture Books

Illustrations

- Are the pictures necessary to tell the story or teach the concept or skill emphasized in the book? Do they contribute to the book's effectiveness?
- Are they aesthetically pleasing, uncluttered, clearly defined? If pictures are murky or faded, is there a definite reason for this style?

Text of Books that Tell Stories

- Is the text developmentally appropriate for students of the age for which it is intended?
- Is there a recognizable theme? Are characters, setting, and plot introduced and developed appropriately?
- Is the story realistic in terms of all story elements, including dialogue? If the story is fanciful, do story elements work?
- Is there a definite style, with appropriate word choice and sentence structure? Does the story sound right when read aloud?
- Is the story close to a childhood experience? Will it introduce children to new experiences and enlarge their vision?

Text of Concept, Alphabet, Number, and Color Books, etc.

- Is the format of the individual pages appropriate to assist students in learning?
- Are illustrations clear, identifiable, and attractive?
- Is content accurate?
- Is the content unambiguous? For example, does it avoid objects that might have several names (e.g., cat, kitty) and silent letters (e.g., knot to illustrate the k sound)?
- Are objects to be counted clearly defined?
- Are all tasks in which students are to participate clearly presented?

(Norton, 1983). Picture books can teach values, behavior, concepts, and skills. They stimulate language development, expand vocabularies, foster intellectual growth, strengthen observational skills, and expand children's perception of art and beauty. Children can enjoy picture books alone, with peers, or with adults. As adults share picture books with nonreaders, they provide many understandings that are prerequisites for children's mastering literacy over time. When adults read to them, children who are themselves starting to read gain both an appreciation for literacy and a model of reading strategies.

Picture books can also be used as integral parts of instruction. Alphabet, concept, and counting books, for example, reinforce instruction; other books can expand students' background experiences and knowledge base. A teacher might present a different concept book each day as part of language arts work; counting books and books on shapes and size differences belong in math work. These books can become models for student-created books. Books with a distinct content thrust, such as Herbert Zim's science books in the Harper and Row I Can Read series, Ryder's *Fireflies* (1977), Brenner's *Wagon Wheels* (1978), or Benchley's *Small Wolf* (1972), another I Can Read book, show learners that factual information can be obtained from books. Such books also help students understand the differences between narrative and expository text structure (see Chapter 7 for more details).

Picture books can be the starting point for many discussions. *There's a Nightmare in My Closet* (Mayer, 1969), *The Runaway Bunny* (Brown, 1972), *Do You Want to Be My Friend?* (Carle, 1971), and *I Like Me!* (Carlson, 1989) can all encourage children to talk about their personal feelings. Children can also be steered toward more "literary" discussions by experiencing and talking about picture books by the same author or on the same theme. Series such as Hoban's Frances, Lobel's Frog and Toad books, Keat's books about Peter, or Wiseman's Morris the Moose series (which has been updated recently) introduce characters with strong, identifiable traits and recognizable problems to solve. Books such as *Black and White* (Macaulay, 1990) can be especially challenging. This book, which presents four stories that may or may not be related and four distinct sets of type faces and illustrations, motivates students to careful inspection and speculation. Through reading and discussion, children learn to like specific characters, make judgments about them, and by extension evaluate how authors craft their stories.

In choosing picture books for their students, teachers should heed the following caveat. Many older picture books have worked their way indelibly into the hearts and minds of generation after generation of children. But many of these books reflect values and attitudes that have, fortunately, changed over time. Teachers need to be aware of inadvertent and subtle signs of racism and sexism in picture books. Consider the concern expressed by the four-year-old son of two professionals: Ben loved trains in general and adored Tommy the Tank Engine in all its manifestations—books, toys, television program; but one day he asked, "Mommy, why is it that the engines are all boys and the train cars are all girls? That doesn't seem right."

Traditional Literature

Mother Goose and nursery rhymes introduce children to traditional literature. Also included in this category are folktales, fairy tales, tall tales, myths, and legends. Traditional literature originated in the oral tradition and has been handed down from generation to generation. The many forms of traditional literature arose from the needs of people in ancient times to speculate about their beginnings, find heroes to emulate and worship, and develop explanations for what they did not understand in the world around them. These people also wanted to spin good tales to entertain themselves. No piece of traditional literature has a specific author, although much credit for our knowledge of these stories must be given to collectors such as the Brothers Grimm or Charles Perrault.

Traditional literature can be both culture-specific and universal. Common themes and recurring structural patterns appear in all traditional literature, with specific manifestations depending on the cultural and social groups in which the story originally developed. Norton (1983) pointed out the differences between stories about King Arthur as told by nobility in the English court and those, such as "Jack the Giant Killer," that were told by peasants. The differences reflect the needs and concerns of the different groups and undoubtedly their varying purposes for spinning stories. But similarities are evident as well. Evil lurks, whether as powerful giants to be overcome or the more abstract subterfuge surrounding the Holy Grail; and mighty, just, and true-blooded heroes emerge to right the wrongs.

Traditional literature should be a fundamental part of students' literary experiences. Teachers can use folktales, myths, and legends for story telling, as part of the study of different countries, and as stimuli for dramatics, art, and writing. In-depth study of the myths, folktales, and legends of one country enriches students' understanding of the peoples they study and augments more factual information presented elsewhere. Teachers can choose from many good renditions of traditional stories for language-rich examples to share with children at all developmental levels. Rudine Sims-Bishop, a noted scholar on children's literature, has frequently pointed out that folktales have long served as the primary literary mode for presenting literature about minority cultures (see discussion later in the chapter).

Another approach to presenting diverse literacy traditions for study is to concentrate on the ways in which individual stories have been translated across cultures. For example, variations of *Cinderella*, *Beauty and the Beast*, and *Sleeping Beauty* appear in numerous cultures; almost every culture has its own creation myths; and "pourquoi tales" that offer explanations for natural phenomena and behaviors are equally abundant. In addition to studying one particular story, students might trace across cultures a theme or plot: the weakling who performs valiant feats, the beautiful girl imprisoned by a witch, personifications of good and bad luck.

As students investigate a story or theme across cultures, they gain insight into how national and ethnic characteristics shape literature and how basic themes and issues cut across cultural differences. These understandings should translate into values of acceptance, respect, and tolerance for people of different cultures. Students also gain literary insight, as they see how basic elements of story making—names, places, magical objects, and evil obstacles—are manipulated through change.

Traditional literature can become stimulus material for many integrative language arts activities. Once they have understood the basic elements to be manipulated, students can write their own versions of traditional tales as prose, epic poetry, or drama. Tall tales are especially good for this purpose. Spontaneous or planned dramatic activities based on traditional literature invite students to become swashbucklers, damsels in distress, gods and goddesses, evil witches, demons, and dragons. Art activities, pantomime, and dance also accompany traditional literature quite naturally. Story telling is also a natural outgrowth of the study of traditional literature; it is discussed more fully in the next chapter.

Any discussion of traditional literature must also be accompanied by a strong caveat. As is the case of older picture books, many editions of traditional literature present ethnic stereotypes and sexist attitudes. Teachers should carefully preview what they present to their students and help their students develop strategies for identifying (and rejecting) sexist and racist stereotyping in the literature they read.

Fiction: Realistic and Fantastic

Two basic kinds of fiction are available for school-aged readers: realistic and fantastic. The two forms differ in many ways but together offer students important opportunities to explore their emerging selves, experience adventures vicariously, and expand their views and knowledge of the world. Table 6–4 suggests evaluation criteria for traditional literature.

Realistic fiction.   Characters in realistic fiction act like real people; animals act like animals; the environment is real; and plots revolve around everyday occurrences and common problems, conflicts, and tensions. The antagonists in these books may be the main characters themselves, siblings or parents, other children or adults, or nature. Even if readers have not had similar experiences, they do not have to suspend disbelief in order to read with comprehension. Indeed, actively constructing meaning from examples of this genre can help children learn to understand life situations and empathize more fully with others; students can also experience vicarious escapades and pleasures and escape into mysteries and adventures. Historical fiction, novels about sports, family chronicles, and animal stories suit other interests and needs.

The genre contains many novels, labeled "problem books," that deal with issues such as drugs, divorce, death, aging relatives, life in the inner city, interpersonal relationships, the search for personal identity, and students' emerging sexuality. While frequently criticized and at times even banned, such books can provide students with very real insight into and strategies for coping with their own lives. Teachers must be careful to respect the diversity of responses students will make to such books. Some students may identify on an intensely personal level with characters like Park in *Park's Quest* (Paterson, 1989), who searches for information about his father who had been killed in Viet Nam; Angela, who learns of her illegitimacy in *Tell Me No Lies* (Colman, 1978); or Flip who mail-orders a red fox after his parents adopt a Korean child through the mail in *Mail-Order Kid* (McDonald, 1989). Others may respond in more abstract, intellectual ways. The value of this kind of literature as a springboard for discussion, writing, and individual reflection cannot be underestimated.

Another category is historical fiction. Examples can be found at all reading levels, from numerous I Can Read books such as *And Then What Happened, Paul Revere?* (Fritz, 1972), to longer works like *Sarah Plain and Tall* (MacLachlan, 1985) and *Johnnie Tremain* (Forbes, 1946). Historical fiction helps students gain a sense of the texture and tone of the past as they read about the peoples, values, beliefs, surroundings, hardships, and successes in different time periods. Historical fiction can also increase students' knowledge and understanding of historical events and figures and of their own and others' heritage. Many teachers may be familiar with historical fiction related to American history; however, the range of historical fiction is much broader. For example, *Sun Horse, Moon Horse* (Sutcliff, 1978) chroni-

Table 6–4
Evaluating Children's Fiction

Plot
- Does the work have a clearly developed plot? Is it original, rather than trite or predictable?
- In realistic fiction, is the plot plausible? In fantasy or science fiction, is it logical and consistent within the framework of the story?
- As appropriate, does the plot have action? Is there a clear problem to be solved?
- Is there a recognizable climax that resolves the story?

Characterization
- Are the characters—whether realistic or fanciful—clearly developed?
- Are the strengths, weaknesses, and other personal characteristics obvious and credible?
- Is there character development and growth, and is it believable?
- Do characters' actions make sense both logically and in terms of the story? Does their dialogue seem natural?
- Are the characters free from stereotype?

Theme
- Is there a recognizable, clear theme? Is it an integral part of the story?
- What values are presented? Does the book avoid moralizing?
- In fantasy, is there a universal truth that underlies the metaphor or other device used to present the story?

Content
- Is the story worth telling?
- Is it developmentally appropriate for the age for which it is intended?
- Is content presented accurately? In historical fiction, are dates, places, events, and so forth correct?
- Within the constraints of fantasy, is the story presented believably? Is the point of view consistent?

Style and Other Elements
- Is the style appropriate for the subject of the book and the age of the students for whom it is intended?
- Is the language realistic and rich? Will students understand it?
- Has the author avoided being condescending to readers?
- Is the book generally well-written and do any illustrations enhance or expand the story?
- Is the book truly at the designated level in terms of students' reading abilities, background knowledge, and maturity?

cles the Iceni tribe before the Roman invasion of Britain, and Haugaard's *Hakon of Rogen's Saga* (1963) and *A Slave's Tale* (1965) take place during Viking times.

Good historical fiction is based on extensive research. Some books present historical characters living through real events in a semi-fictionalized context. In others, fictional characters are presented within an accurate historical setting, often interacting with real historical figures and taking part in actual events; *Johnny Tremain* (Forbes, 1946) is a classic example. Johnny lives in Boston in the days before the Revolutionary War and interacts with John Adams, Paul Revere, and other individuals students should know from their history books. In still other books, fictional characters are placed within a specific context and period in history. Their "world" has historical accuracy, as in *Constance: A Story of Early Plymouth* (Clapp, 1968) or *Slave Dancer* (Fox, 1973); but the other characters and events in the novels are fictional. By making characters, their milieu, and events come alive, this kind of fiction gives students insight into specific historical issues and events. It should play an important part in the social studies curriculum.

Fantasy.   Modern fantasy, like traditional fantastic stories, requires readers to suspend disbelief. Some examples of this genre, such as Norton's The Borrowers series, feature off-sized people; in others, characters are personified toys, supernatural beings, humans with supernatural powers, or animals with human characteristics and behaviors. If the main characters are real people and are introduced within a normal, everyday context, they quickly find themselves transported into extraordinary, imaginary adventures, confronting extraordinary difficulties, and solving superhuman problems.

There are many links between traditional literature and fantasy. Stories such as J. R. R. Tolkien's Lord of the Rings series or C. S. Lewis's Narnia novels continue to be popular because they deal dramatically with the fight of good against evil. Ursula LeGuin's Earthsea series of books echoes the themes, characterizations, and conflicts of earlier tales, as the main character Sparrowhawk, later named Ged, learns that responsibility must always accompany the possession and use of power. Susan Cooper's character Will Stanton learns similar lessons in books that include Celtic and English traditional elements and detail another search for a Holy Grail.

Other forms of fantasy include talking animals who get in and out of very human predicaments. Winnie the Pooh, Peter Rabbit, and Paddington Bear are favorite animal characters for young children, and books like *The Cricket in Times Square* (Selden, 1960), and E. B. White's *Charlotte's Web* (1952), *Stuart Little* (1945), and *The Trumpet of the Swan* (1970), appeal to older students. Because the animal characters possess human characteristics, encounter human difficulties, or launch upon human adventures, children can readily accept their behaviors, responses, and reactions. For example, that Stuart Little is a mouse born to a human family does not faze children, who enjoy his adventures and empathize with his quest for his friend Margalo, the bird.

Science fiction books fall into the category of fantasy as well. Space travel, time warps, monsters, and threats from malevolent forces are pervasive in children's science fiction, giving it interest and universal appeal. Often, as in Madeleine L'Engle's books, one set of characters is followed through several adventures. Thus, in *A Wrinkle in Time* (1962), readers meet Charles Wallace, a brainy little boy, and his family and travel across the galaxy as Charles Wallace does battle with the first of the forces of evil he will encounter. Charles Wallace's life is endangered in *The Wind in the Door* (1973), but of course he survives to reemerge as a fifteen year old trying to keep a mad dictator from destroying the world in *A Swiftly Tilting Planet* (1978).

Nonfiction Books for Children

Many children enjoy nonfiction books, whether they are how-to or informational books, joke and humorous books, books about specific content areas, biographies, or other samples of this genre. These books serve many purposes: increasing children's knowledge about the world, satisfying their curiosity, stretching their imagination through vicarious experiences, and providing insight into the lives of people about whom they read. Children gain confidence in their abilities as they replicate experiments and observations presented in science books, make things according to how-to books, and strive to emulate the people whose biographies they read. Table 6–5 lists criteria for evaluating information books and biographies.

Teachers readily perceive the important roles that nonfiction books can play in content area work. If textbooks are in limited supply, are dated, or are too difficult for students, trade books about the same subject can become the core of instruction. Trade books also allow for more diversity of study, in that small groups of students can read and report on a variety of books. Their advantages do not stop there. Many children who do not enjoy fiction become readers when they encounter nonfiction books. For that reason alone, every classroom library should have a balanced selection of nonfiction books.

Additional advantages include exposure to the wide range of formats, writing styles, text structures, and reading tasks that informational books offer. Many informational books depend on graphic material—charts, tables, maps, lists of procedures, and schematic illustrations—to supplement and often to replace traditional text. To make sense from these books, students must practice and master new reading strategies; they must learn to take information from the printed page in ways that are substantially different from those used for straight paragraphs of text. Illustrations and photographs included in informational texts are usually more important than those that appear in fiction; they carry much of the information that is being conveyed and must be studied very carefully if students are to get the most from what they read. These reading tasks may present a real challenge to some students, and teachers may have to work with them to broaden their reading strategies. But the work is beneficial because broader, more flexible reading strategies will pay off in increased skill in content area reading. Mosenthal and Kirsch have written monthly columns about techniques for developing "graphic literacy" in the *Journal of Reading*.

Table 6–5
Evaluating Children's Nonfiction

Accuracy and Authenticity
- Are facts, procedure, and other elements accurate? Is it up-to-date? Are there any significant omissions?
- Is the author qualified to write about the topic?
- Are differing viewpoints presented?
- Are sexism and racism avoided?

Content
- Is content aimed at the appropriate level?
- What is the purpose of the book? Is coverage appropriate for the intended purpose and level of students?
- Will content area books lead to greater understanding? Can they be used in content area instruction?
- Are activities safe, easy to understand, and meaningful?
- Are joke and humorous books tasteful?

Style
- Is the writing clear and concise?
- Is the format (e.g., narrative or expository) appropriate for the topic and purpose of the book? Is the language clear? Does the format invite reader involvement?
- Does the book stimulate curiosity and further study?

Format, Illustrations, and Organization
- Is the format easy to follow? Where appropriate, does the book include a table of contents, marginal notes, study questions, appendices, index, and so forth?
- Are illustrations clear, easy to understand, and important to the text? Are size relationships, scale, procedures, and so forth made clear?
- Do the type, layout, and use of space contribute to the book's effectiveness?

The range of nonfiction books for children is truly amazing. For example, DeGroff (1990) cites informational books with titles as provocative as *Sam Goes Trucking, Horses in the Circus Ring, The Skeleton Inside You,* and *How To Be an Ocean Scientist in Your Own Home* (see references at end of book). Authors such as Aliki can be particularly popular with students because of the range of topics about which she has written. From her works, students can learn about dinosaurs, how books are printed, medieval life, the senses, and many other topics. Biographies of people in various professions expand students' sense of their own potential, and biographies and historical nonfiction can also introduce students to individuals from diverse ethnic and racial groups. Students can read biographies of Harriet Tubman or Barbara Jordan or books about conflicts between the Aztecs and Spaniards during the conquest of Mexico or almost any other subject.

Magazines for Children

According to the International Reading Association publication *Magazines for Children* (Stoll, 1990), magazines should be a significant part of students' reading. The range of available magazines is truly impressive. Some, such as *Art & Man*, are designed for classroom use; others, such as *Cricket: The Magazine for Children* assume that children will read them independently. Some magazines are content-specific and often highly specialized. For example, *Classical Calliope: The Muses' Magazine for Youth* concentrates on the language, literature, culture, and myths of ancient Roman and Greek civilizations.

Children's magazines are also available in a wide range of difficulty levels. Teachers can provide interesting, appropriate reading material for both weaker and more accelerated readers. It is also important to remember that magazines can enrich the school curriculum, especially if appropriate books are scarce. Periodicals of short stories by and for students supplement language arts anthologies, and content-specific periodicals can reinforce work in science or social studies. Magazines of current events can provide common reading material around which teachers can structure discussions, debates, and writing assignments.

Books to Expand Students' Sensitivity and Knowledge

Some books are designed to broaden students' sensitivity, perception, and knowledge. These books may deliberately strive to instill positive values in their readers or to dispel stereotypes. Or they may simply present stories or information about different ethnic groups, show girls and boys in varied and often nontraditional roles, portray the aged positively, or seek to dispel false information about people with handicapping conditions. In so doing, these books present important models and information to impressionable young readers. Bishop (1990) maintained that such books will help students recognize both the connectedness and the differences between all people. They will also help students understand the effects of social issues and forces on the lives of individuals.

Multicultural/Multi-ethnic literature.   Literature can help students appreciate the multicultural aspects of their society if it meets two major criteria. First, books should present characters from many different cultures and races and present them accurately, realistically, and respectfully. In the past (and unfortunately still in some literature today), story characters often represented the worst kinds of stereotypes, thereby reinforcing or creating erroneous ideas. Books often presented all the individuals from a particular group in a similar way. For example, all people from one group might be depicted as short or round-faced or jovial so that distinctness and individuality within that group are not apparent. Another tactic in some literature and basal readers has been to include "uniracial" characters in illustrations; these are people whose names might be ethnic and whose skin color might be dark but whose facial and body features are clearly Caucasian (Reimer, 1992). None of these representations would further students' sensitivity to cultural diversity.

The second way in which books can positively influence students is to provide good, solid information about different cultures and about people of color. In the past, information has often been primarily about the folklore and traditions of different groups (Reimer, 1992), and some excellent examples are available. Biographies and historical accounts are also useful, as are fictional renderings of how people from different groups actually live. Fiction of this type must be scrutinized carefully, though, because it can overly emphasize the efforts by immigrants and people of color to assimilate themselves into mainstream American life, often at the cost of diminishing the importance of the characters' ethnic and racial heritage (Reimer, 1992). This kind of fiction tends to minimize the distinctiveness of unique groups of people and perpetuate the "melting pot" view of culture.

Finding good literature about diverse peoples is not easy. By the mid 1980s, less than 1% of the children's literature published concerned African-Americans, and there was even less about Hispanics, Native Americans, or Asian-Americans (Bishop, 1987). Appendix A suggests helpful booklists, and Table 6–6 offers criteria for evaluating this kind of literature.

Nonsexist literature.   In attempting to provide students with nonsexist literature, teachers should look for two major attributes. The first is *inclusion*: females

Table 6–6
Questions for Evaluating Literature for Signs of Racism or Sexism

---

Accuracy and Authenticity
- Are characters and situations accurately and authentically presented or are they merely stereotypes or caricatures?
- Do characters take on life as individuals or do they remain stereotypic and similar?

Content
- What set of values does the book seem to espouse?
- What values do characters demonstrate?
- Does the book seem to set forth an ideology, and if so, it is acceptable?
- Are characters presented in diverse roles? Are the roles stereotypical?

Style
- Is language used appropriately? If Black English is used, does it have a negative effect? If accents are represented, do they demean the speakers?
- Are there implied judgments made about characters, their actions, or the situations?

Format, Illustrations, and Organization
- Are illustrations appropriate? Are there any subtle messages in them?
- Are female characters or people of color shortchanged in any way? Do they receive less attention than white male characters? Are they all given appropriate names or are they referred to primarily by pronouns?

should be present in the text *and* in illustrations of books students encounter—in fiction, nonfiction, how-to, and other books. Females should play major roles in the books, for example, as main characters of stories and as subjects of biographies.

The second attribute is *mold-breaking*. Girls and boys, as well as women and men, should be presented in the full range of human diversity that exists in the population at large. Girls should be tough and do interesting, exciting things; they should climb trees, solve problems, excel at athletics, become scientists and doctors. Boys should be nurturing, sensitive, and kind; they should be teachers, librarians, and caregivers to young children. By establishing in literature that girls and boys and women and men demonstrate many different behavioral styles, aspire to many professions, and accomplish wide-ranging feats, teachers are helping students reach beyond stereotypical expectations for who they can be and what they can achieve. Again, see Table 6–6 for guidelines for evaluating this kind of literature.

SUMMARY

No one elementary school teacher is going to be fully knowledgeable about children's literature, but all teachers owe it to themselves and their students to learn as much as possible about the range of books available for children's use. By balancing the classics and newer works, fiction and nonfiction, easy books and more challenging ones, teachers can supplement students' learning in truly meaningful ways.

QUESTIONS AND TASKS

1. Be sure that you understand these terms:
   a. fiction
   b. fantastic fiction
   c. realistic fiction
   d. historical fiction
   e. nonfiction, including informational books
   f. picture books
   g. traditional literature

2. Select several children's books from among those mentioned in this chapter or find others that you like. Share them with several children and carefully record their responses. What do you notice? What relationships might there be between children's gender, age, and book type?

3. This chapter states that many nonfiction books depend on charts and other graphics to supplement text. Find several examples of such books and develop a lesson to teach children how to read this kind of text.

4. Find several examples of fiction and nonfiction that deal with multicultural issues. Analyze them for content, style, and accuracy. In what ways are they good? In what, if any, ways are they inadequate?

5. The first paragraph of this chapter cites Langer's contention that literature is often "considered a way to indoctrinate students into the cultural knowledge, good taste, and elitist traditions of our society." Write your response to this statement, and discuss its meaning with other members of your class.

Literature-Based Approaches to Literacy Instruction

For many years and in many classrooms, children's literature has effectively been consigned to the category of "frills" or "extras" that will be used "if there is time" or when students acquire "basic skills." Even when teachers read to their students daily, the connection between this pleasurable activity and "real" reading instruction may be tenuous at best. Many educators have criticized this approach, but often to no avail (Veatch, 1968; Holdaway, 1979; Sloan, 1984). Jim Trelease, author of *The Read-Aloud Handbook* (1985), acknowledges the need for some skills instruction but suggests that "we balance the scales in our children's minds. It is imperative that we let our children know there is something more to reading than the practicing, the blendings, the vowel sounds, something more to it than the questions at the end of the chapter. And we must let them know this early, before they have permanently closed the door on reading for the rest of their lives" (p. 8).

In recent years, literature has found a more secure niche in some elementary classrooms. Teachers are electing to use literature as the core of their literacy program, and administrators are supporting this choice. The state of California has taken children's literature seriously enough to develop the "California Reading Initiative," the core of which consists of graded lists of books to be read throughout the school years. These "living" lists will grow and change over time and are only part of a reading and language arts curriculum framework designed to ensure the most effective use of literature in all classrooms (Alexander, 1987).

ASSUMPTIONS, ISSUES, AND ATTITUDES ABOUT LEARNING TO READ

Several assumptions underlie the decision to use literature as the core of a literacy program, whether the decision is part of a statewide initiative or is merely the result of a desire for change among a group of teachers. The primary assumption is that students will learn to read successfully without the structured, lockstep progression of basal reader series. Authentic literature, encountered in a classroom where the teacher monitors student progress and provides appropriate instruction, will create strong readers. Writing skills will also thrive in this kind of environment. As Graves (1893) has stated, "All children need literature. Children who are authors need it even more" (p. 67). It is safe to add that children who are expected to *think* about what they read have a particular need for authentic print material as the core of their school activities.

Basal Reader Series and Literature: A Continuing Tension

Teachers in many districts are not given the option of deciding whether to use a basal reader series. This is an example of the lack of "control of literacy instruction" discussed in Chapter 1. Yet, because they believe that a literature program will benefit their students, many teachers seek ways to implement such a program.

Teachers who truly believe in a literature approach try to keep the basal in proper perspective.[1] They work toward integrating the basal reader selectively into a literature approach, rather than using literature to supplement the basal. If they use the teachers' manual at all, it serves as a reference for book lists and activities. Classrooms are filled with books and other print material *as if* a literature approach were the sole instructional method. Inherent in this approach is movement toward flexible grouping, elimination of worksheets and workbooks, and more student involvement in selection of reading, monitoring of progress, and pacing.

---

[1] See Aaron (1987) and Winograd, Lipson, & Wixson (1989) for other discussions of combining basal and literature-based approaches. These sources, however, advocate literature as a supplement to the basal, while this book encourages the use of the basal as a supplement to literature.

To mesh a basal program with a literature-based approach, teachers need first to determine the extent to which the basal contains authentic, full-length literature. Often basals present abridged, homogenized versions of stories, edited to conform to a basal reading level or to simplify vocabulary or syntax (Routman, 1989). Diluting the language of real literature makes it less motivating and less interesting to read. Abridged material can also be more difficult to read because although it is shorter, it lacks the cohesiveness of the original.

The second step in folding a basal series into a literature approach is to gain a full, clear sense of what students are expected to master during a particular school year. The scope and sequence charts and periodic check up quizzes that dominate basal instruction predetermine what students are "responsible" for learning and what teachers will be held "accountable" for teaching. An experienced teacher usually has an internalized set of expectations for a given grade level, but beginning teachers will need to develop a sense of the expected "outcomes" for both reading and language arts. This sense translates into benchmarks for students' learning, which teachers can look for as they observe students work and interact in conferences and small groups. They can also use them to determine content for whole class mini-lessons, small-group work, and individual instruction.

Competencies To Be Gained in a Literature-Based Program

The goal of any literacy program is, of course, to help students become strong readers and writers. Commercial publishers provide a statement of program goals and objectives, usually in terms of the skills to be mastered. Instruction and evaluation are then tied to this statement. When teachers undertake a literacy-based program, their goals and objectives usually encompass much more than what is presented by commercial publishers. Table 7–1 presents global competencies to be gained from a literature-based program; teachers will undoubtedly want to add to the list to suit the grade level and character of each individual class.

Locus of Control in a Literature-Based Program

For a literature program to work well, teachers must be willing to take control of literacy lessons, and to give control to their students as well. Teachers learn to observe students carefully and depend on their own ability to plan instruction without the carefully-sequenced lessons of a basal teachers' guide and language arts teachers' edition. Teachers also develop varied strategies for evaluating students' progress. Students assume responsibility as well—for selecting books, deciding whether they want to read what they select, reading independently and in groups, keeping track of their reading, monitoring their progress, seeking help when needed, and completing follow-up activities as required.

In some ways, the materials in the classroom also have a share of the control. If the materials are varied, developmentally appropriate, and interesting, they will invite students to learning. If there is a mismatch between students and reading selections, learning will not be as effective.

Table 7–1
Competencies to Be Developed in a Literature-Based Program

Students should develop the following competencies through a literature-based program:

1. Ability to read silently and orally in varied texts that are suitable for their age, ability, and background experiences

2. Facility with figurative and poetic language, in terms of recognition, understanding, and use in their own writing

3. Ability to continue to expand their vocabularies for reading, writing, listening, and speaking

4. Ability to add to their storehouse of strategies for constructing meaning from and with text, in listening and in speaking

5. Ability to respond to works of literature in many ways, including mental, intellectual, emotional, sensory, and physical

6. Facility with different types of literary works, including ability to understand
   - characters, events, and sequence of events
   - setting and its impact on characters and events
   - and discuss theme

7. Facility with different text structures, including narration and various structural patterns in exposition

DEVELOPING A LITERATURE-BASED LITERACY PROGRAM

Developing and maintaining a literature-based instructional program is no small task. Teachers must accumulate many materials, plan complex scheduling systems and innovative student activities, and help students adjust to what they may perceive as a bewilderingly loose approach to reading and writing instruction (Routman, 1989, 1991). In reality, the structure should be relatively tight so that teachers and students understand mutual expectations and responsibilities. Within this agreed-upon structure, the kind discussed fully as a workshop environment in Chapter 2, teachers and students can thrive.

Materials in a Literature-Based Classroom

To demonstrate to students that books will play an important part in their instruction, a readily accessible core library, from the very first day of school, is essential. Whether for use in a self-contained classroom or in a departmentalized reading/language arts program, teachers should accumulate a sizable library (75 to 100 books) before the start of school and aim for 400 or so books by year's end (Routman, 1989). Magazines, brochures (those available from the federal government or local agricultural extension services, for example) and other print media may also be appropriate. Teachers might consider having a class subscription to one or more magazines and should encourage students to bring in any magazines they get at home.

In selecting materials, teachers should draw upon evaluation guidelines such as those presented in the previous chapter and on their own mental checklist of what constitutes good literature. It is also wise to try to evaluate books from the perspective of the children they are teaching. Moss (1977) wrote that "a book by itself is nothing—a film shown in an empty cinema: one can only assess its value by the light it brings to a child's eye" (p. 142).

It is important that teachers keep track of the materials in the permanent class library and materials borrowed from other sources. Books and materials might be categorized according to genre or topic—but not according to difficulty. In a literature-based program, students quickly recognize that some books are harder than others, and they select accordingly. Keeping brief notations and cross-references on each book enables teachers to make recommendations to students as needed.

Students should also keep track of what they read and how they respond to each selection. Keeping a literature log (discussed in a later section) or an individual reading roster make this easy (see Figure 7–1). Students should also share their opinions about what they read through weekly or monthly entries on a bulletin board. A class roster stored in a file box keeps a year-long record (and helps teachers evaluate their library). Individual or small groups can compile "reviews" for inclusion in this roster after they have read and discussed particular books.

Figure 7–1
Book Rosters

Name		
Titles	Dates	Comments

(A) Book roster for individual student

Title		
Author		
Publisher		Date
Reader's Name	Date	Comments

(B) Book roster for single book to be filled in by students as they read it

Text Sets in the Literature-Based Classroom

Text sets can be beneficial in assembling materials for a literature-based class-room (Harste, Short, & Burke, 1988). A *text set* is two or more books that are relat-ed according to the dimensions listed and described in Table 7–2. Students who have worked with teacher-assembled text sets can be encouraged to suggest addi-tional combinations of books and indeed to assemble some themselves. Their search can take them into magazines and other sources to round out their own text sets. Compiling, sharing, and critiquing text sets can be beneficial and pleasur-able experiences.

Planning the Literature Workshop

A thoroughly planned and carefully organized workshop environment, as discussed in Chapter 2, is the best classroom management scheme for a literature-based pro-gram. A successful literature workshop must be balanced in several ways:

1. Student self-selection of books is balanced with teacher suggestions for books to read and teacher assignments of books that small groups or occasionally the whole class must read.

2. Independent reading and writing about what has been read are balanced with whole class mini-lessons, small-group instruction, peer conferences, and group or individual conferencing with the teacher.

3. "Quiet" reading and writing work is balanced with oral work during which students discuss books, ask and respond to questions, conduct "book talks," participate in story telling, and use their emerging knowledge about literature in their own role in peer response groups and "author's chair." Teachers need to learn to value and to be able to evaluate this oral work.

4. Independent writing about what has been read, recorded in "literary let-ters" or "literature logs," is balanced with public discussions and public writings about reading selections.

Finally, in a literature workshop, instruction traditionally classified as lan-guage arts work is balanced with and integrated into reading instruction through thoughtful cross-referencing of terms, strategies, and activities. Thus, "lessons during writing workshops feature examples from literature: how authors develop a plot, use interesting language, and create good leads and closings. Discussions during reading help students learn to read like writers" (Strickland, 1987, p. 75). Reading in content area books is also emphasized.

In all classrooms, the components that provide the superstructure of students' and teachers' activities are relatively similar. The major categories of activities are:

1. Instructional interactions

2. Independent, silent work

Table 7–2
Text Sets

Text sets are composed of books that vary along these dimensions:
- presentation of the same story, differing in the form of the retelling, the cultural perspective presented, the author or illustrator, and so forth
- story structures or basic organizational patterns
- thematic similarities, such as books about families, friendships, being afraid, starting school
- text types, such as folktales, tall tales, how-to books, science experiment books
- the same topic, regardless of genre
- the same illustrator or author
- the same character in many different stories or adventures

Possibilities of text sets include:
- books in a series, such as the *Amelia Bedelia, Nate the Great, Frog and Toad, Frances* books
- poetry text set:
    several books of poetry by adults
    magazines that publish poetry by students
    biographies of poets, such as Robert Frost or Emily Dickinson
    The Place My Words Are Looking For: What Poets Say About and Through Their Work by Paul Janeczko, which features 39 poets sharing their work, their lives, and their thoughts about writing
- Boston/Revolutionary War text set:
    And then what happened, Paul Revere? by J. Fritz
    Sam the Minuteman, by N. Benchley
    The Midnight Ride of Paul Revere, by Henry Wadsworth Longfellow
    Johnnie Tremain, by Esther Forbes
    several nonfiction books about the period
    maps about colonial America
    primary documents such as newspaper articles from the period
- works by Arnold Lobel, Daniel Pinkwater, or Maurice Sendak for young readers; Judy Blume, Paula Fox, or Katherine Paterson for older readers
- books' issues, themes, content area topics, and so forth, especially to supplement content area study by increasing independent reading
- books to increase students' awareness about issues, such as possible professions, health, civic responsibilities, cultural diversity

---

3. Focused literature study of numerous forms
4. Activities to follow up reading, whether spontaneous or assigned

These categories of activities, represented on the horizontal axis of the matrix in Figure 7-2, have numerous manifestations in a literature-based classroom. The vertical axis of the matrix shows classroom activities further classified according to

Figure 7–2
Matrix of Activities in a Literature-Based Classroom

Silent/Independent reading activities	Oral/Shared activites	Writing activities
Sustained silent reading (SSR)		Sustained silent writing (SSW)
Independent reading		Making notes on what is read, while reading Writing after reading
Focused literature studies	Book talks Literature response groups Storytelling Drama, puppets, art	Keeping literature logs Writing research reports Story writing, in groups or as individuals Adding to book rosters, other public reviews
	Conferences with teachers/peers Discussions with peers Informal book talks	

their overall purposes. The cells include more specific examples, which are explained in the section that follows and in other chapters.

Thematic Units

In many instances, students themselves select what they will read. In other cases, students read designated material, either in preparation for a session with the teacher or peers or to complete language arts or content area assignments. Teachers also introduce thematic units consisting of several books about a common topic or theme.

Thematic units allow students to study topics in depth. There usually are more books suggested for a thematic unit than for a text set, although the idea of grouping books for focused study is similar. A designated topic might be literary, such as a unit on folktales or science fiction. Or it might be tied closely to work in science or social studies, giving students experience with informational books. Norton (1990) suggested a comprehensive unit approach to teaching multicultural literature that includes many different kinds of reading. Her plan begins with traditional literature to give students a broad view of a culture and to help them form generalizations. In the next phase, the focus is narowed; students read traditional tales from only one area. In phase three, students extend their reading to biographies, autobiographies, and historical nonfiction. Then, students read and evaluate historical fiction based on the sense of authenticity they have gained from previous reading. Finally, students read contemporary fiction, biography, and poetry of the focal area. In this last phase, they look for threads from the traditional literature they have read earlier. This kind of sequence can be a model for other thematic units; its progression allows students to refine their focus as they gain information by reading. They take on manageable "chunks" of study at each phase of the unit.

By now, the importance of a large classroom library must be evident. Without ample supplies of print material, students will not have the rich opportunities that a literature-based approach should provide.

Typical Days in Literature-Based Literacy Classrooms

There is no one day that has a preestablished format in a literature-based classroom because the model is flexible enough to be used in numerous contexts. No matter what the grade, the use of literature as the focus of children's study is the commonality. How teachers structure a typical day varies according to students' skills, prior experiences, and levels of independence, along with availability of materials and amount of time that can be devoted to literacy work. Two week-long schedules are included in Appendix B, one for a self-contained third-grade class and a second for a departmentalized fifth-grade reading/language arts class with a 90-minute period of instruction (that is, two class periods of 45 minutes each). They were first referenced in Chapter 2 on classroom management.

Mini-lessons.   As discussed in Chapter 2, mini-lessons are presented to the entire class at the beginning of the class session. At the start of the year, teachers use the mini-lesson time to acclimate students to the class; that accomplished, teachers present brief, focused instruction. In a literature-based class, the mini-lesson focus may be a new book or author that the teacher thinks the students will enjoy. Mini-lessons of this sort shape students' ability to engage in focused literature study, in that teachers model "literary conversations" or book talks and present terminology for thinking and talking about books. Teachers might also model and discuss strategies for comprehension, literary analysis, or writing, including ways of thinking about characterization, methods for inferring author's tone, or techniques for understanding specific literary devices. Still other mini-lessons might concern use of graphic organizers or strategies for activating prior knowledge before reading.

Building mini-lessons on familiar authors and specific pieces of literature makes them more meaningful. Information presented does not seem abstract because discussion grows from what students know. No matter what the nature of the mini-lesson, teachers tie reading and writing concepts together. A lesson on identifying an author's tone, for example, would not be complete without a discussion on how the students themselves can achieve tone in their own writing.

Another important function of mini-lessons is to provide opportunities for reviewing and reteaching previously taught skills. When appropriate, those students whom the teacher has identified as weak in the skill being presented should be called on to answer questions, so that they are very clearly drawn into the instruction. For them, the work is remedial; for other students, it is review. Small-group work on the same material may be provided after the mini-lesson for these students so that they can revisit the lesson in a smaller setting. Following the mini-lesson, students disperse to various other responsibilities, including working alone, in small groups, or with the teacher.

Independent reading and writing.   Independent reading or writing is one possible activity after a mini-lesson. As indicated on the weekly plans, a sustained silent reading (SSR) period might follow the mini-lesson at least some days of the week. In this scenario, students and teacher read self-selected materials quietly for a period of time determined by the students' familiarity with the approach and grade level.

In another scenario, some students move from the mini-lesson into independent reading some days of the week, independent writing other days, and individual work with the teacher or in small groups on still other days. In this case, independent reading could serve one of several functions: to complete a short-term assignment, to work on a longer-term project, or to prepare for a conference with the teacher or fellow students. Likewise, students might simply read, because in a literature-based classroom, that is exactly what students do: read independently. They read new material and they revisit old favorites. It is good to remember that as suggested in *Becoming a Nation of Readers*, the time students spend reading independently "is associated with gains in reading achievement" (Anderson, Hiebert, Scott, & Wilkinson, 1985, p. 119). Independent writing activities are equally important and will be discussed in the sections that follow.

Focused literature study.   Focused literature study actually begins early, within the "bedtime storybook learning cycle" when a child spontaneously expresses a reaction to the story or the reader poses a thought-provoking question to the young listener. Through these means, the child realizes that it is appropriate to *respond* to literature in some overt and thoughtful way. When children enter school, thoughtful literature study may give way to the "study" of reading, as students spend increasing amounts of time engaged in the practice of discrete skills. Literature is often relegated to recreational reading. It is only later, when students' "skills" have supposedly matured, that they are asked to study and criticize literature for its own sake; but by then, children's motivation to think about diverse aspects of what they read may have diminished. Students may come to think that "the task of people [who study] literature is to unearth the bizarre in a text, to go where no reader has gone before. [Teachers appear to] mechanically . . . set about their business, seemingly untouched by the book, ready to pounce upon unsuspecting pupils with queries regarding hidden meaning" (Saul, 1989, pp. 297-298).

In a literature-based classroom, students have ample opportunities to engage in focused literature study because teachers understand that reading "skills" alone, without thought and discussion about what is read, will never shape students into real, critical readers. Through many different kinds of activities, focused literature study helps students learn to analyze, judge, synthesize, and evaluate; form and express opinions; and compare works across genre, themes, and topics. Teachers know that students' response to the literature is central to their growth and that responses will vary in form—a question or comment, sharing or retelling, or an art form such as an original composition, a drawing, or a dramatization. Literature study is based on the realization that there may be no real right answers to questions posed and no absolutely right way to respond. "Meaning," as explained in the next chapter, "does not reside ready-made in the text or in the reader; it happens during the transaction between reader and text" (Rosenblatt, 1989, p. 157). By using literature study activities in a class, teachers encourage this "transaction" to take place. Groups of students and their teacher share their ideas and interpretations of what they have read.

The major kind of focused literature study are group discussions, student writing (often in literature logs), and interdisciplinary activities such as drama or art. The objects of students' study may be text sets, sequences of books designed to represent a theme, or books that several students merely have read and want to discuss.

Group discussions.   Group discussions may be on-going or short-term, spontaneous or planned. "Talking about a piece of literature with others gives readers time to explore half-formed ideas, to expand their understandings of literature through hearing others' interpretations, and to become readers who think critically and deeply about what they read. Readers need to understand that a variety of interpretations exist for any piece of literature and that they can collaboratively explore their interpretations with one another to reach new understandings" (Harste, Short, & Burke, 1988, p. 293). Basic procedures for group discussions, sometimes called *literature circles*, are presented in Table 7–3.

Teachers play a dominant role in helping students learn general discussion skills and specific methods for talking about literacy. Presenting brief *book talks* to large or small groups is one way to fulfill this role. Teachers essentially talk about a book, telling a little about the plot (if fiction) or the contents (if nonfiction), perhaps a little about the author or illustrator, and any other information that motivates students to want to spend time with a particular book. Teachers also use general questions such as "What is this story about?" or "What did you find out in this book?" as models for more wide-ranging discussions. Teacher questions should always be open-ended so that issues needing further discussion surface and students make links between the current story, their own lives, and other books they have read.

Discussion groups may meet in two ways: (a) as students are working their way through a book, or (b) after all participants have completed their reading. The former method works well with chapter books or text sets because students meet frequently, briefly discuss what they have read, set goals for independent reading, and then meet for intensive discussion after everyone has finished. Students who encounter difficulty with certain parts have peer support in figuring out what they have read. If students are to finish an entire book before meeting, they may do so as part of Sustained Silent Reading, as homework, or during their free time. The teacher must determine a reasonable deadline by which all students should have finished the book.

Table 7–3
Literature Discussion Groups

Participants
Teacher and students
Students without teacher

Materials
Multiple copies of literature that can withstand intensive discussion

Context
Literature-based classroom in which a workshop approach to instruction is used. Several groups of students may be preparing for discussion at one time. In early childhood classes, teachers may read some or all of the story to the students and make a tape of the story available in a listening area.

Duration
One day for a picture book; several days to a week for longer works

Goal
To prepare for and participate in focused literature study during group discussion sessions

Procedures
1. Teacher gives a short "book talk" about several books to stimulate students' interest; students sign up for the book they wish to read.

2. Students prepare for their discussion group by reading independently during workshop time or at home.

3. Students reading long works may meet daily or every few days to discuss several chapters; alternately, students must complete the entire work before the discussion period.

4. When first using the approach, the teacher asks open-ended questions such as "What is this book about?" and serves as moderator and model for discussion. As students become accustomed to the process, the teacher can play a less dominant role. The teacher may want to offer opinion rather than ask questions and should encourage students to question each other and voice what they have found satisfying and/or confusing about what they have read. Throughout the discussion, students are offering their ideas, possibly referring to their literature logs, and contrasting the meaning each participant has derived from reading.

5. At the end of each session, the teacher helps students summarize what has been discussed and sets goals for the next discussion. These goals include what aspects of the book students want to discuss and may prompt students to reread parts already discussed. Students may want to write in their literature

Table 7–3
continued

logs and bring their notes to the next discussion.

6. At the end of the discussion period, students may be asked to make an oral report to the class or to prepare notations about the book to be kept in the class book roster or posted on the bulletin board.

Alternate Approach

If there are text sets available, students may prepare for discussion by reading one or more books in the set. Although not all books in each set must be read, at least two students should read each book that will be discussed. Then, during discussion, teacher and students compare and contrast books according to content, style, format, and other variables.

To use this approach for reading instructional groups, make the following changes to the previous approach.

Participants

Teacher and several students who are reading at about the same level

Materials

Books that students have prepared the night before

Procedures

1. Students take a few minutes to review their reading before the session begins.

2. Teacher leads a discussion of the reading. The discussion seeks to establish common background knowledge, affirm purpose for reading, and check comprehension.

3. Students take turns reading whole pages of text. Teacher asks high-level questions.

4. Teacher may use an overhead projector and masking strategies to engage students in a more focused interaction with difficult parts of the text (see Chapter 4).

5. Students may again take turns reading whole pages of text or the group may read orally together to "get the sounds" of the text.

6. Teacher provides focused instruction on strategies students need, with specific references to aspects of text where they would be useful.

7. Students are given a written cloze to complete independently or in pairs. The exercise consists of several paragraphs in which the teacher has whited out all but the beginning letters of particular words that illustrate graphophonemic, syntactic, or semantic principles that need practice. Any reasonable response is accepted for completing the cloze.

8. The session ends with additional group reading for pleasure.

At the first discussion meeting, students share ideas and raise questions about their reading. In discussing the books and their topics, students are also discussing their processes for constructing meaning, and in a way, giving each other insight into comprehension strategies. They record questions that they want to address before their next meeting.

At subsequent discussion sessions, students revisit issues and questions from their first meeting. Some students may read from their literature logs; others may share the results of rereading sections of the book or story at hand. The total number of sessions devoted to discussing any book or text set will depend on length and richness of the book or text set and on students' experiences with discussion. At the end of the sessions, students should make a brief oral presentation or prepare written summaries about the group's assessment of the book.

Many discussions, especially in a self-contained class, cut across content areas. Because sharp lines between the content areas blur in a literature-based classroom, students do not hesitate to refer to related books and articles they have read; students also offer their own opinions. Books and other reading material can also be brought in to settle disputes, to provide evidence to support individuals' contentions, and to furnish examples to deepen the discussion.

Discussion groups can also work with young children, even prereaders. The teacher reads a book to the group and leads a brief introductory discussion. A taped version of the story is available for individual use, along with multiple copies of the text. After all children have had a chance to listen to the tape, the discussion group convenes and talks about the book.

Teachers should also structure instructional reading groups as discussions. In doing so, they are inviting students to share more of their thinking, both about what they read and how they construct meaning. By talking about reading strategies in this context, teachers can better diagnose who is progressing well and who needs additional help. A plan for such a reading group is also presented in Table 7–3.

Written Responses to Literature

Students also respond to literature in writing in both informal and formal ways. A *literature log* is an informal mechanism to get students to write about and reflect on what they read. It provides a written trail of their processes of constructing meaning from text. It also helps teachers understand what students are learning about reading.

To help students use literature logs well, teachers need to explain that logs are ungraded records of students' thinking about their reading, not private journals. Students are to write down questions about what they read, reactions to ideas and characters, and indications of difficulties they have had. They may use part of the log as a record of vocabulary they need to look up or of ideas they would like to try in their own writing; they may also use it as a personal roster of books read during a school year. Students should be encouraged to write in their literature logs frequently, whether they have read independently, in preparation for a literature discussion, or as part of an assignment. Logs can then be especially helpful in writing about lengthy pieces of prose or in refreshing the memory about specific aspects of what has been read.

Students share their literature logs with their teachers. As teachers read them, they may comment about ideas and questions students have raised, suggest alternative viewpoints, or recommend other books students might like. The dialogue that results should concern the content of what students have read and their overall process of reading, not discrete decoding or comprehension strategies. Still, teachers use the logs as part of their evaluation process by keeping track of the kinds, number, and difficulty of books students read and any problems they seem to be encountering. By combining the raw evidence in students' logs, knowledge of the students, and familiarity with the books being read, teachers can draw preliminary conclusions about the students' current reading skills.

Students may also write *literary letters* to send to the teacher and to peers. These focus on what students have read and on their responses. Because these are more public than literature logs, they must be more carefully crafted.

Reading and hearing many different kinds of children's literature affect students' writing in many natural and positive ways. First of all, the works they encounter become models for their own writing, as they consciously or unconsciously "lift" story ideas, vocabulary, rhetorical devices, and other aspects from books they have liked. Children's attempting to integrate bits and pieces from literature into their own writing is not copying; rather, it indicates that they are stretching toward more sophisticated, complex models of writing. Teachers may also notice traces of movies and television shows in students' writing; these, too, attest to children's attempts to broaden their repertoire of skills and strategies.

Children can also write about literature more formally than in their literature logs. Although teachers definitely want to help students master various modes for writing about literature, it is important that assignments not become formulaic, highly structured book reports. Before asking students to write about literature, teachers devote time in mini-lessons to explain the strategies and format required. In book talks and literature "conversations" with small groups or with the whole class, teachers also demonstrate how to pull ideas about books together. Because students have seen their teacher model the approach and because they have participated orally in similar analyses, syntheses, or evaluations, they are prepared to tackle these tasks in writing.

Literature can also be a starting point for students' own writing. They might rewrite a favorite story to include additional characters, change the ending, or extend the plot into the future. The samples in Figure 7–3 were written by students who had heard the Judith Viorst story *Alexander and the Terrible, Horrible, No Good, Very Bad Day* (1972).

If a classroom library has ample supplies of nonfiction books, periodicals, and other print reference materials, students will come to view literature as a source of information about which to write. They will learn to go to the classroom library to find ideas for stories, information about topics they want to consider in writing, and data to support the points they want to make. For example, a student who has

Figure 7–3

Students' Writing in Response to *Alexander and the Terrible, Horrible, No Good, Very Bad Day*

Sample 1

My Terrible,
Horribe, No good.
Very bad Day

On one morning, I woke up on the
the side of the bed. Then my
mother called me and so I got
up and got ready for school. I
found out that I haded a white sock
and one red so I put them on
and put my loafers one of
them haded ice cream of last
night when I walk it would
make a funny sound. Then
I went down strair and fell
from the top of the strairs.
and sprain my ankle. Then
I ate my breakfast. Then I
went to school I forgot my
homework. Then my friends
weren't my friend anymore

Sample 2

Very Good, Wonderful,
Terrific, fantastic
day

One day my ant
called me, She said,
Jeanette wood you
like to go horebackride
and I said Yes I
wood Mary, So she
tack me to look at
the new pony, and I
rode and rode intill
it was dark, The end

Sample 3

Terible, Terrible, no good very Bas day.

On morning when, I was waking up, I touched my
hair and I had gums on my hair, I had to cut
hair and when got up my brother had left a banana
pil, and when I stepped that pil, I sprain my ankle
And then I said this is going to be a Terierle,
Horrider, no good, very Bad day

Figure 7–3
continued

Sample 4

Terrible, Horruble, No Good, Very Bad Day

Oane Once a time I came out of my bed and insted of the sun coming up I saw the moon in the sky I went and to the Bath room and I was going to take a both but the water was not od warm it was berry cold I put some water in the stove and went and wash my face but the water was not water it was blood I look for the tuthbrush but the tuthbrush was gone and the paste was gone too. I had to go to school I look at the clock and the clock was 10 till 8:00 I dress and put my shoes and went to school I was going to school and it started to rain I went to put my rain coat and I said I am going to be late to school.

Sample 5

My Wondeful, Most, Good Super Day

You know want happen to day When I wokeup I wokeup bight ander lyy befot my. Mommy and Daddy soerly it was 5:00 o'dock I got dresst and ate my brefeest and when. I was thow with at my mommy wokeup and my daddy woke up too. Then at school and I had super work. I noow want a My Wondeful, Most Good super day. and at lunch a good thing happen I had a good dsert.

Table 7–4
Oral Story Telling

Participants
Teachers and students

Materials
Good stories that can withstand oral retelling
Any props that can enhance the story telling

Context
Any classroom, either self-contained or departmentalized

Duration
As long as the story requires and as long as students can maintain their attention

Goals
To provide pleasurable experiences with literature

To foster students' comprehension skills

Procedures
1. Select a story carefully.
    *   Select a single story or collapse several into one.
    *   Consider students' ages, developmental levels, and background experiences in making the selection.
    *   The story should be exciting and capable of sustaining interest.
    *   Traditional literature is often appropriate because it tends to have rich language, enticing beginnings, and strong action that pull listeners into the action.
2. Prepare the story carefully.
    *   Make notes and an outline about what should be included in the oral story.
    *   Decide what parts should be memorized verbatim and which can be spoken more or less spontaneously.

trouble thinking of subjects on his or her own should be reminded that controversial or topical information in classroom periodicals can be the start of their own essays. Equally, a student whose written work contains exaggerated claims about a topic should be encouraged to research and refine his or her work. Using library materials as sources or as substantiation of writing requires critical reading skills, which are discussed more thoroughly in Chapter 9. Long-term research reports are also discussed in Chapter 9.

Other Interactions with Literature

Surrounding children with print is not enough. Even in the upper grades, teachers must surround children with the *sounds* of literature. Teachers should read to

Table 7–4
continued

- Try delivering the story in private; tape-record the effect and make note of timing.
- Wait a day or two and then listen to the tape objectively; make alterations in the content, word choice, pitch, tempo, stress, or timing.
- Practice the story once or twice a day, sometimes in front of a mirror, until the story is memorized and comfortable; some of these sessions may be taped as well.
- Pay attention to points at which to make eye contact, to the body language, and to the whole range of paralinguistic cues that will be needed.
- Tape what seems to be the finished version and check for presentation; make alterations if needed.
- Make or secure any felt boards, costumes, or finger or stick puppets that will be used.

3. Prepare the students for listening.
   - Let students know the kind of behavior that will be expected during story telling.
   - Tell them the extent to which they will be allowed to participate in the experience.
   - Use posters and other displays to heighten anticipation.

4. Present the story telling to the class.
   - With students gathered comfortably around, tell the story.
   - Make eye contact frequently and employ a range of cues such as body language to augment oral language.
   - Use felt board cutouts or other visual aids.
   - Stop at appropriate points to allow students to participate by supplying words, predicting events, making sound effects, and so forth.

5. Plan follow-up activities.
   - Encourage students to retell the story themselves.
   - Plan opportunities for students to try story telling themselves; provide stories to learn, time to practice, and feedback on students' performances.

their students daily, from picture books, chapter books and novels, and informational/expository works. Professionally-produced tapes of stories are also valuable.

Teachers and students should, as is discussed in the previous chapter, become storytellers as well. In many cultures, *story telling* is a central method for communicating history, lore, and wisdom (Au & Jordan, 1980; Kernan, 1977). Children learn to tell stories by listening, and many bring a strong sense of oral narrative with them when they begin school. They may weave bits and pieces of stories read to them or of television shows into the stories they share. Story telling can in fact play a crucial role in a literature-based classroom at all grade levels. It can "bring children into the act of storymaking [and provide] ways of creating stories *with* children and not just *for* or *to* children" (Trousdale, 1990, p. 164).

No matter what at grade level story telling is introduced, teachers will probably be the first official storyteller; but students should be encouraged from the start to participate in the process. Teachers should also encourage students to participate by filling in sound effects, words, or even ideas. Oral story telling allows students to draw on their sense of story grammar (Applebee, 1978) and their sense of fantasy (Chukovsky, 1963) and effortlessly to become a kind of author. Directions for preparing a story for oral story telling are presented in Table 7–4.

Round robin stories can be effective too. The teacher or indeed a student starts a story, and at what seems like a provocative point, stops so that another person can continue. In this way, no one person has to think up the whole tale, but participants do have to maintain a logical story structure. This activity increases students' awareness of story parts and makes them more sensitive to details and transition points in story making. The more students become involved in the story making, the more quickly they will be able to tell stories on their own and to write them fluently as well.

Readers Theater is another approach to increase students' understanding of literature. It involves oral interpretation of pieces of literature or scripts. Even very young readers can participate. A few simple props, such as chairs, a hat, a flower, and so forth, are all that is needed. Children use facial and body gestures to accompany their interpretation of what they read.

Readers Theater has many advantages. To be successful participants in Readers Theater, students must comprehend what they will present, both from the perspective of their "part" and from that of the story as a whole. Consequently, Readers Theater first of all strengthens students' strategies for constructing meaning from text. Second, audiences receive visual evidence of how their peers have comprehended the material they present. Readers Theater may reinforce for the audience their own comprehension strategies, may augment them, or may cause dissonance. If audience members disagree with the presenters' interpretation, which could happen with complex material, the resulting debate could involve high-level, thoughtful literacy analysis.

In addition, the approach enlivens—gives voice to—literature. The auditory component of preparing and listening to the presentation deepens students' sense of the literary "register," which may be vastly different from their own vernacular language. Increasing their sense of the cadence and pattern of "book language" can help students monitor their silent reading more effectively. Procedures are listed in Table 7–5.

Interdisciplinary Responses

Activities that draw on disciplines other than reading and writing allow students to work alone or collaboratively with the ideas in a book or story and turn them into another medium. Whether these activities use art, writing, drama or other media, they allow students to deepen appreciation and to expand their comprehension of what they have read. Table 7–6 lists some of the activities that can be assigned, suggested, or simply made possible for students.

Table 7–5
Readers Theater

Participants
Students in a literature-based classroom

Materials
Multiple copies of literature or scripts
Simple props to enhance presentation

Context
Literature-based program

Duration
A week or so for preparing the script and practicing prior to performance

Goal
To offer an interpretation of a piece of literature in a pleasurable fashion
To foster interpretative comprehension

Procedures
1. Select material to present as Readers Theater.
   - The piece should have an interesting, ideally suspenseful story line, rich language, considerable dialogue, and strong characters. Folktales, especially humorous ones, are good sources.
   - Prepare the script by removing any extraneous parts from the material, shortening long speeches, and eliminating unnecessary descriptions or transitional material. The part of a narrator can be written to provide transitions and maintain flow.
2. Prepare multiple copies of the script. Participants should have the entire script; they should highlight their own parts for easy reading.
3. Gather minimal props such as hats, shawls, jackets, chairs, and lamps, if they will enhance the presentation. Decide upon background music if any will be used.
4. Have students practice their parts and help them adjust pitch, intonation, volume, and so forth for a smooth delivery.
5. Present the Readers Theatre to other class members and to other audiences.

It is important that interdisciplinary activities be perceived as important and valuable opportunities to demonstrate how students think and feel about what they have read; they lose their effectiveness if they seem tangential to the literacy curriculum. Not all books can sustain the kind of rethinking and rereading that such projects demand, so teachers should take care both in helping students select books to expand in these ways and in deciding what kind of activity will be most appropriate.

Table 7–6
Interdisciplinary Responses to Literature

Drama Activities

- Making puppets for favorite characters and presenting their story as a puppet play
- Using puppets to act out events from stories
- Writing scripts to dramatize stories
- Performing improvisational dramatics based on stories
- Mounting presentations of plays that have been read in class
- Performing Readers Theater
- Developing "story boards" for plays or movie scripts

Art Activities

- Drawing or painting to represent what has been read
- Creating murals about individual stories or about several pieces of literature
- Designing cartoon representations of what has been read, either fiction or non-fiction
- Making dioramas
- Designing illustrations for books that have few if any pictures or designing new illustrations for picture books
- Creating shortened versions of stories in the form of picture books
- Drawing what characters look like based on descriptive evidence presented in stories

Writing Activities

- Developing alternate endings for stories, including adding new characters
- Adding or taking out characters and rewriting stories
- Writing letters to authors or illustrators (send in care of their publishers)
- Writing letters to characters in books
- Writing letters, diaries, etc. from the perspective of characters in fiction or non-fiction books
- Turning narratives into scripts; writing scripts about nonfiction books, especially history books
- Writing newspaper accounts of real events

Other Content Areas

- Developing long-term research projects
- Finding other books, newspaper accounts, and nonprint sources to supplement what has been read
- Finding primary sources about what has been read
- Integrating writing, art, and drama with other content areas to create collaborative projects

Students should have opportunities to share their interdisciplinary responses with other classmates and with other audiences as well. If several classes use a literature-based approach to literacy instruction, teachers might stage a book fair at which students could display their favorite books and their literature response activities. Debates, dramatizations, or Readers Theater could be arranged between the classes to give students opportunities to extend their interactions with their favorite literature.

SUMMARY

Literature in all its forms has value in helping students grow as readers, writers, listeners, and thinkers. It adds to their knowledge base and enriches their lives. Well-chosen and thoughtfully used, literature can be the foundation of literacy instruction throughout the elementary years. It provides a motivating replacement for structured basal readers and language arts textbooks and can encourage students to become lifelong readers.

QUESTIONS AND TASKS

1. Be sure that you understand these terms:
    a. book talks
    b. literature logs
    c. Readers Theater
    d. thematic units

2. Begin to think about procedures for obtaining books for a literature-based program. List as many sources as you can—other than bookstores—and compare your list with others in your class.

3. Select a well-known children's author such as E. B. White, Maurice Sendak, Ezra Jack Keats, or Arnold Lobel. Survey their works and try to find out something about their lives. Prepare a brief mini-lesson about the author and works and, if possible, present it to a group of students. Share some of the books with them.

4. Select six to ten books on a common theme, issue, or event and work them into a thematic unit to present to students. Plan as many writing and interdisciplinary experiences as you can.

5. Think about the concept of a literacy workshop. In what ways does this discussion of literature-based instruction change or expand your definition of a workshop environment?

Introduction to the Reading/Writing/Thinking Classroom

This chapter discusses reading, writing, and thinking. It stresses that teachers in elementary classrooms should view the three as interconnected and plan instruction accordingly. Chapter 9 builds on this discussion, providing suggestions for applications of the reading/writing/thinking connection.

THE READING/WRITING CONNECTION

Reading and writing are related behaviors, and both are inherently thinking processes. Clay (1979, p. 124) maintained that the "building up process [of writing] is an excellent complement to the visual analysis of text [in reading], which is a breaking down process." Unfortunately, in many classrooms the emphasis is on reading subskills, grammar, and writing mechanics, which can obscure the reciprocity between reading and writing. Instead of practicing meaningful tasks, many students participate in fragmented drill activities that dilute students' awareness that reading and writing are mutually inclusive processes and discourage thoughtful explorations of writing. The very behaviors that motivate young learners to discover conventions of print in the world around them and to "invent" a spelling system are sacrificed instead of nurtured. When students do not engage in real literacy activities, their positive attitudes toward literacy learning dwindle (Daly, Vangelisti, & Witte, 1988).

This situation need not be the norm. In many classrooms, reading and writing are coming to be viewed more holistically. As discussed in Chapter 1, reading instruction has undergone change in recent years, and an increased understanding of the reciprocity of reading and writing is part of the change. Additionally, writing instruction has changed considerably in the recent past, and in many classrooms, students are writing more and writing more thoughtfully. Interest in teaching critical thinking skills (Costa & Lowery, 1989; Swartz & Perkins, 1989) has also influenced reading and writing instruction, as theorists and teachers acknowledge the role of active, sophisticated thinking in literacy and the ways in which reading and writing support critical thinking.

INFLUENCES ON LITERACY

Many students learn to read at a superficial level, calling out words successfully but rarely comprehending text and even less often truly thinking about what they have read. Equally, many students never progress far enough with writing to become thoughtful writers; they may be able to string words together into grammatically correct and properly punctuated pieces of text, but often their writing is shallow and empty. The variables that influence reading comprehension and thoughtful writing are discussed next. All contribute to students' abilities to think critically about literacy activities.

Background Knowledge

Perhaps the most important elements that influence children's ability to read with high levels of comprehension and to write thoughtful texts are the background knowledge and experiences they bring to their tasks (Langer, 1984). Cazden (1982) wrote, "A critical resource in constructing meaning is the knowledge of people and places, events and ideas, sometimes called scripts or schemata, that the reader brings to any reading task. . . . the internal psychological context of organized semantic networks of knowledge of the world that are in part related to the reader's vocabulary" (p. 417). Background knowledge and experiences give children mental "hooks" on which to "hang" their new thinking and learning.

Purpose for Reading and Writing

Individuals' purposes for literacy can influence reading comprehension and writing both positively and negatively. Determining purpose, for example, to seek information, insight or pleasure, or to clarify ideas, helps readers guide themselves through text. Purpose contributes to the mindset readers bring to the reading act and to their search of text in an effort to construct meaning. If readers do not establish a purpose for reading, however informally, their reading will be inefficient and possibly unsuccessful. They may not attend to important parts of text, miss nuances of language, miscomprehend, or fail to comprehend at all. Teachers can help students learn to determine appropriate purposes for reading and to include within their purpose active, critical thinking about the texts they encounter.

Although a reader's purpose is more than the selection of stance, the two are related. Indeed, a reader's purpose may dictate a stance and stymie full comprehension. As Rosenblatt (1991) wrote, "The reader's own purpose or [previous] schooling that indoctrinated the same undifferentiated approach to all texts may dictate a different stance from the one the writer intended. For example, a student reading *A Tale of Two Cities* who knows there will be a test on facts about characters and plot may be led to adopt a predominantly efferent stance, screening out all but the relevant data" (p. 160).

It is easy to see that writers as well as readers must learn to establish purpose. Designating a particular purpose for writing, along with the selection of an audience, voice, and tone is part of learning to be a thoughtful writer. Students will learn to do this when they are given many purposes for writing and when they write for audiences beyond their own classroom teacher.

Context for Literacy

Finally, the context in which one reads or writes influences success. A personal example will illustrate:

> Within the three weeks preceding this writing, I have read successfully in my own living room, bedroom, kitchen, and office; in a plane traveling across the Pacific Ocean; and in hotel rooms in Hong Kong and mainland China. I also tried unsuccessfully to read in an airport waiting room in Guangzhou, China, as I waited out a typhoon in order to be able to return to Hong Kong. Unable to land in the storm in Hong Kong, my plane had been forced back to mainland China, where I (and fellow travelers) had had to spend the night. Because we had already officially left China when we relinquished our visas and boarded the plane to Hong Kong, we had to "surrender" our passports to immigration officials at the airport. We all sat—apprehensively—hoping the weather would clear so that we could leave. My novel, Tom Robbins' *Skinny Legs and All*, was no longer wonderfully funny. Back it went into my suitcase, and out came my knitting. The *context* was not right for me to read with comprehension, enjoyment, and appreciation; in the airport, the rote skill of knitting was more comforting than "constructing meaning" could be.

For children, the classroom can be almost as inhospitable as the crowded, foreign airport was to me. Waiting to "demonstrate" comprehension by answering questions can be as anxiety-producing as waiting to get my passport back; trying to understand expectations for behavior can be as frustrating as trying to understand directions and information provided only in Chinese. In short, the classroom, as it has traditionally been structured, may not be a positive context for reading comprehension, especially if the prevailing definition of comprehension includes a strong component of thinking critically about text. To think critically means to take risks, to offer one's own ideas; a classroom context to support critical thinking must be accepting, open, and reassuring.

Equally, to write well requires that students take risks, offer their own ideas, and stretch in their attempts to express themselves. A classroom in which neatness, correctness, and adherence to specific assignments are valued above all else is a context that tells students that risk-taking and experimentation are not welcome. In such classrooms, students who conform to predetermined standards may be deemed "successful"; but seldom will they learn to be thoughtful writers.

Cognition and Metacognition

Real comprehension cannot take place without thinking. Literacy users must think about the text they are reading and about the means by which and the context in which this new construction is taking place. Equally, they must learn to think about the texts they themselves construct as they write.

Learning *how* to think about reading and writing gives children control over their literacy behaviors. They can better access appropriate background knowledge, establish purposes for literacy, and monitor comprehension; they can select from their various literacy strategies for the ongoing task of gaining meaning from print. Teachers in reading/writing/thinking classrooms help students become aware of their thinking by focusing on, discussing, and even labeling students' thought processes whenever possible (Costa & Lowery, 1989). These behaviors encourage students to *think about thinking* in new and productive ways.

This kind of thinking involves *metacognition*, the process of deliberately thinking about thinking. "Metacognition is our ability to know what we know and what we don't know. . . . our ability to plan a strategy for producing what information is needed, to be conscious of our own steps and strategies during the act of problem solving, and to reflect and evaluate the productivity of our own thinking" (Costa, 1984, p. 57). The metacognitive tasks in literacy are (a) self-knowledge, (b) task knowledge, and (c) self-monitoring (Swartz & Perkins, 1989). The tasks are summarized in Figure 8–1 and briefly discussed in the text that follows.

An important aspect of self-knowledge is children's sense of efficacy—how they view themselves as literacy users. Children who acknowledge their own strengths and weaknesses as literacy users and who perceive themselves to be making progress in reading and writing are not daunted by the increasingly difficult literacy tasks that confront them; they possess strategies to think their way through new tasks and have the self-confidence to know when they need to seek help.

Figure 8–1
Metacognitive Behavior

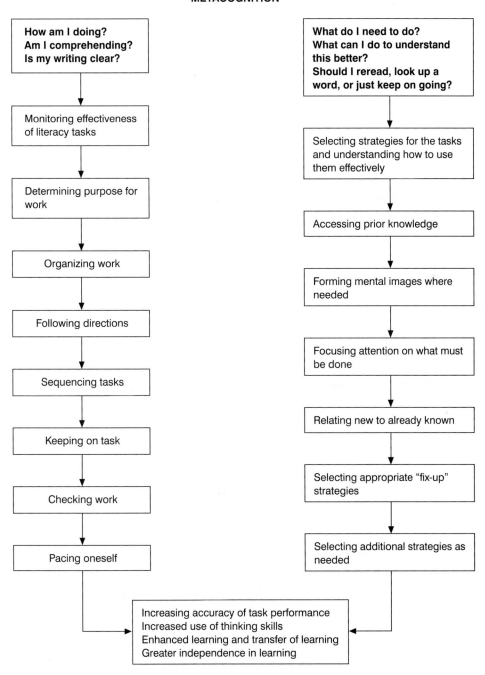

Children who think of themselves as poor readers and writers may place very real obstacles in their path to growth. They may perceive the acquisition of literacy as an impossible task, one that will never make sense and that they can never master. Johnston and Winograd (1985) referred to this situation as "passive failure," stating that, "Once learners view themselves as helpless, they perceive a lack of relationship between their behavior and its outcomes" (p. 291). Children may give up *trying* to make sense of literacy and come to approach reading and writing tasks with a limited, rigid, and often poorly understood set of strategies. They think that comprehending is a matter of luck rather than the result of the conscious application of reading strategies. Instead of trying to understand *how* they can approach literacy tasks, they think that they simply cannot read or write well.

Task knowledge and self-monitoring are closely related metacognitive behaviors. By understanding what a task requires, readers and writers are better able to plan and to make progress toward completing the task. Although students may not be able to state step-by-step procedures for undertaking each literacy task they encounter, they should have some sense that different tasks do require different behaviors and that they, as readers and writers, can select and control their behaviors. Children with a limited view of what literacy is (for example, reading is "saying the words," and writing is "spelling correctly") will have difficulty conceptualizing this point.[1]

Students also need to trust implicitly that reading should make sense and use this trust as part of their self-monitoring. This is true whether they are reading their own work or that of other authors. Writing about his own reading, Mosenthal (1989) stated:

> [M]onitoring refers to checking out how sensible things are. It is not just a concern for failure [to comprehend]; it is also a concern for success. With respect to failure, when I misidentify a word or overlook a transition, an inference is not made or a misinference is made. I say to myself, "That didn't make sense." It is not the lost or misguided inference that brings me to my senses, but the awareness that *no sense is being made*. This awareness is healthy, for it is the result of a desire to achieve certainty. It may prompt reaction, depending on how uncertain I am about the direction of my movement in the text. I may stop to contemplate the significance of a word or section of text. In so doing, I strive to make strong the mesh of relationships that connect me to what has gone before and that guides me into what lies ahead. (pp. 248–249; emphasis added)

Developing and flexibly accessing a repertoire of metacognitive strategies increases students' literacy abilities; however, metacognitive strategies in and of themselves do not produce critical readers and thoughtful writers. Having ascertained that they are comprehending the text at hand, students must engage in a kind of inquiry *about* the text. This behavior becomes a meaningful part of students' approach to literacy when they have thought-provoking texts to read and

---

[1]Interviews used as part of the assessment process give teachers an opportunity to identify students' incorrect ideas. They can then work to correct students' misconceptions and broaden their understanding of what literacy is and what it involves.

authentic writing tasks—and when they have been taught and understand strategies to use in this inquiry. Table 8–1 lists commonly accepted thinking skills and explains their application in literacy work.

Transacting Meaning: The Influence of Louise Rosenblatt

Louise Rosenblatt (1938/1978, 1979, 1985, 1991), drawing extensively on the learning theories of John Dewey, developed a model of *transacting meaning* in reading and writing. She wrote that as readers read, "[n]ew tentative guidelines, new bases for hypothetic structure, present themselves. A complex, nonlinear, self-correcting transaction between reader and text continues—the arousal and fulfillment (or frustration) of expectations and the construction of a growing, often revised 'meaning.' Finally, a synthesis or organization, more or less coherent and complete, emerges, the result of a to-and-fro interplay between reader and text" (1989, p. 158; see also Clifford, 1990).

Inherent in Rosenblatt's conception that *individual readers transact individual texts* is an unmistakable component of critical thinking. Background knowledge, one's purpose for reading, the levels and kinds of thought one exerts, and other highly personal variables contribute to the meaning each reader takes away from text. Rosenblatt (1985) wrote: "Although all students should not be required to give the same sort of expression to their reactions [to text], in most cases a personal experience will elicit a definite response; it will lead to some kind of reflection. It may also lead to the desire to communicate this to others whom the boy or girl trusts. An atmosphere of informal, friendly exchange could be created. . . . When the young reader considers why he [or she] has responded in a certain way, he [or she] is learning both to read more adequately and to seek personal meaning in [text]"(p. 70).

Rosenblatt (1938/1978) further proposed that there are two kinds of reading, represented by an *efferent* or *aesthetic stance*. Good readers consciously adopt either stance as they attempt to "transact" meaning from the text they are reading. Efferent reading is performed when one needs to get information from text. Aesthetic reading serves to provide pleasure, as when one reads a story voluntarily and focuses on what is being experienced during reading. In many situations, readers assume a stance somewhere in the middle of the efferent-to-aesthetic reading continuum and may even shift stances as the text requires. Awareness of the two stances and of the different ways one approaches text to accomplish these kinds of reading are part of the metacognitive behaviors critical readers apply.[2]

Writing also produces transactions, the first of which involves the "residue of past experiences of language, spoken and written," that writers bring to their task (Rosenblatt, 1989, p. 163). Other transactions include those between the writer and

---

[2]Of course, this does not mean that literacy users must know the terms *efferent* and *aesthetic*, nor even that the way in which they approach particular tasks is referred to as *taking a stance*. What is important is recognizing that one must approach literacy tasks in a purposeful way and that there are distinctly different ways in which to be purposeful about reading and writing.

Table 8–1
Thinking Skills and Their Use in Reading and Writing

Knowledge Level
- Determining explicitly stated meanings of words, phrases, sentences, and long pieces of text
- Identifying explicitly stated main ideas, details, themes, and so forth
- Making accurate observations
- Selecting correct words to state ideas explicitly and correctly
- Applying correct rules of mechanics in drafting and revising

Generative Level
- Producing multiple interpretations of text where appropriate
- Linking existing and new ideas in novel ways in both reading and writing
- Generating many ideas for writing

Interpretative/Inferential Level
- Distinguishing fact from opinion, literal from figurative meanings, and cause-effect relationships
- Determining implicitly stated meanings
- Understanding the use of evidence in reading and writing for causal explanations, predictions, and generalizations
- Understanding analogies and using them correctly in writing
- Understanding and using conditional (if . . . then) and categorical (all . . . some) arguments
- Recognizing and presenting logical relationships

Evaluation or Problem-Solving Level
- Drawing conclusions based on data
- Presenting data in a way that leads to logical conclusions
- Evaluating and presenting generalizations
- Carrying analyses of information to all levels of thinking
- Uncovering assumptions and presenting one's own assumptions clearly
- Assessing feelings, attitudes, and values in what is read, including one's own writing
- Presenting feelings, attitudes, and values clearly

---

himself or herself as reader and critic. Writers query themselves on the quality and comprehensibility of what they are producing. Finally, writers and their readers must transact meaning, and thoughtful writers consider the nature of this transaction carefully. "Whether communication [of meaning] is achieved depends largely on the writer's taking into account the resemblances and the differences between what the potential reader will bring to the text and the linguistic and life experiences from which the writing springs" (Rosenblatt, 1989, p. 169).

Although Rosenblatt's primary focus was not curriculum issues, her work has and should continue to influence the decisions educators make. She wrote: "Students' achievement of insight into their own reading and writing processes should be seen as the long-term justification for various curricular and teaching strategies" (1989, p. 173).

Judith Langer (1990a, 1990b) has extended Rosenblatt's concepts of stance to propose four distinct interpretative stances, all of which emphasize readers' movements in, through, and out of the texts they encounter. Langer's stances are not linear; like Rosenblatt's, they exist on a continuum and readers may switch from one to another as they construct meaning. Langer has referred to meaning as "envisionment" or "what the reader understands at a particular point in time, the questions she has, as well as her hunches about how [a] piece will unfold. Envisionment develops as the reading progresses. Some information is no longer important, some is added, and some is changed. What readers come away with at the end of the reading [is] the final envisionment. This includes what they understand, what they don't, and the questions they still have" (1990b, p. 812). Langer's four stances are outlined in Table 8–2.

Langer's model offers teachers a way of understanding how students think when they read critically for varied purposes. Teachers come to see that as readers comprehend, they engage in a series of changing relations with the text at hand and that each changing relationship adds to the depth and intensity of the meaning that the readers are constructing. The movement in, through, and out of a text must be an active process, one that readers themselves must undertake and propel forward. However, understanding these four stances can help teachers develop questions to cue students to the kinds of mental operations they should be using as they read. As will be discussed later in this chapter, the questions become a kind of "scaffold" that supports students as they learn to engage in this kind of reading on their own. As students become familiar with the thinking processes each stance fosters, they interact with text in richer, more reflective ways.

Table 8–2
Stances for Movement In, Through, and Out of Text

1. *Being out and stepping in.* Readers try to make an initial contact with the text, often by surveying what is presented and drawing on background knowledge.

2. *Being in and moving through.* Readers use both text and background knowledge to develop meaning; they ask questions about elements such as motivation and causality in stories and about the accumulating ideas in informational texts.

3. *Being in and stepping out.* Readers reflect on their own lives, on the lives of characters, or on the human condition; text knowledge is used to reflect on personal knowledge.

4. *Stepping out and objectifying the experience.* Readers distance themselves from the text in order to evaluate it, objectify it, and relate it to other texts and to their own experiences.

THE READING/WRITING/THINKING CLASSROOM

Teachers who recognize the interconnection of reading, writing, and thinking make certain decisions about their classrooms and the activities that engage students. These decisions concern the actual classroom environment, the opportunities for discussion about writing, and the frequency and diversity of writing.

As has been stressed before, the classroom must be a literate environment, one in which the value of literacy is demonstrated continually. The classroom also must offer opportunities to share and to discuss reading and writing, reading and writing done by the students and perhaps by the teacher and by the other authors students encounter in the material they read. Students must be allowed to talk about their work with each other and with their teacher in both structured and unstructured settings.

Teachers seeking to establish a reading/writing/thinking classroom must be thinkers themselves. In addition to making many decisions, they draw extensively upon their knowledge base about child development, the acquisition of literacy skills, and the kinds of pedagogical techniques and strategies that can best support and nurture their students' critical thinking. Their knowledge base begins with a thorough understanding of reading comprehension and the many concepts associated with critical thinking.

The importance of creating a sense of community, in which students learn together in an open, accepting environment, has been stressed throughout this book and bears mentioning again here. At any level of development, reading and writing involve a kind of exposure, in that readers divulge constructions of meaning from text that may still be tentative and writers prepare something to be shared with others. In many classrooms, the only audience for students' work is the teacher, who may give feedback but primarily assigns grades. In the reading/writing/thinking classroom, the audience is broader because students' work is shared, discussed, critiqued, questioned, and defended. The tone of the classroom must be one that makes students feel comfortable presenting their works-in-progress and their ideas to their peers and to their teacher. There must be a mutual understanding that when work is discussed, it is the work, not the students themselves, that is the object of discussion. Rules and procedures must be negotiated and agreed upon by all so that discussions can be thoughtful, civil, and productive for all students. Teachers must carefully explain expectations for behavior and required procedural steps for sharing discussions of individual students' work. Teachers must also enforce these expectations to ensure that all students will benefit fully. Among the expectations that teachers present are what Richard Paul, an expert in teaching critical thinking, refers to as "intellectual moral virtues" (1987a, 1987b, 1988). The five "virtues" are presented in Table 8–3.

MEANS TO ENCOURAGE CRITICAL THINKING

Teachers build on their own knowledge base about literacy and thinking by employing specific instructional strategies to encourage students' metacognition

Table 8–3
"Intellectual Moral Virtues"[3]

---

1. *Intellectual Humility.* Students recognize the limits of their own knowledge and are sensitive to the limitations and biases of their viewpoints.

   • "Well, I just don't know enough to judge that idea."

2. *Intellectual Courage.* Students face and deal fairly with ideas, viewpoints, and beliefs against which they have strong negative feelings or to which they have not given enough consideration.

   • "That's an interesting point, I don't think I agree, but tell me more."

3. *Intellectual Empathy.* Students can put themselves in other people's places and understand their points of view.

   • "I can really see how that comment would upset you."

4. *Intellectual Integrity.* Students recognize the importance of being true to their own thinking and also of being consistent in applying standards of evidence and proof to oneself as well as to others.

   • "Well, now, this is what I think the story meant but let me go back and check what the author wrote."

5. *Intellectual Perseverance.* Students will struggle with confusion and questions over a period of time in order to achieve better understanding or insight.

   • "I just don't understand but I'm going to think about it until it makes sense."

---

and critical thinking. They use verbal "scaffolds" to help students learn to think about their reading and writing, participate in carefully designed, structured interactions with students, and offer students numerous "thinking tools" that help them become independent critical thinkers.

Thinking Scaffolds

The concept of *scaffolding* has its roots in the verbal interaction between parents and preverbal offspring, as when parents structure a game such as peekaboo so that the child will learn to participate. Scaffolds are not pat phrases, questions, or scripted statements to be offered at predetermined times. They are instead parts of a supportive verbal framework or scaffold that teachers attempt to provide to help children understand processes they are trying to master.

As they use instructional scaffolds, teachers first assume entire responsibility for instruction and guidance of learning, that is, they provide fully developed verbal explanations to "scaffold" or support students' efforts to think about and complete tasks. Teachers relinquish control gradually as students gain confidence and

---

[3]Adapted from "Critical Thinking, Moral Integrity and Citizenship: Teaching for Intellectual Virtues" by Richard W. Paul, 1987. Paper presented at Seventh Annual Conference on Critical Thinking and Educational Reform, Sonoma State University, Rohnert Park, CA.

skill, until finally students can assume entire responsibility for independent completion of tasks and demonstration of skills. Teachers' role throughout is to gauge the extent to which and the points at which to release responsibility, or to remove components of the initial scaffold and let students figure out what to do themselves (Cazden, 1988).

Instructional use of scaffolds frequently stresses skills mastery; for the reading/writing/thinking classroom, *thinking scaffolds* are proposed. To be most beneficial, thinking scaffolds should be embedded within the fabric of instruction and learning activities so that they become the standard way of interacting between teachers, learners, and texts. Thinking scaffolds involve two teacher behaviors, often used in concert: (a) offering explanations and modeling behaviors, and (b) asking questions. Thinking scaffolds help literacy learners refine and build upon hypotheses about literacy and clarify misconceptions before they become ingrained. Scaffolds also provide new information that children need to extend hypotheses and to become motivated to extend their thinking and stretch to new understandings and mastery.

If we think of school reading activities as consisting of three parts—prereading, reading, and postreading—Table 8–4 makes sense. It shows how teachers can provide literacy and thinking scaffolds at appropriate points in students' interactions with text throughout students' school years. The nature of the interactions between teachers, students, and texts will change, but goals and means of interacting will remain essentially the same. Throughout students' school experiences, the primary goal will be to encourage students to think about their own literacy behaviors and about the texts they encounter. The primary means will be verbal—modeling and questioning, both about what is being read and about the processes used to construct meaning about the text.

Questioning

Much classroom talking—and thinking—involves questions from both teachers and students. Teachers' questioning and subsequent answers and explanations become scaffolds for the kinds of self-monitoring and critical thinking that students must learn to do independently. "Teachers use questions to elicit certain cognitive objectives or thinking skills. Embedded in these questions and in statements are cues for the cognitive task or behavior that the student is to carry out. There is a relationship between the type of thinking [cued by] the teacher's verbal behavior and the type of thinking students use in response" (Costa & Lowery, 1989, p. 22).

Questions should not serve primarily to maintain the momentum of an instructional sequence, although they certainly can be meaningfully used in this way. In addition, teachers must remember that students' correct answers do not necessarily indicate understanding and that incorrect answers should be analyzed diagnostically before instruction moves on. As Cazden (1988) reminded us, "There is a critical difference between helping a child somehow get a particular answer and helping a child gain some conceptual understanding from which answers to similar questions can be constructed at a future time" (p. 108). Questions that help

Table 8–4
Scaffolding for Prereading, During Reading, and Postreading

In each instance, the teacher will use verbal scaffolding to help students understand appropriate tasks.

Prereading Scaffolds
- Using title, illustrations, and other textual clues to activate background knowledge
- Using clues to make predictions about text
- Anticipating text based on knowledge of text structure
- Analyzing illustrations or graphics to gain a preview of the text

During Reading Scaffolds
- Summarizing what has been read so far
- Monitoring comprehension
- Checking on predictions
- Altering predictions based on new evidence
- Checking on accuracy of text, possible biases, point of view, and so forth

Postreading Scaffolds
- Monitoring final comprehension in general
- Monitoring specific aspects of comprehension with reference to aspects of text
- Checking on predictions with reference to evidence in text
- Responding affectively with reference to aspects of text that produced specific feelings
- Aligning new information with previous learning

children gain conceptual understanding and that can be generalized to other situations and diverse content areas are essential for learners to become critical thinkers. Equally important are questions that help students gain strategies for mastering content area material (Peters, 1990).

Questions to stimulate critical thinking are of three distinct types: (a) those that target concepts and strategies; (b) those that address specific pieces of text, however large or small; and (c) those that address content area learning.

When teachers pose worthwhile critical thinking questions about concepts and strategies, they invariably couple them with explanations and expansions. These types of questions are appropriate scaffolding statements. By questioning in this way, teachers attempt to gain insight into children's cognitive processes and provide corrective and elaborative feedback on what children are trying to do. Teachers also try to structure interactions with specific texts so that students have experiences in critically thinking their way through literacy challenges and can generalize the strategies they develop to new texts they encounter.

Questions that teachers ask about texts should be open-ended enough to allow students to express opinions, offer interpretations, and externalize their processes of making sense of what they read. These questions may address organizational patterns of texts, details of what students are reading, or the more global meanings derived from text. Students should always be encouraged to draw upon both text and their own experiences to justify their answers. Teachers might also ask students to reconsider and reconceptualize text, as when they ask students to suggest alternative endings for a story.

Teachers need to ensure that students understand the parameters of questioning. Convincing students that there is *no one right answer* to a question is a difficult task, but this understanding is essential for critical thinking. Norris and Ennis (1989) encourage teachers to "be generous in interpreting students' responses," especially when they are learning to express their critical thinking to others (p. 155). By their very nature, many questions about content area learning *will* have only one right answer, but questions should not be a disguised oral quiz. Questions should strengthen students' skills by focusing their attention on the selection of appropriate strategies for content area reading and by developing alternative interpretations for what they read. In many ways, content area questions combine attributes of question types (a) and (b), discussed previously. Peters (1990) suggested, "The key here is the learner's ability to use content and strategy knowledge in a flexible manner and to transfer it to new learning experiences" (p. 67).

Questions to develop real critical reading are rarely found in basal reader teachers' manuals, anthologies of children's literature, or even content area textbooks. Teachers have to learn to make them up for themselves, recognizing fully that their questions will shape students' purposes for reading. Furthermore, to use questions effectively, teachers must first learn to be good listeners. They need to hear what students say lexically (what words they utter), what content knowledge they present, and what students' utterances imply about their thinking. To ferret out the cognitive implications of what children say, teachers must rely on their own knowledge about the structure and prerequisites of literacy learning. As expert literacy users, teachers can then elaborate upon, shape, or refocus statements appropriately. For example, if a child is grappling with a specific convention of writing or reading, the teacher might pose a question about what the child is trying to do, direct the child's attention to specific aspects of the behavior, and ask what the child thinks she should do next or differently. Using information about what the child claims she is doing and her hunches about what she should be doing, the teacher can determine what the child has figured out correctly, what the child may have misunderstood, and how best to help the child think through the puzzle confronting her. Such a sequence affirms accurate thinking and averts perpetuation of incorrect ideas or inefficient strategies.

SUMMARY

In an ideal setting, students gain competence in reading, writing, and thinking by simultaneously practicing these behaviors in authentic, purposeful tasks. When teachers believe that their students are capable of strong, critical thought, they structure the classroom to provide opportunities to model their own thinking strategies and to challenge students toward higher levels of thinking. Reading, writing, and talking become means by which students externalize, analyze, and hone their own thinking skills.

QUESTIONS AND TASKS

1. Be sure that you understand these terms:
   a. background knowledge
   b. efferent and aesthetic stances
   c. envisionment
   d. metacognition
   e. thinking scaffold
   f. transacting meaning

2. With another person in class, find a piece of prose or a poem that you *expect* to be difficult. Read it silently and then discuss your progress in making sense of the material. Try to separate yourself from the process and analyze the ways in which you transacted meaning independently and together. What does this process suggest about literacy instruction?

3. Consider the relationship between students' emerging expertise as literacy users and as thinkers. How do these aspects of development overlap and support each other?

4. The chapter states that Norris and Ennis advise teachers to "be generous in interpreting students' responses." What does this advice mean to you? How can the generosity of teachers help students become better critical thinkers?

9 CHAPTER

Activities to Encourage Critical Thinking About Literacy

A student in a graduate workshop on reading and critical thinking, responding to a quotation from the writings of Louise Rosenblatt, wrote the work presented in Table 9–1. It shows how she transacted meaning with the quote and then integrated theory and practice. The piece presents an excellent contrast of two classrooms, one in which critical thinking and reading are supported and one in which the opposite is true. Before reading on, first read Table 9–1 to orient yourself to some of the possibilities available to teachers who want to establish reading/writing/thinking classrooms.

In this chapter, approaches to encourage critical reading are presented first, followed by a discussion of writing. Of course, considerable overlap exists in all

Table 9–1
Student Assignment/Critical Reading Class[1]

Students' achievement of insight into their own reading and writing processes should be seen as the long-term justification for various curricular and teaching strategies.

—Rosenblatt, 1989, p. 173

Student's Paper

In contemplating Rosenblatt's ideas the following came to mind:

The whole idea of movie magic is that interweave of powerful image, and dialogue, and performance, and music that can never be separated. . . . But only a generation of readers will spawn a generation of writers.

—Steven Spielberg, excerpt from his acceptance speech at the Academy Awards ceremony, 1987.

The following dialogue illustrates a number of Rosenblatt's ideas translated into classroom actualities.

Setting: The middle school students are Dick and Janie. Each is emerging from his/her respective English class. They converse as they walk to the cafeteria.

Janie: Ho-hum. I'm starved. Heading for lunch, Dick?

Dick: I've already eaten, but I'll join you for dessert. How was your English class?

Janie: Well, Dick. Another lit class over. Only 130 to go. Will I ever make it?

Dick: Janie, you don't sound excited. What are you reading?

Janie: We're reading *Bridge to Terabithia,* I think. All Mr. Smith does is ask, "Who are the main characters? Who can find where the foreshadowing occurs?" Then Sam Jones answers all the questions, and we all go back to sleep. B-o-o-ring. What are you reading?

Dick: We're reading that, too, but we all love it. Before we started, before we even had the book, Mrs. Miller divided us up into groups of four. Then, we were each given five statements to think about, agree or disagree with, and discuss.

Janie: And you didn't even have the book yet?

Dick: Nope. I remember one of the statements was "In matters of importance, young people should agree with what their parents tell them." Others were "One of the scariest things is to have a close friend die" and "It is usually wrong for young people to make up imaginary friends or places."

Janie: I could get into that. When I was in second grade, my closest friend was in

---

[1]This dialogue was prepared by Karen Mechem, for the Summer 1990 Institute on Critical Thinking held at Pine Manor College, Wellesley, MA; it is used by permission with only minor changes.

Table 9–1
continued

a car accident, and she was in the hospital for a long, long time before she finally died. Anyway, after you all discussed these, what then? You got the book, right?

Dick: Nope, not yet. Then Mrs. Miller read the first few pages of the book on an overhead as we followed along. She "thought aloud" as she went down the notes she'd take if she were a student reading the book.

Janie: Then you got the book, right?

Dick: Yeah. Then we got the book and our own small notebook to take notes in, just for this novel. We talked about writing down characters' names and their descriptions and significant events as what would make good notes. We also had graphic organizers to help us keep theme and plot straight, and we were told to include our own personal thoughts and reactions as well.

Janie: So, then you had silent reading and the teacher grades papers at her desk, right?

Dick: Janie, Janie, Janie! Will you ever learn? Remember, we were still in groups of four. Mrs. Miller said we could *either* read silently or we could take turns reading aloud to each other. Then we did our group *think alouds* about what was a significant event or character to note. Sometimes we disagreed about what was important, so we talked about it and gave reasons. We had some questions about one part, so we asked Mrs. Miller. She was walking around, ready to help anyone who needed it.

Janie: Let's get back to the reading. I would have thought most kids would have read by themselves. No, huh?

Dick: From listening to Mrs. Miller's first reading of it, we remembered it was fun to read and listen to each other in small groups. So we did that, but only those people who wanted to had to read out loud. There wasn't any pressure.

Janie: Let's go back to the paper you first got with the statements. What did you finally do with that?

Dick: We found evidence in the book about whether the main characters, Jess and Leslie, would have agreed or disagreed with each statement, and we kept track of the evidence as we read.

Janie: You did that in groups, too?

Dick: Oh, sure. We discussed it. But then, on our own, each kid had to choose one statement and expand on it. You had to tell whether you thought Jess or Leslie would agree or disagree with the statement and you had to quote parts of the text to support your idea. Then you stated whether you

Table 9–1
continued

	agreed or disagreed yourself and told why from your own experience, as much as possible.
Janie:	Sounds like your teacher has it all together. I suppose you read each others' papers and corrected grammar and stuff.
Dick:	Well, yes and no. Everyone had to read two papers: one of a person who wrote on the same statement as you did and one written on a different statement. But we didn't really pay attention to grammar or spelling because these are only drafts. We'll fix them up later.
Janie:	It sounds like this is all taking a long time.
Dick:	Well, we're into six class periods and we're about halfway through. But, that's OK because everyone loves the book. Plus, we learn a lot from being in both a "writer's seat" and an "editor's seat."
Janie:	What do you mean?
Dick:	Well, you have to defend your own writing; but when you read another person's paper that is about the same statement and you make editorial comments, you learn a lot about reading and writing. Lots of times, another person finds a reference or has an idea that can make your own paper better.
Janie:	Isn't that cheating?
Dick:	Mrs. Miller has a different attitude about that. She says we learn by reading, writing, talking to each other, and even by listening—all in a giant mish-mosh.
Janie:	That sounds great! What are you doing next in class?
Dick:	We're going to listen to a professional recording of the parts of the story we haven't read yet, and Mrs. Miller is going to read to us from some of the autobiographical stuff the author has written. We're going to complete a set of graphic organizers about the relationships between plot, setting, theme, and character development, and then we're going to dramatize some of the important scenes, like between Jess and his family. And we're going to try to figure out how the story might have changed if Jess had been a girl and Leslie has been a boy. . . . But, Janie, where are you going? I thought you wanted lunch.
Janie:	I'm going to see my guidance counselor to see if I can switch into your class.

The contrast between Dick and Janie's classes illustrates the differences between classes where students are given assigned reading to do and those in which they are invited to transact their own meaning from text.

schoolwork; students realize that strategies learned for reading work are equally valuable both in writing and in studying content area material. The discussion in this chapter is based on the assumptions that the curriculum is integrated as much as possible and that students recognize the need to consciously choose to use the described approaches to critical reading and thoughtful writing.

APPROACHES TO FOSTER CRITICAL READING

Talking about their reading, their thinking, and their processes for constructing meaning from text is essential if elementary school students are to become strong critical readers. The activities described next all involve talking and can be categorized as verbal interactional.

Think Alouds

A *think aloud* is a procedure used to externalize the thought processes involved in reading comprehension (Davey, 1983, 1985). Think alouds help students "develop flexibility of thought and an appreciation for the variety of ways to solve the same problem" (Costa & Lowery, 1989, pp. 61–62). When teachers introduce the think-aloud approach, they use modeling rather than direct instruction to encourage students' critical reading skills. After teachers have modeled the approach several times, they encourage students to engage in their own think-aloud sessions in pairs or in small groups to gain mutual support in their comprehension process. Procedures for think alouds are presented in Table 9–2.

When students understand the think-aloud approach, they can begin to use it themselves in small, interactive reading groups. Two or three students reading together and sharing their thought processes provide peer instruction and support as critical thinking strategies emerge. Students should also be encouraged to adapt the think-aloud approach as part of their silent reading, so that they use it to "think through" reading tasks and employ fix-up strategies as needed. Such a sub-vocalized think aloud promotes metacognition.

The Directed Thinking About Reading Activity

The think-aloud approach is an excellent way to prepare students for the *directed thinking about reading* activity or *DTAR*—a group reading session that encourages critical thinking about text.[2] Because DTAR activities take time, they are most appropriate for selections that can withstand analysis, such as interesting short stories or expository material.

The power of the DTAR activity resides in its flexibility. Teachers may conduct DTAR sessions with small or medium-sized groups of students; skills can be pre-

---

[2]This approach is also called the Directed Thinking Reading Activity, but the emphasis on *thinking about reading* seems to have a broader meaning that is more in line with the objectives of a reading/writing/thinking classroom; see Sardy, 1985.

Table 9–2
Directions for Think Alouds

1. Teacher creates or selects a passage to read aloud.
   • The passage should contain difficult, ambiguous, or unfamiliar words; contradictions; unfamiliar literary devices; or other puzzles to be solved. As an introduction, using an overhead transparency of the passage often works well.
2. Teacher models strategies by reading passage aloud while students follow silently. Teacher pauses and verbalizes aspects of the comprehension process such as:
   • making predictions
   • creating imagery
   • puzzling over confusing points
   • making links to prior knowledge, especially by using analogies and "like a" or "like when" statements
   • using fix-up strategies such as rereading or context clues
3. Teacher summarizes passage, checks predictions, and responds affectively when appropriate.
4. Teacher models procedure several times, involving students in discussions of what is read and how strategies were used.
5. Students practice think alouds with partners.
   • Again, passages should be carefully selected; they should illustrate reading problems students may encounter.
6. Students practice silently and keep track of the strategies they use as they read.
   • Students may want to keep a checklist handy as they read, both to tally their strategies and to remind them of others they might use (see number 2 above).
7. Students begin to apply the think-aloud procedure with daily school assignments in reading and content areas.
   • Students may still keep a checklist and should be encouraged to compare strategies with each other to gain insight into how peers tackle similar reading tasks.

Think alouds demonstrate to students that reading should make sense and that readers can use fix-up strategies when reading does not make sense.

sented through direct instruction or indirectly as students demonstrate misunderstanding or need. As will be discussed later, the approach can be used as the framework for long-term group activities such as unit projects. The phases of a DTAR activity are summarized in Table 9–3.

The emphasis in the DTAR is to teach students to view a "text as a set of problems to be solved rather than as a final word on a subject. [Students] learn that they are entitled to criticize and evaluate a text for the extent to which it succeeds

Table 9–3
Directed Thinking About Reading Activities

Prereading

1. Teacher finds a well-written text selection that is worth studying in some depth.

2. Teacher determines objectives for the DTAR.

3. Teacher surveys the text for novel or unusual vocabulary, jargon, unfamiliar words, unfamiliar literary devices, and graphic cues.

4. Teacher divides the selection into logical segments to determine points at which students' reading will be interrupted in order to direct or focus their thinking toward the text.

5. Teacher develops several questions or statements to introduce the selection, set a purpose for reading, and help activate background knowledge. These should stimulate higher levels of thinking.

During Reading

1. Teacher delivers opening questions or statements and encourages students to make predictions about what the text will present.

2. Teacher presents information to build background knowledge where needed.

3. Students read first segment of text silently to test predictions and purpose for reading.
   • Teacher and students discuss first segment of text; students answer questions and perhaps raise new ones.
   • Students adjust predictions and purpose for reading as needed; students generate new questions to guide further reading.

4. The preceding procedures are repeated for each segment of text.
   • Teacher asks questions to help students identify the main idea or theme of what they are reading, determine the author's purpose, and clarify their own purpose for reading. Students' input to the discussion is invited and valued.

Postreading

1. Teacher asks questions and leads discussion to determine if objectives for reading have been met and if students have comprehended selection.

2. Students may do extension activities to reinforce learning.

3. Students apply procedures in other reading activities.

(The Directed Thinking About Reading activity is a model for teacher-led, small-group reading and discussion that encourages students to think critically about what they read.)

---

in communicating to them as individual readers" (Sardy, 1985, p. 214). An important part of the approach is balancing questions about content, text, and reading strategies. As teachers ask questions, they model the variables students should consider as they read. Questions should be directed primarily at complex, interesting, or puzzling aspects of text. Literal/recall or yes/no questions should be avoided except to clarify miscomprehension or focus students' attention at significant details they may have missed. Specific questions may ask readers to refocus at the word, phrase, sentence, or paragraph level or activate prior knowledge; all questions should require students to integrate information across text. In addition, students should be encouraged to raise their own questions.

Part of the flexibility of the DTAR is that the postreading phase allows for review and expansion. Provocative questions from teachers and students can spur discussions. In such exchanges, students draw on evidence from the text and their experiences to defend or reshape their ideas. By collaborating, they expand their strategies for evaluating and analyzing what they read. Questioning is only one form of postreading activity. Some texts lend themselves to critical thought through dramatization, puppets, art, pantomime, or choral or dramatic reading— what Jim Trelease (1985) refers to as the "third dimension" of students' reading. Analysis of art in children's books can influence postreading discussion, especially when the art contributes to setting, mood, or tone.

Students should also be encouraged to respond to text at an affective level. As Rosenblatt wrote, "Teachers and pupils should be relaxed enough to face what indeed happened as they interpreted the printed page. Frank expressions of boredom or even vigorous rejection is a more valid starting point for learning than are docile attempts to tell `what the teacher wants'" (1975, p. 70).

Reciprocal Teaching

As in DTAR sessions, reciprocal teaching involves a dialogue between a teacher and students; but in reciprocal teaching, students assume the teacher's role of formulating questions about text. This approach has been referred to as a strategy to get students to "read with their minds." Its goal is for students to learn to construct meaning efficiently from text and to self-monitor as they read. Four strategies are involved: generating questions, summarizing, clarifying, and predicting (Palinscar & Brown, 1984). Procedures are presented in Table 9–4.

Reciprocal teaching must be introduced carefully so that students understand how this new approach expands their responsibilities. Participating in think alouds and DTAR activities should have familiarized students with verbal interactions about text, content, and reading strategies; as a result, students should be able to express aspects of their own metacognition.

Researchers have found that reciprocal teaching can be very effective with students of varied ability levels. Because this approach allows students to exert control, weaker students feel less apprehensive about raising questions. In addition, observing their peers as they model questioning and comprehension strategies may make more sense to students than teachers' oral explanations. Using the approach with literature can lead to spirited discussions about interpretations of text, and using it in content areas can significantly enhance students' repertoire of critical reading strategies.

Table 9–4
Directions for Reciprocal Teaching

1. Teacher introduces the reciprocal teaching procedure by stating that it will help students self-monitor and read with comprehension.
2. Teacher explains the strategies students will use:
   - *Generating questions*. Pointing toward specific information in text that readers can think about in many ways.
   - *Summarizing*. Focusing on important information and involving readers actively.
   - *Clarifying*. Directing attention toward confusing aspects of text and applying fix-up strategies.
   - *Predicting*. Anticipating what will be found in text based on clues provided by the author and on background knowledge of the genre and content.
3. Teacher selects appropriate, short passages for students to study silently.
4. Teacher models four strategies presented above by focusing on specific sections of text. Students take part in discussion and form their own questions.
5. Students practice generating their own questions as though they were the teacher while the teacher guides the question formation and gives feedback.
   - Teacher helps students develop more focused questions and find answers in text.
   - Teacher answers questions and demonstrates strategies for finding answers.
6. Students practice procedure in pairs or small groups, with individuals taking turns being the teachers. Teacher monitors and participates in dialogue.

Reciprocal teaching creates a dialogue between teachers and students about texts. Students must formulate questions about what they read.

Individual Reading Conferences

A reading conference allows students to demonstrate what they know and can do while the teacher observes and interprets behavior in a focused, intense way. Based on teacher observation, specific instruction, often in the form of scaffolding, may be offered on the spot or in the future. Teachers keep various kinds of anecdotal records during each conference to help them in instructional planning.

Unlike writing conferences, where work in progress is discussed, children prepare a reading selection prior to the conferences. Students read and talk about their selection, and as a comprehension check, teachers ask students to engage in a think aloud or pose thought-provoking questions. Students' responses during a think aloud or answers to difficult questions reveal how thoroughly and thoughtfully students have prepared their reading—that is, whether they have left preparation at the decoding level or have truly gone on to think critically about the text.

Teachers' responses and explanations provide immediate scaffolding to help students achieve higher levels of critical thinking.

Conferences can also be used to gather information about students' ability to read unfamiliar material. Teachers can keep a running record for insight into students' many decoding strategies and conduct an interview to determine students' perception of their reading abilities (see Chapter 3).

Mapping and Other Graphic Organizers

No discussion of reading/writing/thinking classrooms is complete without a mention of graphic organizers. Teaching students to use some sort of a graphic representation of their thinking greatly enhances their ability to read critically (Heimlich & Pittelman, 1986). Graphic organizers supplement classroom discussion and students' independent reading in several ways. First, they allow for abstract or implicit information, concepts, and relationships to be represented in a concrete, that is, graphic, way. Graphic representations can aid students in organizing and elaborating on ideas before, during, and after reading and in so doing show relations between new information and students' existing, or prior, knowledge. Further, they help students store and retrieve information more efficiently than traditional outlines or note cards. Finally, graphic organizers can help students visualize and thereby understand text structure.

Many different kinds of graphic organizers are recommended for use in reading and content area classes. These include Venn diagrams, sequence chains, main idea tables, story maps, character analysis charts, comparison tables, criteria grids, decision-making charts, and concept maps. Whatever its form, a good graphic organizer illustrates both the key parts of a whole and the relationship between those parts, resulting in a holistic understanding of the theme, concept, or idea presented. Differences in student-developed graphic organizers often indicate differences in perspective, attitudes, analysis, and interpretation; these differences can serve as a springboard for fruitful discussion as students explain and defend their work. Figures 9–1 and 9–2 show several graphic organizers and explain their use, and Table 9–5 presents procedures to introduce the concept and purpose of graphic organizers and specific steps to help students understand their use.

An especially useful graphic organizer is the "Know, Want to Know, Learn" or K-W-L strategy (Ogle, 1989), which allows teachers and students to keep track of learning in an efficient, graphic way. The K-W-L approach includes considerable prereading work. First, teachers ask students to brainstorm what they know about a topic; students compile this information in the appropriate section of the graphic organizer.

Next, students are asked to anticipate the categories of information they will find as they read. Thus, they approach their reading "already thinking of higher order categories and ways to organize the myriad of facts that often drown young readers and kill their interest in expository text" (Ogle, 1989, pp. 213–214). Airing

Figure 9–1
Graphic Organizers for Narrative Texts

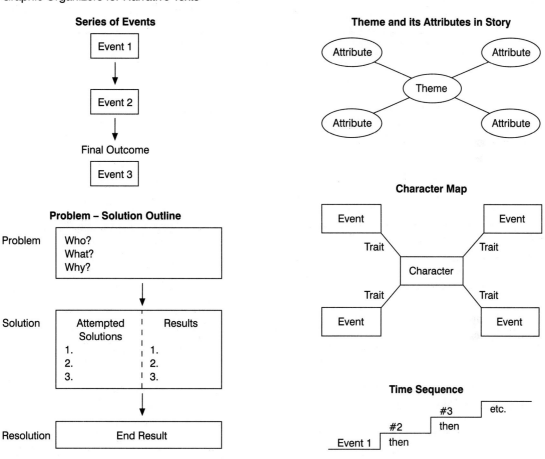

A story map can be used to track what students read or to plan a story they will write.

Figure 9–2
Graphic Organizers for Expository Texts

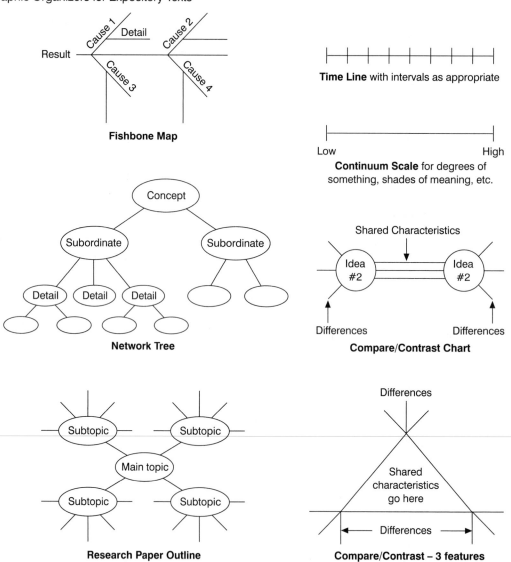

Fishbone Map

Time Line with intervals as appropriate

Continuum Scale for degrees of
something, shades of meaning, etc.

Network Tree

Compare/Contrast Chart

Research Paper Outline

Compare/Contrast – 3 features

what students know and what they expect is beneficial because false assumptions
or understandings can be corrected and conceptual gaps can be filled before
reading and study commence. Ogle cites an example from science instruction: "If
students think wolves are likely to kill humans, this assumption needs to be elicit-
ed so that it can be refuted directly. If teachers ignore the assumptions of their students, little learning can be expected" (1989, p. 206). Further, real thought, in all its

Table 9–5

Using Graphic Organizers

For each graphic organizer that students are to use, teachers should do the following:

1. Describe how the graphic organizer can be useful for organizing information and relating ideas.

2. Demonstrate the graphic organizer, its purpose and form, and steps for filling it out.
   - Complete first with familiar material or a familiar story.
   - Then complete with unfamiliar material or a new story.

3. Have students construct their own representations, possibly in small groups, with new but easy material.

4. Have students share their graphic organizers with each other, discuss the differences and similarities, and evaluate their efforts.

5. Encourage students to use the graphic organizer with different material to see how it works.

6. Repeat steps with each new graphic organizer; help students understand the similarities and differences in the various graphic organizers that are presented.

7. When students feel comfortable with several different graphic organizers, discuss how certain ones are best suited to certain kinds of material.

8. Continue practicing with graphic organizers so that students see their value as part of the ongoing learning process.

If students are going to use graphic organizers successfully, they must realize their value and feel confident in their own ability to construct and interpret graphic representations of information.

---

forms, will be stymied by incorrect ideas. Finally, students complete the K-W-L chart with what they learn. Figure 9–3 shows a K-W-L chart.

It is important for students to realize that graphic organizers are authentic documentation of their reading and thinking. They may not look like traditional paper-and-pencil work, but they are just as serious. Deciding which graphic organizer to use and what to include in one makes students stretch their thinking in new and productive ways.

APPROACHES TO FOSTER THOUGHTFUL WRITING

Classroom approaches to bring writing, reading, and thinking together are explored next. Like the reading activities already discussed, many writing activities require students to talk extensively to the teacher and to each other. Students must also explore different modes of writing, different voices, and different audiences if

Figure 9–3
Know, Want to Know, Learn (K-W-L) Graphic Organizer

This is what I know . . .	This is what I want to learn . . .	This is what I have learned . . .

This is the kind of information I expect to find.

1.

2.

3.

4.

they are to progress beyond a basic, superficial, although technically correct, level of writing competency.

Writing-to-Learn Activities

For students to become strong writers and thinkers, they must write often. The *writing-to-learn approach* advances this goal; it can be easily integrated into self-contained classrooms or language arts and content area programs.

The writing-to-learn approach stresses the importance of writing in all curriculum areas to enhance the development of thinking skills. Activities help students stretch their thinking toward unconventional, creative, and new ideas; write and think about topics and ideas in new ways; and record thoughts for analysis, evaluation, and expansion at a later time. In such activities, there is no right answer, no one best way to approach the task at hand. De-emphasis on right answers may be disconcerting for students at first, but in time, they will become risk takers who, recognizing the fluidity of the writing process, are able to bend their minds and pencils around ideas in novel ways. Just as thinkers can and must change their minds many times, students using the writing-to-learn approach will realize that their writing can be changed in substantive ways. They will also learn how to approach diverse writing tasks efficiently because they will have had many experiences with writing in different contexts and for different purposes.

The writing-to-learn approach includes activities such as keeping journals, using some graphic organizers, writing notes and lists, engaging in nonstop writing, and completing other focused activities that require students to take a particular stance, assume a role, or otherwise stretch their thinking about the topic at hand (Berthoff, 1988; Elbow, 1981; Flower & Fulwiler, 1980; Juell, 1985; Rico, 1983).

The "products" that result in writing-to-learn can be analyzed and evaluated by their writers, who then expand, extend, or elaborate upon the emerging ideas and knowledge with more writing, reading, or thinking. As intellectual juices begin to flow, fluency, accuracy, and quality of expression are not so much devalued as placed in perspective as students learn to recognize writing as both a tool to explore, organize, and test their thinking and also a means to enhance comprehension of reading assignments (Gere, 1985). Students learn to separate the actual producing process from the revision process because they are using what has been referred to as a kind of writing "push-up" (Elbow, 1981).

Furthermore, one of the most important instructional purposes for using writing-to-learn strategies is that as students write about a topic, they may identify conceptual or informational gaps that they can fill with additional reading and thought. They will "see" their thinking on paper, with all its rough edges and false starts, and with successful merging of ideas. Many writing-to-learn activities are listed and explained in Table 9–6.

Opportunities To Share Writing

An essential part of critical thinking during the writing process is a kind of role reversal: writers must assume the role of the intended reader and evaluate their work from that perspective to determine if their work is in fact communicating meaning as intended. This is a sophisticated task, for it requires that students distance themselves from what they are doing so that they can in fact evaluate their efforts. To learn to view their own work critically, students need opportunities both to prepare writing to share with teachers and with peers and also to read and respond critically to each other's work. "Going public" by sharing motivates writers to think long and hard about what they have written. In addition, the "audience" who read a peer's work use many critical thinking skills as they decide what

Table 9–6
Opportunities for Using Writing-to-Learn Activities

1.	Daily log entries of ideas, random thoughts, verbal rambles
2.	Double-entry journals, in which students record • observations on their reading and study • comments or reactions to what they have read
3.	Process/learning logs, in which students comment on and think their way through their learning in all content areas
4.	Focused "quick writes," an assignment in which students try out unique voice, perspective, or tone
5.	Letters that will not be sent, again in order to try out new voices, stances, or perspectives
6.	Notes or lists of ideas, thoughts, and so forth, as raw material for future work

comments to make and questions to ask about the piece. Conferences can provide one means of sharing writing, and the classroom can be structured to allow for frequent peer interaction at all junctures of the writing process.

Interactions with teachers.   Writing conferences between teachers and students help students reach toward greater levels of clarity and fluency. While teachers may use the opportunity for some on-the-spot instruction, the real goal is to help students think critically and creatively about work at hand and work to be done in the future. Teachers can model the thought processes needed for this level of interaction with text and help students find and change pieces of text that are confusing. Discussion focuses on what students have been trying to do in their writing and how well they are accomplishing their goals. Students and teachers share ideas about written work, and teachers guide students to higher levels of thinking. Part of this thinking may even be to decide to abandon a piece of work for a while because it does not seem to be working. The student puts it back into the writing folder, to be analyzed later for possible reworking.

Interactions with peers.   It is also important for peers to discuss their work, share ideas, and externalize thinking about works in progress. More competent writers will often share their expertise with novices in child-to-child terms rather than in the formal language of instruction (Morris, 1986). Writers hone their critical thinking skills as they consider and respond to peers' comments and questions. Many educators and researchers have suggested procedures for establishing peer response groups and teacher-student conferences (see Appendix A). If teachers' goals are to encourage writing growth *and* to foster high levels of critical thinking about writing, three levels of peer interaction can be most beneficial. The different levels involve students' thinking together about their writing as it emerges from its initial draft form, in almost-final form, and as a completed piece. Each level serves a specific purpose, requires distinct preparation, and focuses critical thinking on different aspects of the writing process. Steps for each form of interaction are listed in Table 9–7; examples of procedures are discussed next.

The first level of peer interaction, sometimes referred to as *Authors' Circle*, brings together in small groups students who want to share works in progress and get feedback on what they are trying to do. "Authors' Circle demonstrates to writers that their first concern is with the meaning of what they want to say, not with the conventions of writing. . . . This process gives authors the opportunity to shift from the perspective of writer to reader to critic and so to take a new look at their compositions" (Harste, Short, & Burke, 1988, p. 221). Ideally, works have already been revised somewhat, perhaps as the result of teacher or very informal peer conferences.

At first, only one student may present a piece of writing; but as students become familiar with the process, two or more may bring to a session pieces to think about with their peers. Students who participate must understand that the questions and comments made during the session should relate to meaning, so that the authors gain a sense of what is and is not working in their writing and of how to clarify what they are trying to communicate.

Table 9–7
Levels of Interaction about Student Writing

Mode	Participants	Teacher	Status of Writing	Focus of Discussion
Authors' Circle	Several students	Sets tone	In progress, draft	Is the writing conveying meaning?
Editorial Conference	Designated "Assistant" and peer	Sets limits and responsibilities; selects "Assistant"	Somewhat polished	How can the piece be polished? What mechanical features can be changed? What word or phrasing can be changed?
Peer Conference	Author and other students	Sets tone, helps shape language to be used	Nearly finished	How well has the piece conveyed meaning? What, if anything, is confusing? What is ambiguous? What has the author done well?

Teachers' responsibilities in establishing Authors' Circle procedures include setting the tone for an open exchange of ideas and modeling the kinds of questions students should ask. After students read their piece, teachers pose the first few questions and perhaps use a think-aloud procedure to explain the questions asked. If the student-writer hesitates in responding, the teacher might pose additional questions to prompt the kind of thinking the writer should be doing as he reconsiders the piece before him. As other students begin to question the author, the teacher can redirect questions that are poorly stated or even declare certain questions inappropriate if they will not advance the purpose of clarifying what the piece is communicating. As students gain proficiency in the necessary skills, teachers may decide only to "drop in" on the sessions or to allow students to meet and discuss works by themselves.

Through Authors' Circle, students' writing becomes the "basal" material for teaching high-level thinking skills. Critical reading skills developed by reading one's own and others' work will readily transfer to subsequent writing tasks and to reading commercial material, as students bring the same kinds of questions to bear during independent work.

At the second level of interaction, students present work in a more polished form. Harste, Short, and Burke (1988) suggest that teachers set up a formal editorial board. Students wear visors, arm bands, buttons, and other paraphernalia, provided by the teacher, to identify themselves as members of the board. Other students consult them about their writing at the "Editors' Table." The Editors' Table idea can also work on a simpler, less formal level, called, perhaps, an *Editorial Conference*.

As students work through the process of bringing a piece of writing from draft to publication form, they should be encouraged to turn to their peers for editorial assistance. Certain students can be designated as editors during each writing session. In establishing the procedures for interaction of this kind, teachers make sure that students understand the limits and responsibilities involved. They remind students of the kinds of questions and interchanges that have taken place in teacher-student conferences and emphasize that students should use the same approaches in working with each other.

This process is less formal than those in Authors' Circle or other conferences, in that students simply request help from a fellow student when they find themselves struggling with a writing puzzle. The puzzle may concern mechanics, means to structure an idea, or complex issues about communicating meaning. In any case, the student writer seeks help from a peer, and together they attempt to find the most effective way to state the writer's ideas.

The seemingly impromptu nature of editorial conferences belies their value in encouraging critical thinking about writing. Because student writers turn to their peers to solve writing puzzles *as they occur*, the experience of thinking together about a piece of writing is authentic and purposeful. If students have learned what are essentially protocols for thinking about writing, the immediacy of the Editorial Conference challenges them to use their skills and strategies on their own, without teacher instruction or intervention. When students serve as editors for each other's work, they "develop an appreciation of audience and the communicative commitment [writers] make to their readers" (Harste, Short, & Burke, 1988, p. 257). How well students can apply what they have learned about thinking about writing will be reflected in the extent to which the piece of writing succeeds in communicating to others.

When students complete a piece of writing, they may want to present the work to a group of peers to see how they—a real audience—actually respond. When children get together to share pieces of finished writing, they interact as authors and audience; and they again exercise their critical thinking skills. This can be thought of as *Peer Writing Review*.

Before initiating this kind of peer interaction, teachers must again assess the sense of community shared by students and the degree to which they have in fact learned appropriate strategies for talking about each other's work. All students must realize that productive discussions should focus on the writing itself, not on the writer, and that questions asked should concern the text presented for review. The goal of discussions is to help the student writer identify any final changes needed to make his or her piece as successful as possible.

Underlying peer review at this level is the realization that every piece of writing is composed by an author. Thinking critically about text involves formulating questions that could be posed *to the author*. During Peer Writing Review sessions, the author is present and is questioned directly about his or her attempts to construct meaning in print. He or she can respond by clarifying intentions, explaining needed references, and requesting suggestions for how to improve the comprehensibility of the written piece. This kind of interaction differs from an "Authors' Circle" session in that the piece being discussed in a Peer Writing Review session has been revised extensively and is thus richer and more substantial. The student authors who present their work experience their writing through the eyes of others and hone skills that will be applied in their next writing effort. Members of the response group share their experiences of reading the piece, compare their interpretations with each other, and affirm their thinking as the authors respond. They too hone skills they can apply to their own reading and writing work.

Writing Across the Curriculum

The term *writing across the curriculum* is often used to describe the approach that exploits every opportunity to allow children to write in varied ways, in all their curriculum areas (Tchudi & Huerta, 1983; Thaiss, 1986). They can write factual reports, letters, diaries, or logs; they can develop math problems and write science reports; they can create fanciful, imaginative efforts *as long as the writing presents information accurately.*

The writing-across-the-curriculum approach emphasizes several objectives: to process content information correctly, to think critically, and to write fluently. To that end, teachers must realize the importance of providing students with opportunities to acquire ample content knowledge and information to process (Peters, 1990). Without ample domain knowledge, writing-across-the-curriculum activities do not ensure that students become writers *and* thinkers. Indeed, the idea of writing across the curriculum can be easily contorted into activities that do generate some writing but do not encourage real thinking. Too often, teachers ask children to write as a follow-up to content area work but have not provided enough information to produce a valid writing experience. If information is merely spoon-fed to children and their follow-up writing assignments ask them to "feed" the information back to their teachers, the writing experience is invalid. Consider a second grader who had been studying Germany, Korea, and India in social studies and wanted to write a report about those countries, but was confused about the assignment. She couldn't write from personal experience, so she started her paper bravely and honestly. Realizing, perhaps, that her paper was considerably different from her peers', she tried to pull herself into line. She wrote: "I don't no abwt germany but I am riten abwt germany. I want to go to germany. To see wat it is like" (Salinger, 1988, p. 258). Contrast that with a second grader's report about trout, presented in Figure 9–4. The trout report is factual and honest, authentic in its representation of the child's research. Having mastered the ability to integrate reading, writing, and thinking skills to achieve this effort, the child is well-prepared to go on to more thoughtful, analytic reading/writing tasks.

Writing across the curriculum gives children opportunities to process information in a wide variety of ways. Table 9–8 presents five specific kinds of student responses and suggests how each could be used in a writing-across-the-curriculum program. From time to time, few children may find some of the assignments silly or have trouble handling a full research report; but because there are varied

Figure 9–4
Report on Trout by Second Grade Student[3]

TROUT

Trout eggs are vary tiny. 14 to 16 trout eggs can be as big as 1 penny. When they are 1 or 2 weeks old they're called eyed eggs because you can see the fish's eyes. A look up close shows the whole embryo. They will hatch in about two months.

When trout are young thay have up and doun lines called parr marks. The parr marks camouflage the fish in tall grasses. When the trout gets older insted of the parr marks it has spots. The spots help the fish blend in with the pebbles at the bottom of the stream. The trout has 8 fins. It is red, yellow, blue and sometimes green. It eats minnows, insects, wrms, tadpoles and even frogs. The trouts tealth are tiny and sharp. They are used to keep prey inside the trout's mouth. The trout has good senses to catch its food. It has good eyesyht and color vision. The trout uses its nostrils to small its pray.

It has ears inside its head. It can still hear very we66. The trout could even hear a worm wiggling at the bottom of a stream. Moste fish have a sense that humans don't have. It is called the lateral line. It helps the fish know when something is near by. One other way the trout catches its food is that it is a fast swimmer.

opportunities for writing, the whole class, from avid story writers to meticulous fact seekers, can accomplish something. Through writing-across-the curriculum assignments, students gain valuable practice thinking about a topic from various points of view, adopting a particular perspective for their writing, and writing in

[3]From *Language Arts and Literacy for Young Children* (p. 259) by T. Salinger, 1988, New York: Merrill/Macmillan. Copyright 1988 by Macmillan Publishing Company. Reprinted by permission.

different modes, for different purposes, and to different audiences. The writing-across-the-curriculum approach places writing, along with reading, at the very center of students' work, and answers teachers' frequent questions about when they will find time to allow their children to write. Their students write as part of instruction, as a follow-up to instruction, and as a means for teachers to evaluate learning both in the content areas and in language arts.

Writing Across the Curriculum and Student Long-Term Projects

Students need considerable support in learning how to complete thoughtful, long-term research projects. The emphasis here is on *thoughtful*, for without a guiding idea of how to proceed, students often complete long-term projects almost mindlessly, with routinized, derivative but potentially very attractive "products" emerging at the end. However, direct instruction, coupled with teacher guidance and feedback, will make such projects the ideal mode for developing critical thinking skills. Table 9–9 presents questions teachers should ask themselves before introducing long-term research projects, along with teachers' responsibilities as pro-

Table 9–8
Student Response Patterns

1. Expressive: biographical or autobiographical

   Students write about a time or incident or feeling from the perspective of someone who had direct experience that can be reported; student may assume the role and write in the first person or extend the writing into the third person. Information should be accurate.

2. Literary: story, play, poem

   Students write a literary piece in a specific genre that presents information accurately but elaborates as needed to maintain the genre selected.

3. Expository: reporting information

   Students prepare a factual report that synthesizes information accurately.

4. Expository: interpretative

   Students prepare a report on factual information but add interpretation, explanation, analysis, or comparisons. Information must be accurate and verifiable.

5. Persuasive: speculative, problem-solving, or evaluative

   Students prepare a report that includes accurate information but goes on to add hypotheses, judgmental analysis, or other speculative interpretation from either the students' or some other perspective. These efforts offer a "kid's eye view" of the world with substantiation to support the writer's ideas.

   Students may assume these response patterns as they write to fulfill assignments in writing-across-the-curriculum programs.

Table 9–9
Questions to Ask Before Assigning Long-Term Research Projects

Student Preparation

1. Are students ready for the required level of independent work?
2. Are students ready for the required level of collaborative work?
3. Do students possess adequate reading and writing skills to undertake such a project?
4. Do students need review in library and reference skills, skimming and scanning, taking notes, developing graphic organizers, and so forth?

Content Knowledge

1. Have students learned enough content to be able to do an adequate job preparing their projects?
2. Will the topics selected for study advance students' content knowledge?

Logistics of Long-term Projects

1. Will there be adequate time to devote to students' projects?
2. Will the teacher be able to act as a resource person?
3. Are there enough books and other materials to allow students to do successful research?
4. Will the pressures of other academic demands make the long-term project seem less important than it should?

jects get under way. If the answer to these questions is negative, the experience of long-term work may be frustrating for students and teachers alike.

Long-term research projects allow students to pursue their interests in depth, pose and seek answers to their own questions, analyze and evaluate various sources of data, and make decisions over time about how information will be selected, organized, and presented. This is clearly a heavy order for elementary school students, but teachers often report that students become quite self-sufficient as they work through an extensive project (Weis & Stewart-Dore, 1987). Research projects can easily take four to six weeks to complete. They give students experience managing resources over an extended period of time and encourage collaboration. While a finished product in some form is expected from a long-term project, the shape it takes is less important than the learning about content, process, and critical thinking that takes place during the project.

Once students have mastered the research and study strategies described in Chapter 5, they are ready to do a research project. The foundation of successful long-term *research* projects is the selection of appropriate questions to guide reading, writing, and thinking. Filling out a Know, Want to Know, Learn or weblike graphic organizer can be very beneficial in formalizing question generation and helping students begin to focus their research. The criteria for deciding what form an end product should take include the topic to be investigated, the questions to be answered, the age and experience of students, the resources available, and the time to be expended.

As students work on a long-term project, teachers serve as resources. They help students solve problems, demonstrate decision-making procedures, and guide in the composing and editing processes. It can be beneficial for teachers to model each step by completing a research project themselves. Table 9–10 shows a rough chronology of such a project.

At the end of a long-term research project, finished reports, handwritten or typed on a classroom word processor, should be bound together as a published book. Other written efforts, like scripts for plays or outlines of presentations, can also be published or presented orally. If children's efforts have not led to extensive writing but are instead a series of pictures with annotations, those captions should be read and shared with the same enthusiasm as a full report. It is up to teachers to encourage children to do as much writing as possible within this kind of activity but not to make writing seem to be a burdensome chore. The process of selecting topics and reference materials, sorting through data, conferencing with others, and evaluating the final product provides the means for encouraging critical thinking.

Presenting the results of their projects to their classmates provides an additional vehicle to promote critical thinking.

SUMMARY

Verbal interaction between teachers and students and between groups of students provides the means to help students develop critical thinking skills. The kinds of questions and comments teachers present shape students' ways of thinking about their own and others' texts. With teacher support and encouragement, students learn to analyze and evaluate what they read and write and to justify their ideas in logical, thoughtful ways.

QUESTIONS AND TASKS

1. Be sure that you understand these terms:
    a. Authors' Chair, Editorial Conferences, Peer Writing Review
    b. Directed Thinking about Reading Activity
    c. reciprocal teaching
    d. think alouds
    e. writing across the curriculum
    f. writing to learn

Table 9–10
Chronology of a Long-term Research Project

Week 1

1. Teacher introduces concept of long-term project and explains scope of work.

2. Teacher and students brainstorm possible topics. Teacher helps students identify workable topics. (This process will vary depending on students' grade and experiences, resources available, and grouping plans; if students are to work in teams, topics may be more ambitious than if they are working independently. So, too, a good school library encourages ambitious projects.)

3. Teacher provides instruction/review about library methodology, use of reference books, noting what has been read, skimming, scanning, etc.

4. If students are to work together, they are assigned to or elect to join together in work teams.

5. Individuals or members of each work team begin a "Know, Want to Know, Learn" or other graphic organizer about their proposed topic.

6. Students make first trip to library.

Week 2

1. Students commence work independently or as team members; if working in teams, they allocate resources and assign tasks.

2. Teacher proveds mini-lessons as needed.

3. Teacher serves as resource person.

4. On Thursday or Friday, teacher conducts small-group meetings to determine progress, help students redefine topics as needed, and set new priorities for future work.

5. Students assess their progress, develop new graphic organizers, and update their K-W-L chart.

Weeks 3 and 4

1. Students continue to work more or less at own pace but with reminders that

2. Select a short children's book or story. Using the class described by Dick in Table 9–1 as a model, develop a plan to introduce and use the book with students. Note where you could most effectively use thinking scaffolds.

3. Select a piece of children's literature and ask two or more children to "think aloud" as they read it. The piece should be challenging conceptually but at an appropriate reading level for the children. Make note of similarities and differences in what the children say and compare inferences you can make about their use of strategies to construct meaning.

Table 9–10
continued

---

they should be well into their work. They assume increasing amounts of responsibility and independence.

2. Teacher continues to serve as resource person and to offer mini-lessons as needed.

3. On Friday of each week, teacher checks progress. Students evaluate own progress, redefine goals, and set new priorities. Students collate assembled notes and graphic organizers to identify what else needs to be researched.

Week 5

1. Students begin to visualize finished product and make decisions about how the project will be brought to conclusion.

2. Students may begin to write, record data, and or assemble "evidence" to reflect their work.

3. Students collaborate and consult with teacher as their work progresses.

4. Teacher continues to serve as resource person and to offer mini-lessons as needed.

5. By Thursday, students should have at least a rough draft of their finished product and be ready to discuss their efforts among themselves.

6. On Friday, teacher checks with each team privately, *or,* on Thursday and Friday, teacher holds conferences with students working independently.

Week 6

1. Teacher provides support as students assemble their final products.

2. Students assemble their projects, which may be handwritten, produced on a word processor, or rendered in some multimedia format.

3. If students are to give an oral presentation, they practice their respective parts.

4. On Thursday and Friday, students present their work to their classmates through visual display and oral presentations.

---

4. Select a topic that would be taught in social studies or science in the elementary school. Design as many writing-across-the-curriculum activities as you can that would be appropriate for the topic. Be sure that each activity would truly enhance students' learning.

10 CHAPTER

The Home-School Connection

Teachers, school administrators, and the public at large all accept as truth that home involvement is essential for quality education. The National Assessment of Educational Progress routinely includes questions about "home support" in its student background questions and routinely finds that academic achievement and home support are linked.[1] Public interest pieces on radio

---

[1] Part of each NAEP assessment is a five-minute general-background questionnaire and a five-minute subject-specific questionnaire. Information is gathered about students' in- and out-of-school habits and behaviors, including television viewing, homework, number of books in the home, and extent of parent involvement in activities such as helping with homework or listening to children read.

and television urge parents[2] to read to their children, and billboards advocate involvement in school activities. Professional and lay literature resounds with statements about the positive results of parent and community involvement in schools and suggests ways of accomplishing this goal.

Although many teachers acknowledge the value of home-school connections, some are reluctant to make more than cursory overtures to students' caregivers, especially if there is no schoolwide initiative for home involvement. Reasons cited include lack of time for meaningful involvement, mistrust of parents' intentions or abilities, past failures to involve parents or other caregivers, and the resulting indifference to the whole idea (Fredericks & Rasinski, 1989). At the same time, caregivers may be reluctant to seek involvement, often for the same reasons. Many variables, including cultural differences, inhibit the communication that is necessary between school and home.

FACTORS TO CONSIDER

There is no one right way for teachers to create a home-classroom connection and no one right way for family members to support their children's learning. Some efforts are relatively informal; others are more structured. Teachers should continually seek to enlist parental support for educational goals, all the while recognizing the overarching societal realities that recently have begun to work against traditional home-school interaction patterns. And, as teachers seek to establish ties with their students' homes, they must consider many complex factors.

Lifestyle and Demographic Shifts

The first complex factor to consider in attempting to establish parental support concerns shifts in lifestyles and demographics. The populations of schools are changing rapidly; and, indeed, the very concepts of "family" and "home" have been redefined in recent years. The variables that have contributed to these changes are listed in Table 10–1. The pressures of modern life, the ambitions parents have for their children, and the social realities of our world preclude for many children the gentle memories Eudora Welty recounted in *One Writer's Beginnings* (1983):

> I learned from the early age of two or three that any room in our house, at any time of the day, was there to read in, or to be read to. My mother read to me. She'd read to me in the big bedroom in the mornings, when we were in her rocker together, which ticked in rhythm as we rocked, as though we had a cricket accompanying the story. She'd read to me in the dining room on winter afternoons . . . and at night when I'd got into my own bed. I must have given her no peace. . . .
>
> Neither of my parents had come from homes that could afford to buy many books, but though it must have been something of a strain on his salary, . . . my father was all

---

[2]Throughout this chapter, the word *parent* is frequently used as a generic term for any adult who takes care of children in the home environment.

Table 10–1
Demographic and Life Style Shifts

Changing Characteristics of Schools
- more preschool programs
- more day-care and extended-day programs
- more need for English-as-a-second-language (ESL) programs
- more whole language and workshop approaches that may be unfamiliar to parents

Changing Characteristics of Families
- more single parent homes, especially single mothers
- higher divorce rates
- greater incidence of split custody, with children dividing time between parents
- more working mothers
- more children receiving care from surrogate caregivers

Changing Racial and Ethnic Characteristics
- more children of color in schools, representing varied ethnic and cultural groups
- increased immigration, especially from Latin American and Southeast Asia
- greater language diversity, with more children not speaking English when they enter school
- greater cultural diversity, with differing values held for education and differing definitions of the role of school

Other Realities
- increased rates of teenage pregnancy, resulting in nontraditional parenting practices
- increased use of drugs, resulting in an increase in babies born addicted to drugs
- increased homelessness, resulting in greater student mobility and failure of many students to establish solid beginning skills, identification with school, and supportive relationships with teachers and peers

---

the while carefully selecting and ordering away [the books] he and Mother thought we children should grow up with. They bought first for the future. . . .

I live in gratitude to my parents for initiating me—and as early as I begged for it, without keeping me waiting—into knowledge of the word. (pp. 5, 6, 9, 10)

Constraints of time, energy, and money preclude more traditional forms of home support. Teachers must learn to look for and encourage workable alternative patterns that will make parents feel welcome and valuable.

Stereotypes

In greeting each class, teachers must expect the unexpected, because truly homogeneous classes may be somewhat a thing of the past. Statistics on demographic shifts illustrate important trends but do not personalize the range of diversity in terms of home life, academic preparation, language, and expectations that can cohabit in one elementary classroom.

To be useful, discussions of demographic changes must lump individuals into groups, a practice that can lead to stereotypes. Stereotyping contributes to the formation of a set of expectations for background experiences, attitudes, abilities, inclinations, and behaviors that nongroup members cannot personally verify and that they may come to accept as truth. Stereotyping depersonalizes group members so that their idiosyncratic, individual characteristics are not readily perceived by nongroup members, whose expectations and attitudes have been shaped by what "they have heard" or what "research shows." This blindness may result in prejudging or misjudging children or caregivers and always blocks genuine communication (Purcell-Gates & Salinger, 1990). Writing specifically about working with children from single-parent homes, Ritty (1991) stated, "Teacher expectations for and attitudes about students can be transmitted directly and indirectly. Expectations are conveyed by the values presented in a teacher's language and the curriculum content" (p. 604). Attitudes and expectations expressed in school are carried home, where they may be shared with parents and caregivers who then feel even more alienated from the school environment.

Teachers have to recognize that they are often the outsiders, the nongroup members in the communities where they teach; and they have to acknowledge the stereotypical ideas that they may hold about the students and the expectations that accompany those ideas. Only then can they begin to prepare the way for solid communication between the home and school. Parents, of course, probably have their own set of stereotypes and expectations for teachers, based on economic, educational, ethnic, political, and even age differences. Parents may filter their interactions with teachers and their expectations through their predetermined set of stereotypes, thus increasing the obstacles to communication.

Binding teachers and parents together and motivating them to overcome potential difficulty is a desire for their "shared" children to be successful, especially in reading and writing. Parental manifestation of this desire may differ widely, especially in the increasing number of nontraditional or nonmainstream homes, and teachers may not be fully aware of its existence. I will never forget the morning during midwinter in 1971. I was teaching first grade in a depressed inner-city neighborhood in Brooklyn, New York. Nathan walked in late as usual but clutching a note from his mother. The note reminded me that Nathan was one of four children, apologized for his tardiness, and asked my indulgence. "The hot water has been turned off in our building," she wrote, "and I have to boil water for the children to wash in the morning. It is very important," this mother emphasized, "for them to come to school clean."

IMPORTANT RESEARCH

Two significant studies have depicted home support for literacy through lengthy, fine-grained investigations of several vastly different homes. The contrast between them is interesting. The author of one of these books, *Family Literacy* (1983), is

Denny Taylor, who researched the subject by studying the literacy development of several children living in middle-class homes and contrasted home and school-based literacy practices. She found that the "transmission of literacy styles and values was viewed as a social process in which the reading and writing experiences of children [were] mediated by the individual members of the family. . . . Within the context of the family [this] transmission . . . [was] a diffuse experience, often occurring at the margins of awareness" (pp. 25, 20). The parents, as literacy users, supported the goals and objectives of their children's school; and because certain behaviors already existed in the lives of their older siblings, young children fell into established patterns of talking about school, requesting help with homework, and reading to parents. Parents did not seek to teach their children or compensate for perceived deficits in children's instruction; instead, they embedded interactions about school, especially about reading and writing, into the social structure of the families' time together. Taylor did note, however, that parents actually tried to teach younger children those skills that older siblings had found difficult. Also, she noted that older children were "able to share [with younger siblings] . . . many school-related literacy experiences that would have smacked of teaching if [parents] had attempted them" (p. 22).

Taylor's book was significant because it so thoroughly documented the fabric of homes where school-based literacy experiences were supported. Still, her subjects were middle-class and white. The profiles she presented have been further enriched by descriptions contained in *Growing Up Literate: Learning From Inner-City Families*, written by Taylor and Catherine Dorsey-Gaines (1988). Using the ethnographic methodology of the first book, Taylor and Dorsey-Gaines investigated several low-income, nontraditional homes in a northeastern urban area. What they found defied the stereotypes of such homes as places where school is suspect, books are absent, children are neglected, and literacy is devalued. Because the homes they studied were often stressful, "the parents' provisions of a literate environment and support of their children's education [were] somewhat balanced (however precariously) with the strong need for the children to become independent survivors in a sometimes hostile world" (p. 15). Still, the researchers observed that the "families spent time together, that there was a rhythm to their lives, and that they enjoyed each other's company. Friends visited. Children played. People helped one another. Sometimes there was sadness and grief, at other times there was anger and resentment, but there was always a quiet determination in the way in which they approached the difficulties that confronted them" (pp. 191–192).

Additionally, parents in this study made many efforts to get children ready for school and supported what the schools offered. Indeed, the researchers contended that the parents were "taking the necessary steps to enable the children to succeed at the tasks that were set for them. The children learned their lessons well, and [there were] at least some indications that school literacy was meaningful" (p. 95). Equally important, Taylor and Dorsey-Gaines observed many instances of parents using literacy independently and sharing reading and writing with their children. In these homes, literacy was clearly valued as a purposeful tool in the parents' interaction with the world around them, and both the value and purposefulness were routinely modeled for the children to see. Some of these behaviors are listed in Table 10–2.

Table 10–2
Examples of Literacy Behaviors Found in Families Studied in *Growing Up Literate*[3]

Instrumental reading, documents related to public agencies or dealing with daily life such as recipes or television guides

Social-interactional reading and writing, for building and maintaining relationships; for example, greeting cards

News-related reading, newspapers and magazines

Recreational reading and writing, reading mysteries, love stories, newspapers, magazines, and so forth; doing crossword puzzles, writing letters

Confirmational reading, checking, confirming, or announcing facts or beliefs and gaining support for attitudes and beliefs already held; for example, family trees in a family Bible, birth certificates, financial records, loan notes, and wills. The researchers "found that the families saved all kinds of print that became archival materials to be referred to when necessary or read on special occasions" (p. 147).

Writing as a memory aid, preparing schedules, lists, calendars, and so forth

Critical/Educational reading and writing, reading textbooks, journal and magazine articles, and so forth; practicing skills learned in classes, such as shorthand; writing to fulfill assignments

Writing to reinforce or substitute for oral messages, such as notes to school, messages left by adults for children, and so forth

Writing for financial purposes, to record numbers and accounts and other purposes of expenditures

Sociohistorical reading, in order to explore personal identities and the social, political, and economic circumstances of their lives; for example, autobiographies and biographies of African-Americans, or the writing efforts of the children in the families studied

PARENTAL PARTICIPATION, INVOLVEMENT, AND SUPPORT

Among the complex factors facing teachers in establishing the important home-school connection is the task of finding out how much parents can be involved in the classroom and then determining the extent to which involvement will be beneficial. An initial letter sent home early in the school year should let them know that there are many ways of becoming active partners in their children's education. There are three basic forms involvement can take: (a) participation, (b) involvement, and (c) support, all of which are discussed in the following sections. Ideally, all parents and caregivers will be *supportive*; but not all can become actively engaged in the life of the classroom, and many may need strong encour-

---

[3]Adapted from *Growing Up Literate: Learning from Inner-City Families* by D Taylor and C. Dorsey-Gaines, 1988, Portsmouth, NH: Heinemann.

agement to venture forth into this new level of involvement with their children's learning.

Participation

Parents must make large commitments of time and energy if they are going to participate regularly in their children's classrooms. Those who can devote one or more days per week to working in the school can become real partners in the learning process. They can take on specific responsibilities, roles, and tasks by serving as aides, tutors, or resource persons. By being in the classroom often, parents observe children interacting with peers, learning, struggling, wasting time, failing and trying again; they come to appreciate issues of classroom management, lesson planning, and group dynamics; and they provide opportunities for children to accept the authority of adults other than their teacher and to turn to other adults as learning resources. Adults who come to know a class in this way can play an important role in instruction and decision making and can help teachers personalize the literacy curriculum.

What teachers can do.   If teachers want parent participation on a regular basis, they must be willing to spend time nurturing and encouraging these volunteers. They will need support in developing ideas, learning how to organize and present materials, and handling discipline problems. Expecting too much too soon is perhaps the biggest mistake teachers can make. Parents' skills and abilities will vary widely, as will their understanding of the literacy curriculum with which they will assist. A gradual, sensitive, and supportive introduction to the class is necessary if parents are to become successful classroom participants. Table 10–3 suggests some of the activities and roles parent participants can perform on a regular basis.

Involvement

Some parents and caregivers may not be able to help regularly but want to be involved in the class from time to time. Perhaps they can devote a morning or day to the class on an infrequent basis; perhaps they would like to read to the class, discuss an important issue or topic, share a skill, or be an occasional "celebrity" visitor. Deciding how best to use their involvement is a challenge to teachers because these parents will not have the continual interaction with the children needed to establish their authority and role as a resource person. They will also lack the insight into the rhythms and routines of the class and will not be able to pitch in as readily as a more frequent visitor. In addition, they may not be able to participate in any training teachers provide for volunteers and will feel insecure about taking on substantive tasks with the children. Still, their presence should be encouraged and welcomed.

What teachers can do.   If the teacher knows that some parents will be available on an infrequent basis, he or she can set aside for them specific, discrete tasks that

Table 10–3

A Sampling of What Parents Can Do in the Classroom

Parents who participate on a regular basis can:
- read to and with individuals
- read to and with small groups
- listen to children read
- transcribe children's dictation
- supervise art activities
- participate in ongoing projects
- share their own skills and talents in ongoing projects, such as sewing, weaving, bookbinding, woodworking, and writing poetry
- take children to the school library

With training from the teacher, parents who participate regularly can:
- lead Authors' Chair or literary conversation groups
  (see Chapters 9 for details)
- conduct small-group instruction on an ongoing basis
- offer remedial or enrichment work to individuals

Parents who participate infrequently can:
- read to and with individuals and small groups
- listen to children read
- play learning games with students
- talk to and with students about their work or topics of interest
- share their skills in special, short-term projects
- go on class trips
- judge contests

Parents who visit only on rare occasions can:
- be a "celebrity reader" in small groups
- share a special skill, talent, or interest
- judge contests
- go on trips
- listen to children read

The individual schedules, talents, and inclinations of parents, coupled with the needs and characteristics of individual classrooms, will dictate the extent to which parents can play active roles in their children's education in school.

are not essential to the daily routines of the literacy curriculum but that can be enriching and meaningful for both adults and children. Reading to or with individual children is one example. Also, teachers might survey this group of parents to determine interests or skills they might be able to share with small groups or with the whole class. Students can do background reading in preparation for a "celebrity parent" visit or prepare a list of questions or issues to discuss. For example, a mother of a student in my first grade class many years ago was a talented handweaver; she donated about two days a month to an on-going weaving project that the students could also pursue in her absence. Students learned how to weave, researched weaving and the production of wool, and learned important vocabulary as well.

Even if their visits are not frequent, parents should be led to some understanding of the curriculum objectives and classroom routines so that their work can support students' literacy growth. A brief brochure about the class, in addition to the parent letters discussed below, can provide this needed orientation. Again, see Table 10–3 for tasks for the infrequent parent volunteer.

Support

Many parents want to support their children's literacy growth, but their personal schedules and needs keep them away from school, except possibly on parents' night. However, conversations that take place on parents' night might be brief or hurried and never address parents' real concerns about helping their youngsters.

Teachers can often gain support from this group of parents and caregivers by openly communicating expectations and possibilities to them. There is often not enough appreciation for what might be called the "curriculum of the home"; both parents and teachers fail to realize how influential it can be in supporting academic learning. Included in this curriculum are conversations about everyday events, schoolwork, leisure reading, and even television viewing. It is indeed sad when caregivers and older siblings do not recognize the important ongoing role they can play in students' academic lives and when they miss opportunities for even casual discussions about school-related topics. The parents studied by Taylor and Dorsey-Gaines fell into this kind of interaction easily and naturally and provided support and incentive as powerful as any that could be provided in more affluent, better-educated families.

What teachers can do.   When parents cannot participate in the classroom, they may feel alienated from their children's life at school and may simply not know how to offer effective assistance and support. Frequent, informal but informative letters sent home can offer suggestions, encouragement, and concrete ideas about how to support children's learning. Teachers might, for example, send a note home before a particular television miniseries and suggest that family members not only watch it together but also discuss its contents. Explanations of long-term projects and activities let parents know what is going on so they can discuss schoolwork with their children. Setting up a regular classroom lending library can encourage parents to read with and to their children regularly. Steps for formalizing such a library appear in Table 10–4.

BRINGING ABOUT A SUCCESSFUL HOME-SCHOOL CONNECTION: THREE STAGES

Achieving a successful home-school connection is a difficult task. It requires thoughtful communication, patience, sometimes tact, and always time; but a well-planned program can empower parents and teachers. Although some parents may

Table 10–4
Steps for Setting Up a Home-School Library Exchange

1. Beg, borrow, or buy books for the classroom to offer as wide a representation of topics as possible and an appropriately wide range of difficulty levels.

2. Arrange a convenient library area in the classroom; it does not need to be fancy but should be both inviting for browsing and easy to keep organized.

3. Mark each book to indicate that it belongs to the class.

4. In cooperation with students, devise an organizational system for the library. The library can be organized in many ways, such as:
   - by topic
   - by author
   - by genre
   - in alphabetical order

5. Devise a checkout system as similar as possible to that of a real library.
   - Use library envelopes and cards that can be removed from the book.
   - Affix a sheet to each book to stamp the due date.

6. Let parents know that the lending library program will begin, what it will involve, and what is expected from them.
   - They will share the books with their children.
   - They will remind children to return the books.
   - They will sign a form indicating that their child has listened to a parent or sibling read the book or that the child has read the book with someone or to himself or herself.
   - When books are routinely shared with parents, as in the younger grades, parents will write a one- or two-sentence comment about the sharing experience

7. Let parents know how you will go about recording children's reading. For example, you might give certificates or prizes for reading and sharing a certain number of books.

8. Thoroughly discuss with students their responsibilities. These include:
   - sharing the book with people at home
   - returning the books within a designated time period
   - discussing the book in class

9. Let students select books. Check them out, using a stamp or other device, as in a regular library.

10. Send books home, providing plastic bags for younger children; be sure to include paperwork that parents must sign.

11. Celebrate success in bringing the books back to school.

12. Let children discuss books and their parents' responses.

13. Award prizes or certificates or hold a party to celebrate the students' use of the library.

volunteer to help from the very first day of school, many will be reluctant, will think they are unwelcome, and will wait to be invited. A letter sent home at the very beginning of the year is a good first step. It can affirm the value the teacher places on home support and may suggest specific family activities to help the children. Furthermore, such a letter can introduce the literacy curriculum in which children will participate and invite parents to become an active part of their children's learning. Additional letters and notes throughout the year reaffirm the teacher's ideas, hopefully initiate dialogue, and repeat the invitation for parent involvement. Teachers might also consider developing a brochure to explain their literacy program to parents. Samples of a parent letter and suggestions for the contents of a brochure are presented in Appendix D.

The best possible home-school program is one that encompasses an entire school and seeks to involve as extensively as possible parents and caregivers in all aspects of school, from program planning to implementation (Rasinski & Fredericks, 1989). All school personnel, including specialists and administrators as well as teachers, should be involved. Ideally, plans extend beyond a single parent night or special event, so that the level of commitment, involvement, and sophistication of parents steadily increases. Parents and teachers will come to know and trust each other more as they negotiate long-term plans, attend workshops, and even socialize together.

Welcoming Parents and Caregivers.   As family members begin to come forward with questions and concerns or with offers to help, they must be made to feel welcome and competent. When the instructional program differs from the traditional basal reader/workbook approach, communication with parents is especially important because their expectations may be severely violated when children bring home papers with invented spelling, talk about spending a period "just reading a book," or state that they have no formal grammar textbook. The very idea of a curriculum in which children *read and write a lot* instead of doing extensive subskill activities may be totally bewildering to parents. The level of independence children demonstrate may falsely suggest a lack of teaching to parents accustomed to a more traditional approach. A careful explanation of goals, objectives, methodology, and routines—presented in plain language—is a necessary first step in integrating parents into the classroom and gaining their support. Teachers may want to host brief afterschool meetings, or parents may be receptive to suggestions of readings from journals like *The Reading Teacher* (see Appendix A). Parents also need time to observe the children in action before jumping in to work with individuals or groups. As stated previously, a brief brochure can serve as a reference as parents acclimate themselves. This period of learning about and observing the program is *Stage One* in establishing a home-school connection.

Explaining.   *Stage Two* involves careful explanations of the policies, organizational procedures, and routines of the classroom, explanations that allow parents to realize how teacher decisions and plans are designed to foster children's literacy growth. By understanding how their children's classroom is organized—and the rationale for the organization—volunteers better envision the place they will occupy there. Again, teacher discussion and brief readings can explain the curriculum. Teachers may communicate this information in a detailed newsletter, in individual parent conferences, or during parents' night.

Preparing.   In *Stage Three*, parents prepare to work with children. Actual involvement with students should be suggested only when everyone feels comfortable. Rushing volunteers into an assistant or tutor role too quickly limits the contributions they can make to children's learning.

So far, discussion has centered on individual teachers reaching out to parents of children in their class. In some school systems, efforts to secure parent participation, involvement, and support are more widespread and formalized. The school system of Norfolk, Virginia, has such an approach, which is summarized in Appendix D.

COMMUNICATING WITH THE HOME

As has been stated, home-school communication is vitally important. Letters and brochures are only some of the communications written during the course of the school year. Throughout the year, additional letters, written without "educationese," keep family members informed. Communicating frequently helps teachers demonstrate their concern and lends authority to suggestions for activities family members can undertake with their children. Part of the strength of the schoolwide effort in Norfolk, Virginia (see Appendix D) is the clarity and regularity of its parent communications. Sharing group letters with students helps them understand why it is important to bring letters home. Requesting that a signed tear-off slip from a letter be returned emphasizes teachers' seriousness and provides a means for comments or questions from the home.

Homework

A more subtle form of communication is the kind of homework teachers assign. Teachers can encourage home support by making homework assignments clear, challenging, and unambiguous. This too is especially important for those parents who do not spend time in the classroom itself. Homework reflects the kinds of work that students do in the classroom and extends the learning begun during the school day. If the literacy curriculum is one in which students work more or less independently, their homework assignments may seem quite individualized. Still, there should be some consistency in what students are asked to do at home, even if each child accomplishes the tasks in a unique way.

Teachers who are implementing a workshop approach might consider assigning homework as a weekly "contract." This approach ensures that all students have homework daily (or however often it is deemed appropriate), but it allows students to make choices about how they will fulfill their obligations. Students might, for example, have to read a certain number of chapters in a book and write in a literature log; they might have to bring a paper from draft to final form over the course of a week; or they might have to make a certain amount of progress on a long-term project. The major disadvantage of a contract system is that students may let their assignments pile up until the end of the week and hurry through them on Thursday night. The remedies for this include setting a midweek due date for some work or discussing with students their responsibilities and time management techniques.

Of course, parents and caregivers are not supposed to *do* homework for the children; but they may have to explain it and, ideally, discuss what children have done. If the assignment is merely a worksheet, there is little incentive for dialogue; if the homework assignment is vague, discussion may center on its ambiguity rather than its content. Clear, worthwhile assignments provide parents with a window into their children's school life and give them a topic for discussion. Parents also need to understand the responsibilities involved in a homework contract. In addition, teachers may need to educate parents about homework assignments that seem to be "just reading," rather than completing worksheets and workbook pages.

Reporting on Progress

Communicating about the literacy curriculum, student activities, or strategies for home support is easy in comparison to the task of reporting each student's progress. Filling in grades on a report card and writing a brief sentence about each child has always been a time-consuming task, but it is one that is relatively noncommittal in comparison to the in-depth kind of reporting that best suits the approaches to literacy instruction advocated in this book. The richness of the experiences students encounter cannot be captured in single grades and certainly is not reflected in a standardized test score. Nor can a few sentences at a parent-teacher conference convey students' overall progress.

Parent conferences may be the only face-to-face contact between teachers and those who care for their students, and as such, they are tremendously important. Organizing an agenda, gathering materials, and making notes about each child can make conferences more beneficial for all concerned. A "Letter to a Teacher" published in *Learning Magazine* (Gerritz, 1983) captures parental anxiety about these crucial interchanges. It is reproduced in Figure 10–1.

To be successful in communicating with parents, teachers must be willing to present as complete a picture as possible of how students have progressed. Flood and Lapp (1989) suggested a "comparison report," which can be thought of as a parent equivalent of the student portfolios discussed in Chapter 3. The contents of a parent portfolio are suggested in Table 10–5. One of the most valuable aspects of a parent portfolio is that it provides real examples of what students are doing and can handle successfully.

Flood and Lapp point out that in some schools, parent conferences are held only once, usually early in the year. This need not inhibit teachers from keeping parent portfolios. Initial material can be accumulated for each child prior to the parent conferences; the material and the portfolio concept are then discussed at

Figure 10–1
Letter to a Teacher by Kalle Gerritz[4]

Dear Mrs. McCrea, About That Conference Next Week . . .

A parent's letter to a teacher points out ways to make parent-teacher conferences easier–and more helpful–for all concerned.

BY KALLE GERRITZ

It's a week until our conference about David, and I already have a knot in my stomach. Even having sat behind the desk as a teacher doesn't make it any easier when it's *my* child. I still have a knot.

I guess I'm like most people in that I don't deal very well with the unknown. I start weaving dreadful fantasies, anticipating the worst. Oh, I know David is a terrific kid. The question is, do *you*? I also know I shouldn't get anxious; when I'm anxious, I don't listen very well, and that's not a great way to go into a conference that's supposed to be for my benefit, is it? So I've been trying to think of ways to make our getting together a little easier for me, and maybe for you too. Here are a few suggestions:

Information in advance about what we'll be talking about would definitely help loosen that knot in my stomach. You might send a general note to all the parents outlining the topics you usually cover—and maybe even ask us what we'd like to hear about on a tear-off at the bottom (that way you won't have to wait and wonder what *I'm* going to spring on *you*!). If I have a sense of what's on the agenda, I can pull my thoughts together and formulate reasonable-sounding questions (my words just get jumbled up if I don't have a chance to plan a bit). I could also talk with David's father about his ideas, and bring them along, since he can't always get away for daytime meetings.

It would help if you went over, at the outset of the meeting, what you plan to cover during the meeting—as well as what you don't plan to discuss. That way I'll know what to expect and can dispel those dreadful fantasies right from the start. At the same time, it would be useful if you told me how you want to structure the meeting. Should I interrupt with questions or wait until you ask for them? Will there be things for me to look at or read? How much time will we have? Much as I hate to admit it, we parents are a bit like students when it comes to parent-teacher conferences. The more that's laid out for us at the beginning of the lesson, the more we're apt to learn.

What I really want to know about David is how he's doing—both in relation to his own ability (and certainly I want to know if he's slacking off), and in comparison with other children. I know comparisons aren't supposed to be important, but I do wonder where he stands. Eventually he'll be getting some kind of comparative grades; I don't want to be taken by surprise. Hearing for years that "he's working up to his ability" in spelling won't prepare me for his first official low grade in the subject. I want to know as much as you can tell me about my child's schoolwork.

If you do have bad news for me, tell me at the start, so I don't have to spend my time waiting for the other shoe to drop. Let me know exactly what you see to be the problem. Show me the papers, tell me the episodes, put everything out for me to look at. I'll probably be upset, but I'll react more calmly if I get clear, specific information. I'd like to know how serious you think the problem is, too. Is it a big issue that you think will have long-term effects, or do you see it as a minor annoyance that will go away by itself? Is it part of a larger concern, or is it an isolated event? Help me to keep my perspective by telling me just how worried I should be.

Please tell me, too, what you plan to do about any problem David is having—and how I can help. The worst feeling for me is helplessness. If you can give me some guidance about what David needs (a special tutor, *less* help with homework, whatever), I'll have something to do besides worry.

Which brings me to another point. Even though I think I know what "fine motor skills" and "set theory" mean, some real-world examples will help me to be sure we agree on their meaning and purpose. I like seeing David's work. I'm also interested in what you see in his writing and art. Don't worry about boring me with lots of examples; where my child's progress is concerned, I'd rather see his work than listen to lots of fancy talk about it.

Finally, please plan to reserve some time to listen to me. I want to be able to tell you how *I* think David's doing, to ask you some questions, to respond to what you've told me. I know that I do go on at times, so I won't mind if you remind me that we have only a few minutes left and ask if I have any *last* things to say. If I feel there's a lot more to talk about, I hope we can schedule another conference.

If all this makes you think I'm an overconcerned parent, well, maybe I am. I admit I'm something of a zealot where David's skills, competence and progress are concerned. I want what's best for him, of course. I've put him under your care and tutelage for six hours a day. Now I expect to know what's been going on during that time, how he's doing, and what I can do to help. I think we can be a terrific team—if I can just untie that knot in my stomach.

Kalle Gerritz is a parent and former teacher.

Table 10–5
Contents of a Parent's Portfolio

Classroom-based, Informal Measures
- running records collected throughout the year
- writing samples showing mastery of various stages of the writing process
- informal comprehension measures, such as writing about what has been read

Standardized Measures
- norm-referenced and criterion-referenced tests
- explanations of scoring, e.g., scores based on percentiles rather than percents

Self-assessments
- logs, journal entries, and any other self-assessments students have prepared and have selected for inclusion in the portfolio

Reading and Writing Log Sheets
- indicators of extent of voluntary reading
- student-kept record sheets such as those presented in Appendix B

Illustrative and Comparative Data
- samples of the kinds of reading students do to show parents the difficulty level students can handle (this shows much more than citing a grade level)
- samples of reading from the beginning, middle, and end of the year to show growth
- writing samples from throughout the year, again to show growth
- sample items from standardized instruments to show parents what is being measured and how it is measured (this can be especially helpful if students are successful in a literature-based program and are being assessed on subskill measures)
- if possible, samples of previous standardized measures to indicate growth in the kinds of material students can handle
- graphic presentations to show changes, such as a chart of the months of the school year showing the number of books and the kinds of books read each month; a child might begin the year reading extensively in short books but progress to fewer, longer books later on

Actual samples of students' work can convey more to parents than grades or standardized test scores.

the parent conferences. Collecting material for a parent portfolio should continue throughout the year. The students themselves should be involved so that "a portfolio becomes a joint project for the teacher and the student—[thus] there will be two voices capable of and willing to explain progress" (Flood & Lapp, 1989, p. 514). If teachers then keep the portfolio relatively current, they will always be ready to discuss students if parents request conferences. At the end of the year, the portfolio is sent home as a record of each student's experiences and progress. Brief notes attached to work samples help parents understand what they are seeing.

SUMMARY

Parents and other caregivers can be valuable partners in children's learning. However, there are no easy formulas for establishing links between the home and school. It is often up to teachers to initiate these links, to make the contacts that let family members know that even if they cannot become regular classroom volunteers, their support and involvement are welcome. Because teachers are not always from the same background as the students they teach, reaching out toward children's homes may take extra effort and planning; but the benefits are tremendous in terms of immediate support and long-term effects on students' learning.

QUESTIONS AND TASKS

1. Be sure that you understand these terms:
   a. home-school connection
   b. participation, involvement, and support from the home

2. Think about the brief excerpt from Eudora Welty's *One Writer's Beginnings* and the summary of research by Taylor and Dorsey-Gaines. In pairs or small groups, share memories of home literacy experiences that you had while you were in elementary school. See how many different kinds of experiences (possibly both positive and negative) you can all remember. Categorize the experiences.

3. If possible, interview a teacher whose class is ethnically, racially, and linguistically mixed. What experiences and advice can this teacher share?

4. Refer to Table 10–2 for examples of literacy behaviors observed in the families studied in *Growing Up Literate*. Keep a log for five days of your own literacy behaviors and of those of your family (if you do not live alone). See how many of the same behaviors you engage in. Do you think your being a student limits or expands the list?

5. If you are a parent, keep a log for a week of the literacy interchanges you have with your children.

6. In activities 4 and 5, you are conducting brief ethnographies in your own home. Spend some time during a class session comparing the logs prepared in these two activities.

11 CHAPTER

Fostering Professional Growth

Throughout this book, the term "community of learners" has been used to describe the best kind of environment for children's learning. The term is an equally appropriate descriptor of an environment in which teachers can grow professionally and personally. Within a community of professionals learning together, teachers benefit from collaboration with others and explore new ideas on their own. As they and their colleagues search for the best possible models of instruction to foster students' literacy growth, they refine their abilities as kid-watchers, decision makers, and researchers.

The sense of a school as a community of professionals learning together can come from many sources. Strong administrators who respect and value their staff can encourage the development of such an environment by providing ideas for instructional change, time for discussion, and support as teachers reach for new models of interaction with students. Administrators may allow release time for special workshops or courses or finance teachers' trips to professional meetings. In such an environment, teachers cannot help but respond enthusiastically. Unfortunately, this kind of school setting is not as common as it should be, often because of circumstances far beyond the administrators' control.

But teachers have other ways of creating a community of learners, and many of the most dynamic and supportive school environments have emerged from teachers' own efforts to grow professionally (Routman, 1989, 1991).

TEACHERS AS KIDWATCHERS, DECISION MAKERS, AND RESEARCHERS

A three-part model of the roles of teachers was presented as Figure 2–1 and discussed in Chapter 2. The three roles suggested for classroom teachers are kidwatcher, decision maker, and researcher. Even if they are not consciously aware of what they are doing, all teachers engage in some level of kidwatching and make many decisions as part of daily classroom life. Some teachers may be more aware than others of the value of kidwatching and may draw more deliberately on multiple sources of data for their decision making; but all successful teachers engage in these behaviors.

It is the decision to become a teacher-researcher that can set teachers fully on the path to professional growth and satisfaction. Some teachers make this decision consciously because they have read or heard about this facet of classroom life; other teachers become researchers as they carry out assignments for graduate courses; and still others seem to fall into a research mode as they discover issues and questions about their students' learning (Bissex & Bullock, 1987; Goswani & Stillman, 1987). Whatever induces teachers to become researchers, the result is changes in attitudes toward teaching, increased professionalism, and enhanced abilities as kidwatchers and decision makers. Atwell (1987), citing Donald Graves (1983) maintains that teacher-researchers are "no longer a victim of 'our profession's energy crisis.' When we [as teachers] change our role to that of an inquirer, we become learners, too. We no longer feel drained by the demands we impose on ourselves when we view our classrooms as contexts we motivate, orchestrate, and evaluate. Instead, we are energized as our students . . . assume new control and responsibility" (pp. 90–91).

Teachers, especially those just beginning their professional life, may wonder how they can actually become teacher-researchers. Kutz (1992) suggests a simple answer: "We can begin our teacher research with any informal question that arises from our own daily classroom experience" (p. 196). This means that the process of kidwatching can help teachers identify questions that merit more intense investigation and research. Kutz also recommends "making notes, keeping a journal, recording bits of conversation, and saving artifacts of students' literacy" (p. 196) as part of the methodology of teacher research. These behaviors are recognizable parts of a classroom-based assessment system, activities that all teachers should engage in anyway if their observations and conferences are to be used to fine-tune instruction.

As teachers identify questions to be researched, keep track of relevant data, and begin to draw conclusions about what they have observed, they may begin to alter their decision-making processes. Always keeping track of results, they may tinker with classroom variables to see what will happen if certain constraints are modified. Students can be valuable informants in this process of research. Certainly their behaviors must be recorded as data to be analyzed, but their comments and observations are also important sources of information. Kutz (1992) stated: "It is not enough for us, as teacher-researchers to do research *about* our students and their learning. We must do research *with* our students, working together to discover answers to the questions that arise in our classrooms" (p. 196, emphasis added). Teachers conducting classroom research can make their students part of the process by deliberately alerting them to what is going on, what is being investigated, and what changes are being tried. Students can report their perspective orally or in writing and can make suggestions for ongoing research projects.

Table 11–1 presents a sampling of the kinds of questions that teachers can ask about their classrooms as starting points of classroom-based research.

THE IMPORTANCE OF PROFESSIONAL READING AND WRITING

One of the best ways for teachers to continue to grow as professionals is to keep up on their reading. Often what teachers read can immediately lead to innovations in instruction or formation of questions for classroom-based research. Articles in journals such as *Language Arts*, *The Reading Teacher*, and *The Journal of Reading* blend theory, research, and classroom practice in ways that stimulate reflection and provide practical suggestions for classroom use. Regular columns in these journals increase teachers' knowledge about children's literature, computer software, assessment, and other issues. Because these journals are published by professional organizations, the cost of subscribing carries the added benefit of membership in the National Council of Teachers of English or the International Reading Association. These organizations are discussed in the next section.

Difficult though it may be, teachers should try to find time to read professional books as well. Many of the current books have been written or edited by classroom teachers who share with their readers their theories, philosophies, ideas, successes, and disappointments in clear, lucid language. These books make vital connections between current literacy research and classroom practice. Students' sustained silent reading time would be an ideal time for teachers to read every day; doing so would model for students the value teachers place on reading as part of their own lifelong learning.

Table 11–1
A Sampling of Questions That Can Lead to Teacher Research

Which students seem to adopt most readily to a literature-based approach to instruction? What instructional background experiences seem to prepare students most effectively for this kind of approach?

How does the introduction of a new kind of book affect students' reading? For example, what would happen if a teacher infused a series of nonfiction books into a library that had consisted primarily of fiction?

What effect does the introduction of more emphasis on critical thinking have on students' responses to instruction and activities and on their attitudes toward learning? What, if any, dissonance is evident as students are asked to do more and more thinking on their own and less rote work? How can any dissonance be eliminated or lessened?

What congruence or discord exists between the teacher's philosophy of education and the expectations of students and parents? What specific steps can be taken to achieve communication and accord among all the stakeholders?

What matches or disparities are there between teacher's assessment of students' literacy achievement and the scores students obtain on standardized tests? Which measure seems to be more accurate? What steps can teachers take, individually or as a group, to improve their own record keeping and thereby endow their records with more validity as evaluation data? In what ways can students be actively involved in this pursuit?

What changes, if any, are there in the way students talk about (and think about) their literacy work when the curriculum is altered along lines suggested in this book? In what ways does the introduction of a classroom-based assessment approach influence students' talking about their work?

What results can be observed when students are asked to write more often and in more diverse ways as part of their content-area work?

How do second-language learners fare in a literature-based or critical-thinking approach to literacy instruction? What assistance seems more beneficial in helping them achieve to their fullest potential in such situations?

Just as they encourage their students to use writing as part of their learning processes, teachers should become writers themselves. Keeping a log or journal can encourage self-analysis and insight. It is always difficult for first-year teachers to find the time to keep an actual journal, but even brief notes can be stimulating raw material for reflection. As teachers look back over their notes, trends, patterns, and general themes will emerge. These strands of thought and behavior help teachers recognize the dynamics of their classroom, the kinds of behaviors that are positive and negative, and even the areas that merit teacher research. Excerpts from teacher's logs are among the most illuminating parts of excellent books by Routman (1989, 1991).

Learning rarely thrives in a vacuum, and as is the case with students who are learning to read and write, teachers need to be able to discuss journal articles and books with others. The kinds of interchanges discussed next broaden teachers' sense of classroom practice and professionalism.

OTHER SOURCES OF TEACHER SUPPORT AND GROWTH

Involvement with other professionals who share a vision of how students learn is essential for true teacher growth. Fortunately, opportunities for this kind of professional interaction can take many forms. Beginning teachers and those seeking to change their teaching styles need to know where to look for support and encouragement.

Mentoring and Collaborative Teaching

The two situations described here can be ideal for sharing ideas and supporting mutual growth. The first is the assignment of beginning teachers to a mentor teacher. Beginning teachers assigned to a mentor teacher work closely with an experienced professional who guides them during their first year of full-time teaching. Individuals fresh from teacher training may bring new ideas about literacy instruction, and the resulting dialogue about teaching and learning can be beneficial for beginners and mentors alike. It is possible, of course, that new teachers may encounter mentors or fellow teachers who ascribe to a more traditional basal-reader approach to instruction, and beginners may find themselves having to defend and support their emerging sense of how reading and writing growth occur. Such external pressures represent the flip side of the supportive mentor-assignment situation, and they speak to the need for beginners to seek support groups such as the ones discussed later in this chapter.

Collaborative teaching situations can also be productive. Teachers work together to plan instruction, often in several content areas, for a large group of students whom they all teach. Ideas from literacy instruction implemented in science, social studies, and math will result in students reading and writing in diverse situations. Students' learning is enhanced by the authenticity of their practice activities; teachers learn from each other and from mutual reflection on classroom practice.

Study Groups

As teachers discover the vast array of professional literature offered in journals and in books, they often establish study groups to discuss what they read (Routman, 1991). A study group can actually begin with a meeting of only two or three teachers who share what they have read and what they want for their classrooms.

In ideal situations, administrators may encourage these groups and help subsidize purchase of the materials that will be read. A study group may start with two or three interested teachers and grow to larger numbers. Its purpose is for participants to discuss what they have read and to generate ideas for incorporating new approaches and strategies into classroom practice. In some circumstances, one or two individuals may read material and present their ideas to other group members. Attendance should be voluntary, but all participants are expected to read and think about material that will be shared. Table 11–2 is a brief recollection about how one school district used study groups as the starting point for extensive growth and change.

Study groups should be scheduled to meet on a regular basis but with enough time between meetings for participants to complete reading tasks and possibly try out new ideas in their classrooms. Groups may meet early in the morning, during

Table 11–2
The Story of One District

The district was mixed racially, ethnically, and economically; it was primarily rural and suburban. Change in the district started and in many ways was motivated by one significant administrator, the assistant superintendent in charge of instruction. This particular person has been referred to as the district's "intellectual nudge," and the term can be aptly applied to any visionary who sees different ways to instruct students and who takes the initiative to move teachers toward those new ways.

The first changes were made in the secondary school English program. They reflected the thinking of the Writing Project movement—toward process writing and holistic evaluation of students' work. The administrator provided relevant books, supported involvement in professional organizations, and encouraged experimentation. Gradually, the English teachers adopted newer ways of thinking about instruction, and curriculum changed significantly and positively.

The administrator then turned her sights on the early childhood grades. The teachers were, by and large, good; but the prevailing view of grades kindergarten to third did not completely reflect the exciting research about how students learn during their early years in school. This was especially true in terms of literacy learning. The administrator moved slowly but consistently. She identified several interested and committed teachers as a key group or "task force" to look for and make suggestions for curricular changes in the early grades. This group was asked to meet during the summer—and members were paid for meeting. Their work continued throughout the school year, and they were released from class to participate (substitutes covered for them). In many ways, this core group became a study group. They read and discussed anything that seemed relevant. Books were purchased by the district and kept in a central location for all interested teachers. Teachers were encouraged to attend classes at a nearby university and were given tuition assistance; conference participation was encouraged as well. A researcher was brought in to serve as observer, resource, and facilitator, especially as the teachers began to realize that curriculum changes would necessitate changes in assessment procedures.

free or lunch periods, after school, or in the evening, although it is perhaps best to schedule meetings at times when teachers will not have to leave abruptly to meet a class.

Teachers involved in study groups see among themselves the same kind of growth that occurs when students are allowed to talk about what they read. Participants heighten their critical thinking skills as they try to ferret out the nuggets of ideas that will have immediate impact on their classroom and as they form long-term objectives for innovation; shared ideas encourage the construction of new thinking and new approaches to teaching. Teachers cannot help but personalize much of what they read, so they share observations about and difficulties with individual children. As they discuss their students in light of what they have read

Table 11–2
continued

> The administrator was very supportive of assessment change and helped the teachers work toward a classroom-based system based on analysis of students' behaviors and work samples. With the researcher helping, the core group of teachers, augmented by some new additions, developed and tried out checklists, scoring rubrics, and teacher-administered tests of initial concepts about print. These methods were introduced in the kindergartens and gradually extended to grades one, two, and three. Teachers met to score and discuss the results and realized that they were on their way toward a highly reliable, valid assessment mechanism that matched their teaching far better than a standardized test. The administrator supported the efforts and pledged to do the appropriate research to consider dropping standardized testing entirely in the early grades. Interest in portfolio assessment led the teachers to refine their documents and procedures and to formalize their scoring sessions. Gradually, teachers who were not initially interested in the changes began to make their own interpretations of what was going on—and changes began to occur district-wide. All the while, the administrator supported, suggested, bought books, provided substitutes to cover classes while teachers met or attended conferences—and nudged them toward professional growth and expansion. At the same time, the administrator was bringing local and national attention to her district. Educational programs from Lincoln Center in New York and other cultural programs enriched the curriculum; the district became invovled with the Coalition for Essential Schools.
>
> Changes in the early grades have been positive for teachers and students, and the spillover into other classes has been beneficial as well. Many teachers have been encouraged to become involved in professional organizations, both as members and presenters at conferences. Some have begun to give workshops and teach classes about their instructional and assessment practices. Teachers who do not want such active involvement are affirmed for their competence as well. The district has truly become a community of professionals learning together.

and listen to colleagues' reactions, their insight into their own students cannot help but grow.

Support Groups

Support groups may also begin with just a few concerned teachers who share a common vision of what learning should be about. As they grow in size, support groups usually meet more frequently than study groups, often once a week before school, during a common lunch period, or after school. Their purpose is more global than that of a study group, although articles may be distributed for reading prior to a meeting. The agenda of each meeting reflects participants' expressed needs and may range from viewing a relevant videotape to discussing a topic of concern such as initiating portfolio assessment or watching a demonstration of how to perform a specific function such as taking a running record (Routman, 1991). In some cases, the same agenda may extend over a period of several weeks. In the best of cases, one person, often a reading teacher who has some release time, serves as an organizer and facilitator for the support group.

Setting up a schoolwide support group is not easy but has substantial benefits. Routman (1991) wrote about the process:

> We began haphazardly. The first year our district made a commitment to more mean-
> ingful approaches to reading and writing through literature, our agenda was fragment-
> ed and scattered, reflecting our own confusion and disorganization. Most of our con-
> cerns were related to practical and organizational matters—materials, activities, and
> management. . . . Looking back, that seems quite normal for the change process. We
> needed time to find our own way. . . . By the second year, we knew our needs better
> and, quite naturally . . . began to focus in depth on issue[s] and concern[s]. . . . One of
> the surprising outcomes of our weekly meetings has been seeing ourselves as experts. .
> . . Another unexpected outcome has been finding out that when teachers act responsi-
> bly, we have some power. . . . Perhaps most important, we have become teacher
> researchers—reflective inquirers who have enough theoretical knowledge to look at
> our own teaching, ask and explore our own questions, and begin to trust and value
> what we are observing and finding. (pp. 466–467)

Another model for teacher sharing and growth is the district-wide support group that meets once every month or so. Often started by teachers from several schools who find out about each others' concerns, shared values, and common commitments, district-wide support groups usually meet in the evening in a member's home. The agenda is similar to that of a school support group: sharing ideas from recent reading; discussing issues, frustrations, and concerns; and sometimes focusing on a particular topic such as informal assessment methodologies. Again, it is helpful to have an organizer and facilitator who can make sure things go smoothly.

Among the values of school and district support groups is the sharing of ideas across grade levels and disciplines. The recent movement toward establishing school-based support groups probably grew out of specific changes in literacy instruction (just as support groups developed during the Open Classroom movement in the 1960s and 1970s), but participants bring issues and concerns that cut across all content areas. For example, discussions about reading in science can be enriched by a teacher who has discovered excellent ways to get her students to read in social studies; likewise, a strong language arts teacher can synthesize ideas to comment perceptively about writing across the content areas. When district-level support groups include teachers from elementary, middle, and secondary schools, and regular classrooms and special education programs, discussion can be especially lively and helpful. Cross-fertilization of ideas around the common theme of getting students to become better readers, writers, thinkers, and learners enhances everyone's teaching.

Some highly specialized support groups focus attention on whole-language instruction (Salzer, 1991). Called TAWL (Teachers Applying Whole Language or Teachers Attempting Whole Language) groups, these support groups have provided many teachers with the impetus to begin changes in literacy instruction. Several national groups, including a special-interest group of the International Reading Association, disseminate information about TAWL groups. See Appendix A for addresses.

Support from Other School Staff Members

Teachers seeking to change their instruction often overlook the support that they can gain from school support staff. Librarians, reading and language arts specialists, and many administrators would welcome opportunities to be more closely involved in instructional change. The pressures of their jobs often keep these staff members more isolated from classroom life than they would like, and teachers' overtures to them to be part of a change process may be just the invitation they need to bring about their own professional expansion and growth.

Inservice and Other Workshops

Many states mandate that teachers participate in inservice training; unfortunately, teachers often do not have options about the content or focus of the workshops that meet state requirements. To the extent possible, teachers should select inservice training that will meet their own needs—workshops in children's literature, portfolio assessment, critical thinking. Also to the extent possible, they should request that their needs be considered in selecting workshop leaders. For example, school- and district-based support groups should be encouraged to make suggestions about topics and speakers. In addition, when inservice workshops do not meet teacher needs, teachers should voice their complaints and present their own list of requirements and suggestions for better programs.

If teachers can meet inservice requirements by attending workshops outside of their school district, they often have a wider range from which to choose relevant topics. Unfortunately, many workshops are too packaged and slick to be as meaningful as they could be; teachers are therefore advised to get recommendations from others who have attended workshops prior to enrolling themselves. The best kinds of workshops are those that allow for real interaction between presenters and participants.

Professional Organizations

Involvement in professional organizations can be an important part of teachers' lives. The International Reading Association and the National Council of Teachers of English are especially relevant to those interested in literacy instruction. Both have state and local affiliates and many special interest groups that span diverse topics of relevance to elementary school teachers. Both IRA and NCTE publish journals, brochures, newsletters, and professional books that synthesize current research, theory, and instruction (see Appendix A). Increasingly, many of the articles in IRA and NCTE journals are written by classroom teachers. IRA offers a members' book club that publishes numerous books each year.

Both IRA and NCTE have yearly state, regional, and national conferences. These meetings offer teachers opportunities to attend workshops, talks, and symposia given by literacy researchers and specialists and by teachers who want to share their own classroom-based research. Increasingly, many conference sessions feature talks by teachers who have by themselves, with colleagues, or often with a university representative, investigated aspects of students' literacy learning.

Teachers involved in a professional organization have access to a ready-made network of other teachers and a source of relevant reading material. Working on IRA or NCTE committees at the local, state, or national level can enrich teachers' professional identities and ultimately enhance the lives of their students.

SUMMARY

The changes that are occurring in literacy instruction nationwide have had tremendous impact on curriculum, students, and, of course, teachers. Being part of these changes can be both frustrating and exciting for beginning and experienced teachers alike. Finding support for one's convictions helps alleviate some of the frustration; sharing ideas and successes is part of the excitement.

Teachers need to look within their own schools and to their profession as a whole in order to find people with whom to form communities of learners. Just as students perceive themselves to be members of a community will be more willing to take risks in their learning, so too will teachers reach for new and more productive ways to help their students acquire literacy. The feeling of well-being that comes from membership in a community of professionals learning together enhances teachers' professionalism, their self-esteem, and ultimately their effectiveness with their students.

QUESTIONS AND TASKS

1. Be sure that you understand these terms:
   a. mentoring
   b. teacher study group
   c. teacher support group

2. With two or more of your fellow students, discuss the extent to which a support group has developed in your class. How has this kind of group enhanced your learning?

3. Review any log, observational notes, or general notes you have kept during this class and identify three questions or topics that you might investigate as a teacher-researcher.

4. Review outside reading that you have done during this class. Find out if anyone else has read the same book(s), and discuss your reactions among yourselves. Discuss your reading in a more general way in medium size "study groups" or as part of a whole-class discussion.

Sources of Information About Topics in This Book

BACKGROUND AND GENERAL INFORMATION

Atwell, N. (1987). *In the middle*. Portsmouth, NH: Heinemann.

Bloome, D. (Ed.). (1989). *Classrooms and literacy*. Norwood, NJ: Ablex.

Cazden, C. B. (1988). *Classroom discourse: The language of teaching and learning*. Portsmouth, NH: Heinemann.

Clifford, J. (Ed.). (1990). *The experience of reading: Louise Rosenblatt and reader-response theory*. Portsmouth, NH: Boynton/Cook.

Duffy, G. G. (Ed.). (1990). *Reading in the middle school* (2nd ed.). Newark, DE: International Reading Association.

Edelsky, C., Altwerger, B., & Flores, B. (1991). *Whole language: What's the difference?* Portsmouth, NH: Heinemann.

Harman, S., & Edelsky, C. (1989). The risks of whole language literacy: Alienation and connection. *Language Arts, 66*, 392–406.

Heath, S. B. (1983). *Ways with words: Language, life, and work in communities and classrooms*. Cambridge: Cambridge University Press.

Meek, M., Warlow, A., & Barton, G. (Eds.). (1977). *The cool web: The pattern of children's reading*. London: The Bodley Head.

Meek, M. (1982). *Learning to read*. London: The Bodley Head.

Routman, R. (1991). *Invitations: Changing as teachers and learners, K–12*. Portsmouth, NH: Heinemann.

Routman, R. (1989). *Transitions*. Portsmouth, NH: Heinemann.

Samuels, S. J., & Farstrup, A. E. (Eds.). (1992). *What research has to say about reading instruction* (2nd Ed.). Newark, DE: International Reading Association.

Shannon, R. (1989). *Broken promises: Reading instruction in twentieth-century America*. Granby, MA: Bergin & Garvey.

Torbe, M., & Medway, P. (1981). *The climate for learning*. Upper Montclair, NJ: Boynton/Cook.

ASSESSMENT ISSUES

Barrs, M., Ellis, S., Tester, H., & Thomas, A. (1989). *The primary language record: Handbook for teachers*. Portsmouth, NH: Heinemann.

Harp, B. (Ed.). (1991). *Assessment and evaluation in whole language programs*. Norwood, MA: Christopher-Gordon.

Kamii, C. (Ed.). (1990). *Achievement testing in the early grades: The games grown-ups play*. Washington, DC: National Association for the Education of Young Children.

Tierney, R. J., Carter, M. A., & Desai, L. E. (1991). *Portfolios in the reading-writing classroom*. Norwood, MA: Christopher-Gordon.

Wolf, D. P. (1989). Portfolio assessment: Sampling student work. *Educational Leadership, 46* (7), 35–40.

LITERATURE

Cullinan, B. E. (Ed.). (1987). *Children's literature in the reading program*. Newark, DE: International Reading Association.

Cullinan, B. E. (1989). *Literature and the child*. San Diego: Harcourt Brace Jovanovich.

International Reading Association & The Children's Book Council. (1992). *Kid's favorite books: Children's choices 1989–1991*. Newark, DE: International Reading Association.

Johnson, T. D., & Louis, D. R. (1987). *Literacy through literature*. Portsmouth, NH: Heinemann.

Roser, N., & Frith, M. (Eds.). (1983). *Children's choices: Teaching with books children like*. Newark, DE: International Reading Association.

Ryder, R. J., Graves, B. B., & Graves, M. F. (1989). *Easy reading: Book series and periodicals for less able readers* (2nd Ed.). Newark, DE: International Reading Association.

Stewig, S. W., & Sebesta, S. L. (Eds.). (1989). *Using literature in the elementary classroom*. Urbana, IL: National Council of Teachers of English.

Stoll, D. R. (Ed.). (1990). *Magazines for children*. Newark, DE: International Reading Association.

Trelease, J. (1985). *The read-aloud handbook*. New York: Penguin.

THE READING/WRITING/THINKING CLASSROOM

Brandt, R. S. (Ed.). (1989). *Teaching thinking: Readings from Educational Leadership*. Alexandria, VA: Association for Supervision and Curriculum Development.

Costa, A. L., & Lowery, L. F. (1989). *Techniques for teaching thinking*. Pacific Grove, CA: Midwest Publications.

Heimlich, J. E., & Pittleman, S. D. (1986). *Semantic mapping: Classroom applications*. Newark, DE: International Reading Association.

Norris, S. & Ennis, R. H. (1989). *Evaluating critical thinking*. Pacific Grove, CA: Midwest Publications.

Swartz, R. J., & Perkins, D. N. (1989). *Teaching thinking: Issues and approaches*. Pacific Grove, CA: Midwest Publications.

EMERGENT LITERACY

Adams, M. J. (1990). *Beginning to read: Thinking and learning about print*. Cambridge, MA: MIT Press.

Butler, D., & Clay, M. (1987). *Reading begins at home*. Portsmouth, NH: Heinemann.

Butler, D., & Clay, M. (1988). *Writing begins at home*. Portsmouth, NH: Heinemann.

Goodman, Y. (Ed.). (1990). *How children construct literacy*. Newark, DE: International Reading Association.

Harste, J. C., Woodward, V. A., & Burke, C. L. (1984). *Language stories and literacy lessons*. Portsmouth, NH: Heinemann.

Salinger, T. (1988). *Language arts and literacy for young children*. New York: Merrill/Macmillan.

TEACHER-RESEARCHERS

Bissex, G. L., & Bullock, R. H. (Eds.). (1987). *Seeing for ourselves: Case-study research by teachers of writing*. Portsmouth, NH: Heinemann.

Calkins, L. M. (1991). *Living between the lines*. Portsmouth, NH: Heinemann.

Goswami, D., & Stillman, P. R. (Eds.). (1987). *Reclaiming the classroom: Teacher research as an agency for change*. Upper Montclair, NJ: Boynton/Cook.

Olson, M. W. (Ed.). (1990). *Opening the door to classroom research*. Newark, DE: Heinemann.

BOOKS OF GENERAL INTEREST FOR DISCUSSION AND DEBATE

Kidder, T. (1989). *Among school children*. New York: Avon.

Kotlowitz, A. (1991). *There are no children here: The story of two boys growing up in the other America*. New York: Doubleday.

Kozol, J. (1991). *Savage inequities: Children in America's schools*. New York: Crown.

Rose, M. (1989). *Lives on the boundary*. New York: Penguin.

RECOMMENDED JOURNALS AND NEWSLETTERS

The Reading Teacher and *Journal of Reading*

These journals concern elementary and secondary/adult reading issues respectively. Articles are a mix of theory and practice, and regular columns in each journal are diverse and extremely useful. Published by:

> International Reading Association (IRA)
> 800 Barksdale Road
> PO Box 8139
> Newark, DE 19714–8139

Language Arts

This journal is directed toward elementary teachers. Its contents tend to be more theoretical than that of IRA journals; many report teacher-researcher studies conducted in single classrooms. Published by:

> National Council of Teachers of English (NCTE)
> 1111 Kenyon Road
> Urbana, IL 61801

Teachers Networking: The Whole Language Newsletter, published by:

> Richard C. Owen, Publisher, Inc.
> Rockefeller Center, Box 819
> New York, NY 10185

Whole Language Special Interest Group of IRA Newsletter, published by:

> WLSIG
> c/o Pat Jenkins, Secretary/Treasurer
> 2801 West Broadway, # F6
> Columbia, MO 65203

FOR INFORMATION ABOUT HOME SUPPORT FOR LITERACY

Both IRA and NCTE publish numerous booklets about home support for literacy growth. Topics range from emergent literacy to reading to students to helping adolescents become lifelong readers. IRA also distributes short videotapes that have been developed by various state affiliate councils.

FOR INFORMATION ABOUT CHILDREN'S LITERATURE

Sources of Information and Bibliographies

Children's Book Council
67 Irving Place
New York, NY 10003

Journals Devoted to Children's Literature

The New Advocate, published by:

Christopher-Gordon Publisher
480 Washington Street
Norwood, MA 02062

The Horn Book Magazine, published by:

The Horn Book
14 Beacon Street
Boston, MA 02108

Major Textbooks

Huck, C. S., Hepler, S., & Hickman, J. (1987). *Children's literature in the elementary school* (4th ed.). New York: Holt, Rinehart, & Winston.

Norton, D. E. (1991). *Through the eyes of a child: An introduction to children's literature* (3rd. ed.). New York: Merrill/Macmillan.

Stewig, J. W. (1988). *Children and literature* (2nd ed.). Boston: Houghton Mifflin.

Checklists, Record-Keeping Forms, Questions, Rubrics, and Instructional Plans

These checklists, forms, and other materials are samples that have been developed without reference to specific classes. Teachers who wish to use these outlines are strongly advised to use them as a starting point for their own materials. They are also advised to consider any record-keeping form or rubric as fluid, that is, as something that will be altered to accommodate changing needs.

CHECKLISTS FOR RECORDING STUDENTS' PROGRESS

Sample 1: Checklist for Individual Student

Name _____

Focus of Checklist _____

	Dates	Yes	No
1. Selects appropriate topics • when given choice • when general topic is selected Comments			
2. Demonstrates strategies for planning (e.g., brainstorming, etc.) Comments			
3. Demonstrates understanding of drafting processes Comments			
4. Revises work • adds/deletes information • reorganizes • considers vocabulary/word choice • considers grammar Comments			
5. Other (Add other relevant criteria.)			

Sample 2: Checklist for Group of Students

Focus of Checklist: _____

Date Compiled: _____

	A = Always S = Sometimes N = Never	Student Name	Student Name	Student Name	Student Name	Student Name	Student Name
1. Reads familiar material fluently							
2. Reads with appropriate intonation							
3. Reads with appropriate expression							
4. Self-corrects							
5. Uses punctuation to guide reading							
6. Takes risks in pronouncing unfamiliar words							
7. Demonstrates strategies for decoding unfamiliar words							
• Skips word and continues to read							
• Rereads entire sentence							
• Uses picture clues							
• Uses context clues							
• Sounds word out							
• Asks for help							
• Other strategies evident							
8. Other (Add other relevant criteria.)							

ANECDOTAL RECORD FORMS

Sample 1: Individual Student

This record can be kept over an extended period of time.

Student _____

Date	Reading	Writing	Oral Language	Spontaneous Uses of Literacy	Other (Add more spaces as needed.)

Sample 2: Small Group or Whole Class

This record is best limited to a single observation or observations conducted over a short period of time, such as one week.

Date(s) of Observation _____

Reading _____   Writing _____   Other activities _____

Name _____	Name _____	Name _____	Name _____
Name _____	Name _____	Name _____	Name _____

QUESTIONS TO ASSESS STUDENTS' ATTITUDES AND STRATEGIES

Administer these questions in an informal conference with students. Make notations of answers or tape record the conference for later analysis. Change questions to suit students' needs, levels of understanding, or interactional styles.

Do you like to write? What do you like to write?

When do you like to write?

Do you ever write at home? What do you write there?

Do you think you are a good writer? What makes you think so?

What does someone do to get to be a good writer?

How do you decide what you will write about?

When you can't think of something to write, what do you do?

When you can't think of how to spell a word, what do you do?

What would you say to help someone who is just learning to write?

Do you like to read? What do you like to read about?

When do you like to read?

Do you ever read at home? What do you read there?

Do you think you are a good reader? What makes you think so?[1]

How do you select books you read? What kinds do you like?

How does someone get to be a good reader?

What do you do if you don't know a word in what you are reading?

What do you do if you don't understand what you read?

What would you say to help someone who is having trouble learning to read?

RUBRICS FOR EVALUATING STUDENTS' WRITING

In all probability, only some of the descriptors at each level will apply to any set of student papers. Each descriptor must be qualified with the statement that the students display these characteristics in a developmentally appropriate manner.

Best Paper:

- is about interesting, unusual topics or presents standard topics in an interesting way

---

[1]Answers to questions about what makes students think in certain ways or say certain things can be especially telling because of students' attributions. They may attribute their competence or incompetence to the grades they receive, to the amount of skills they have accumulated and their proficiency or weakness in using them, to external sources such as "my teacher says I am," or to their own feelings about reading and writing, such as "I like to write, so I'm a good writer." When students attribute competence to skills or grades, they often do not fully recognize their own contribution to achievement, and do not fully appreciate the control they can have over their own learning. Discrepancies between students' assessment of their competence and teachers' assessment must be dealt with—directly, immediately, but tactfully. If students are to become truly engaged in their learning and if they are to be able to evaluate their own progress, they must become realistic about their own skills and strategies. This kind of accurate self-awareness is an aspect of metacognition.

- demonstrates some awareness of point of view, feelings of writer or others, and includes intent or motivation
- is well organized with correct paragraphs, regardless of the paper's length
- demonstrates control of sentence construction, including punctuation, pronoun use, subject-verb agreement, and transitional words
- uses a variety of sentence patterns
- uses well chosen, varied, and appropriate words
- includes dialogue, figures of speech, and other devices to make writing interesting to audience
- is written with awareness of needs of audience
- shows control of grammar and mechanics to an extent that errors are minor and do not detract from content
- is legible
- may or may not be accompanied by related art work

Average Paper:

- presents unoriginal ideas, inventories, or clichéd story
- shows at best only a little intent or motivation of characters; does not show awareness of point of view
- may be repetitive
- is not well organized in presentation of story or main points
- may include individual sentences not grouped into paragraphs
- has unelaborated sentences with few descriptions or details
- shows limited control of sentence structure by including primarily simple sentences and/or run-ons
- does not use transitional words or phrases
- lacks control of grammar, mechanics, and spelling to extent that errors make comprehension difficult
- may have handwriting that is difficult to read
- may or may not have art work; may depend too much on art to convey message

Poor Paper:

- presents generally uninteresting ideas
- usually lacks details or description to convey message

- usually does not present writer's point of view or other psychological components
- may have "flat," unemotional writing
- lacks organization as a means to help readers understand writing
- lacks sense of audience
- may have random presentation of ideas, that is, writing "does not make sense"
- lacks control of sentence structure and may include fragments and/or run-ons
- shows severe lack of control of grammar and mechanics
- has spelling errors, including low levels of invented spelling, that interfere with comprehension
- has poor handwriting
- may or may not have artwork; artwork may not be related (e.g., random doodling)

INSTRUCTIONAL PLANS

Sample 1: Early Childhood Class

Assumptions. Class is self-contained and heterogeneously grouped. The instructional day begins at 8:30. No specific time has been designated in these plans for pull-out or special programs such as art, music, or physical education.

8:30–8:40   Students go about daily business of checking supplies, communicating with each other, possibly writing notes for each other's mailboxes. Teacher collects money as needed, takes attendance, etc.

8:40–9:00   Class meeting, to include:
- checking homework
- relevant class discussion and news
- "status-of-the-class" report on what students are working on
- brief oral reading by teacher (poem, very short story, etc.)
- mini-lesson, focused specifically on reading
- clarification of day's work

9:00–10:30   Reading-writing workshop, to include the following activities, varying according to the day of the week and students' needs:
- small-group instruction with teachers

- conferences with teacher
- independent reading and/or writing work
- peer conferences about reading or writing
- working independently or in small groups on long-term projects
- preparing for conference with teacher

Students know the limits of the activities that they may engage in during workshop; they are free to schedule their own time to a certain extent, as long as they are able to complete assignments given by the teacher.

10:30–11:30	Math instruction and practice activities
11:30–12:15	Lunch
12:15–12:35	Teacher reads to students.
12:35–12:45	Mini-lesson on handwriting, grammar, punctuation, or other topic related specifically to writing
12:45–1:45	Social studies, science, health, or other content area instruction and activities; students work on projects related to these subject areas.
1:45–2:15	Shared-book and/or literacy-related activities, to be sampled from the following:

- Sustained Silent Reading or Writing
- shared book experiences in which students discuss and share their favorite books
- book talks, Readers Theatre, or activities
- guided reading
- student-teacher conferences
- small-group sharing of writing

These are only a few of the kinds of activities that may take place. On some days, teachers may work with the whole class, while on other days, students may work in small groups or independently.

2:15–2:40	Students write in journals.
2:40–3:00	Teacher reads to students.
3:00–3:10	Wrap-up: discussion, assignment of any homework; students may read what they have written during the day.
3:15	School day ends.

Sample 2: Mid-Elementary Class

Assumptions. Class is self-contained and heterogeneously grouped. The instructional day begins at 8:30; no specific time has been designated in these plans for pull-out or special programs such as art, music, or physical education.

8:30–8:40	Students go about daily business of checking supplies, communicating with each other, possibly writing notes for each other's mailboxes; teacher collects money as needed, takes attendance, etc.
8:40–9:00	Class meeting, to include:

- checking homework
- relevant class discussion and news
- mini-lesson on reading, writing, specific author, or other literacy topic
- "status-of-the-class" report on what students are working on
- teacher and students set objectives for day's work; they generate a list of required and optional activities and write it on the board

9:00-10:30   Reading-writing workshop, to include the following activities, varying according to the day of the week and students' needs:

- small-group instruction with teachers
- conferences with teacher
- independent reading and/or writing work
- peer conferences about reading or writing
- working independently or in small groups on long-term projects
- preparing for conference with teacher
- independent, silent reading
- working in small, student-directed reading groups

As in the early childhood class, students know the limits of the activities that they may engage in during workshop; they are free to schedule their own time to a certain extent, so long as they are able to complete those assignments designated as "required." Many such assignments will take several days to complete, so students must gauge their time carefully.

10:30–11:30	Content area instruction and practice activities: math, science, social studies; this time may include considerable independent work as students work alone or with small groups on relevant projects and write in learning logs; teacher provides instruction or assistance to small groups.
11:30–12:15	Lunch
12:15–12:35	Teacher reads to students.
12:35–12:45	Group sharing of morning work, especially students reading their writing to others
12:45–1:45	Content area instruction and activities; students work on projects related to these subject areas; this time period includes writing in learning logs for specific subjects; teacher provides instruction or assistance to small groups.
1:45–2:15	Shared-book and/or literacy-related activities, to be sampled from the following:

- Sustained Silent Reading or Writing
- shared-book experiences in which students discuss and share their favorite books
- book talks, Readers Theatre, or activities
- guided reading
- student-teacher conferences
- small-group sharing of writing
- word processing
- working on interdisciplinary projects

	Again, these are only a few of the kinds of activities that may take place. On some days, teachers may work with the whole class, while on other days, students may work in small groups or independently.
2:15–2:40	Students write in journals; they include self-evaluations.
2:40–3:00	Teacher reads to students.
3:00–3:10	Wrap-up: discussion; students may share what they have written, read, or learned during day.
3:15	School day ends.

Sample 3: Upper-Elementary/Middle School Class

Assumption. Class is heterogeneously grouped. It covers both reading and language arts and hence spans two class periods (100 minutes total). Students meet five days a week and are familiar with the reading-writing workshop approach.

8:00–8:05	Students enter classroom, get folders from storage spaces, gather any needed supplies; they turn in papers in designated place.
8:05–8:15	Teacher listens to students report their progress and fills in a "status-of-the-class" report; together students and teacher set objectives for the day and/or week; modifications to plans are made as necessary.
8:15–8:30	Students share writing, make comments, conduct short discussions as need arises; teacher presents short mini-lesson on reading, writing, or literature topic.
8:30–9:15	*Reading-writing workshop period.* Students work on assigned or optional activities, making sure that they prepare for any conferences, and make progress on assigned work. Workshop activities may include:

- small-group discussion and sharing of favorite books
- book talks, Readers Theatre, or activities
- guided reading
- student-teacher conferences
- small-group sharing of writing
- word processing
- small-group instruction with teachers
- independent reading
- independent writing in any stage of progress
- peer conferences about reading or writing
- working independently or in small groups on long-term projects
- preparing for conference with teacher
- independent, silent reading
- working in small, student-directed reading groups

Teacher warns students five minutes before the workshop is to end so that they can put completed work in designated places and put away materials they have taken out during work time.

9:15–9:35	*Group sharing time.* Students read work they want to share with entire class; students discuss what they have read; plans for week may be altered.
9:35–9:45	Teacher reads to students.
9:45	Teacher dismisses students to their next class.

Possible Assignments

Teachers may elect to give two kinds of work assignments: those that are required and those that are optional. Students then are responsible for completing *all* required assignments and selecting from among the optional assignments those they are most interested in. The teacher's responsibilities are to check on the completion of required assignments and to make sure that students are using their optional assignments in ways that will further their literacy growth.

Possibilities, may be required or optional:

- doing an interdisciplinary project
- completing some kind of art-related project about what has been read
- responding to reading in a creative way
- preparing for Readers Theatre or other "production" based on reading work
- illustrating a student-written book

Possibilities, usually required:

- reading and responding to a designated or self-selected piece of literature
- drafting, revising, and completing a designated writing task
- writing in logs or journals
- preparing for a conference with the teacher
- preparing for peer response to writing
- completing any skills-related work

APPENDIX C

Terminology and Concepts About Phonetic and Structural Analysis

PHONICS

Vowels

The letters, *a, e, i, o,* and *u* are vowels; *y* is sometimes a vowel.

Long vowels. The vowel "says its name." Long vowel sounds may be made by the letter itself alone in a word or in combination with other letters. See digraphs below.

Short vowels. The vowel sounds in *cat, egg, sit, cot,* and *cut* are short.

Vowel digraphs are made up of two vowels together when one vowel is sounded and the other is silent. Usually, the first vowel is voiced, but not always, as in *build* and *fruit.* Usually the voiced vowel is long, as in *boat,* but this is not always true, as in *bread.* Examples:

> *ai* (pain); *ay* (hay)
> *ea* (weather, bread, each); *ee* (tree); *ei* (weight, either, receive)
> *ie* (piece, either)
> *oa* (boat); *oe* (toe); *ow* (low); *ou* (tough)
> *ue* (true, blue); *ui* (build, fruit)

Vowel diphthongs are made up of two vowels together whose sounds make one new sound different from the sound made by either individual vowel. These can be very difficult, especially for dialect speakers. Examples:

> *au* (haul); *aw* (hawk); *ew* (few); *ey* (they)
> *oo* (book, school); *oi* (soil); *ow* (cow); *oy* (boy)

R-controlled vowels are vowels or vowel combinations that are followed by an *r*; they are neither long nor short. Again, children who speak dialects that drop or add *r* sounds have trouble with these sounds. Examples:

> *star, ear, tire, ore, or, lure*

Silent vowels are vowels that are not voiced. Examples:

> *sail*, where the *i* is silent
> *sale*, where the *a* is long and the final *e* is a "placeholder" to indicate that the previous vowel "says its name"

Medial vowels are vowels that come in the middle of words, also called "middle vowels." They include C-V-C combinations. *C-V-C* refers to the pattern of words that begin and end with a consonant (single, digraph, or blend) with a short vowel in the middle. Examples:

> *cat, fish, dog*

Medial vowels also include C-V-C-E combinations, which demonstrate the "silent *e*" principle. Examples:

> *cape, bake, hope*

Consonants

Letters that are not vowels (or functioning as vowels) are called consonants.

Initial or *beginning consonant sounds* are the first consonant in a word. The "initial consonant sound" may be made by single, double, or triple combinations of consonants. Examples:

> *sit, shut, school*

Medial consonants are consonants in the middle of a word.

Final, end, or *terminal consonants* are consonants at the end of a word.

Consonant digraphs are made up of two adjacent consonants that make one sound that differs from the sound of either consonant by itself. These are the last elements to appear in children's invented spelling. Examples:

> *ch* (church); *sh* (ship); *th* (that); *wh* (what)
> *gh* (cough)
> *ph* (graph, phone)

Silent consonants are consonants that make no sound. Examples:

b (lamb); *p* (psalm); *h* (ghost); *w* (wring); *l* (walk); *k* (knife)

Consonant blends or *clusters* are made up of two or more adjacent consonants whose sounds *glide* together while the individual sounds remain somewhat distinct. Think of words *b-b-b-lend, c-c-c-luster*, or *g-g-g-lide* to help remember rules about consonant blends. Children use blends in their invented spelling. Blends can appear at the beginning, middle, or end of words and should be taught in clusters according to the first letter of the blend. Teaching them as part of spelling instruction is effective. Examples:

b-blends: blue, brown
c-blends: clown, crown
d-blends: dress, dwell
f-blends: flower, from
g-blends: glue, grow
p-blends: plate, pretty
s-blends: skill, slow, small, snail, spin, story, swam, school, screen, shrink, splash, squash; past, crash
t-blends: tree, trash, twelve, three
n-blends: friend, sing, sink
r-blends: work, hurt

Hard and *soft consonants*. *C* or *g* followed by *e, i,* or *y* usually makes a "soft" sound as in *city* or *gem*; "hard" sounds are those of *cat* and *game*.

MORPHEMIC AND STRUCTURAL ANALYSIS

Roots or *stems*. These terms refer to whole words onto which an affix is added (e.g., *like* is the root of *likes, dislike*, or *likelihood*). They can also refer to Greek and Latin roots, the smaller word parts from which many of our words are built (e.g., the Latin *multus*, meaning many, is the root for *multiply*). Knowing that affixes can be added to words is useful for word attack, but memorization of extensive lists of "word parts" serves little purpose for beginning readers; it forces them to look too closely at individual words and can slow them down. Instruction as part of spelling is best.

Affixes are word parts that are added onto the beginnings or ends of words. They change the meaning of the words in specific ways.

Prefixes are elements added at the beginning of words. Fifteen prefixes account for more than 80 percent of all common words that have prefixes (Herr, 1982). Examples:

Negatives: *dis-, im-, in-, un-*
Directional: *ab-, ad-, de-, en-, ex-, pre-, pro-, re-, sub-*
Combinational: *be-, com-*

Suffixes are word parts added to the ends of words. Examples:

Plural markers: *-s, -es*
Verb markers: *-s,* for third person singular; *-ed, -d, -t,* for past tenses
Adjective or adverb markers: *-er* for comparing two things; *-est* for comparing three or more; *-less* (meaning *without*); *-ful, -full* (meaning *full*)

Noun suffixes include *-er, -ist, -or,* meaning *one who; -tion, -sion, -ment, -ness,* meaning *state of*

Compound words are made up of two little words put together to make one, new, longer word. Children enjoy compound words because they can usually figure them out and feel proud to read big words. However, children must realize that some compounds have a cumulative meaning, as in *lunchroom*, while some may be more deceptive, as in *hot dog* or *eggplant*. Compound words make good spelling lists.

Contractions are made up of one word formed by deleting letters from two other words, inserting an apostrophe to show the deletion, and then used to stand for the two other words. Contractions are most easily learned in conjunction with oral-language work. When children write contractions, they often forget which letters to leave out and where to place the apostrophe (e.g., *is'nt* for *isn't, hsn't* for *hasn't*). Some regional dialects omit additional letters in oral use of contractions, causing additional confusion as children try to spell them in their writing. Spelling instruction is the best place to study and learn contractions.

In teaching phonics and word structure, teachers must remember the following:

1. Children need extensive repetition and practice in varied situations before use of these concepts and skills becomes automatic.
2. Children need to tie these concepts and skills to their oral language and learn ways in which their oral language may mislead them.
3. Practice that reinforces these concepts through auditory and visual channels is best. Writing further reinforces these skills as long as children are using the skills purposefully rather than on fill-in-the-blank worksheets.
4. Many of these concepts and skills can best be introduced through structured "word study" as part of spelling instruction.

CHILDREN'S STEPS FOR FIGURING OUT UNFAMILIAR WORDS INDEPENDENTLY:

1. Look at the word carefully and say the sound of the first letter, blend, or digraph. Then read to the end of the sentence to see if you can figure the word out from context clues.

2. If the preceding technique has not worked, attack the word by trying vowel sounds. A vowel in the middle is most often short; a CVCE construction usually indicates a long vowel and silent *e*; if two vowels are together, often the first vowel is long, except in *oi, oy, ou, ew,* or *ui.*

3. Say the word again after applying the vowel rules. If it still does not make sense, read to the end of the sentence to try context clues again.

4. Try consonant rules next, remembering especially hard and soft *c* and *g* rules and silent consonants.

5. Say the word one more time after applying the consonant rules; again read to the end of the sentence.

6. If the word still does not make sense, write it down to ask the teacher or to look it up in the dictionary at a later time.

7. *Go on reading* because context clues later in the passage may help you figure out the word.

APPENDIX

Home-School Support

SAMPLE LETTERS TO BE SENT HOME

Letter to Parents of Children in an Early Childhood Class

Dear Parents:

This will be an exciting year for children in this class because we will be working to strengthen reading and writing skills. Your child probably already knows a lot about literacy; you have probably heard him or her "read" signs and package labels or letters he or she has written to someone in the family. These behaviors are the beginnings of strong literacy skills, and we plan to build on this foundation.

As children learn anything, including reading and writing, they make many false starts and many mistakes. They need support and answers to questions about what they are doing. I want to ask for your help in supporting growth by continuing to answer questions your child may ask, by continuing to read to him or her as often as possible, and by engaging him or her in conversations about what is going on in school. Your child will bring home books to share with you; let him or her read as much of the book as possible and discuss the story. He or she will bring home beginning writing efforts, which may appear strange and misspelled to you. Don't be put off! These early efforts lead rapidly to control of the mechanics of writing, and your child will want to share them with you. Be enthusiastic about what is brought home!

Your interest in your child's progress is important. Children know when their parents support what they are doing in school. Your help with and acceptance of beginning literacy efforts are also important because you, too, are an important teacher. Let your child see you reading and writing, show him or her that literacy is an important part of your life.

Letter to Parents of Children in Middle School Grades

Dear Parents:

Fifth grade presents some exciting challenges to your children. They change classes now, and I will be their reading and language arts teacher. The children stay with me for two periods each day, and I want to let you know some of the things we will be doing and some of the ways you can support what goes on in school.

Our classes will be set up as "workshops" in which the children will be doing a lot of reading and writing. Each day will begin with a small group meeting that includes a brief lesson on important skills, but mostly students will be working independently at their own rate or in small groups. Having them work this way will allow me to give them individual attention, to hold conferences with them about their reading and writing, and to pull small groups together when they need extra instruction.

My goal is for the children to become independent readers and writers, and to do that, they must *practice a lot!* As you will notice when you visit the classroom, we have a lot of books and many places to keep children's writing. Everyone will have opportunities to select what they want to read, as well as reading the books we discuss as a class. Everyone will do a lot of writing of many different kinds, and they will be graded on work that they have drafted and revised several times.

Even though your child will be reading and writing extensively in school, please encourage him or her to read at home as well. Make sure he or she goes to the library often; encourage him or her to buy books; if possible, give books and magazine subscriptions as gifts. And talk to your child about what we read in school and what you yourself read. These conversations are very important in helping children understand what they read and in recognizing that significant adults in their lives enjoy and value literacy skills.

BROCHURE FOR CAREGIVERS ABOUT THEIR CHILD'S LITERACY DEVELOPMENT

Purpose: to give parents a brief overview of what their children are learning

Characteristics: short, colorful, written in easy-to-understand language, well illustrated

Contents:

Introduction. States goal for children's academic work, expectations of what will be accomplished.

Role of parents. Stresses importance of home-school connection.

Steps caregivers can take. Briefly but clearly states activities that caregivers and children can engage in and suggests routines (such as book talks or homework) that should be established.

Materials. Suggests the kinds of books and materials parents should try to provide.

Other readings. Either provides or suggests other sources of information about the home-school connection and reading and writing growth.

Such a brochure should be prepared in as informal a way as possible so that it is not perceived as "educationese." It should be neat and attractive, possibly with cartoons as illustrations.

PARENT INVOLVEMENT PROGRAMS FROM NORFOLK, VIRGINIA

According to Marycarolyn France of the Norfolk, Virginia, public schools, the following four programs are in place to encourage parent involvement in the schools.

1. *The Home Learning Program,* which includes 17 learning packets designed to foster language development in kindergarten students. Children take packets of about 10 pages home, complete them with their parents, and bring them back to school. Distributed twice a month, the packets include activities to strengthen reading, vocabulary, story telling, handwriting, math, science, and social studies. Parents are asked to return a checklist for each packet. An index of the Home Learning Packets is reproduced as a sample of the activities.

2. *The Pre-kindergarten Home Learning Program,* which is a series of 9 three-page activity packets focused on separate nursery rhymes. Their purpose is to encourage meaningful interaction between preschoolers and parents and thereby to establish the habit of talking about schoolwork. A parent checklist is included with these as well.

3. *My Thinking Book,* which is a series of 8 two-page activity packets, centered on a nursery rhyme and intended to foster thinking skills. Packets are sent home once a month, beginning in November.

4. *Making Friends with Books*, which is a series of intergenerational workshops designed for two purposes: to improve the reading skills of participants and to help them learn strategies to strengthen the prereading skills of their youngsters. The intended population has been parents with minimal literacy skills, those who lack confidence in their ability to help their children with school work. During six-week-long workshops, parents are taught different read-aloud techniques: echo reading, choral reading, paired reading, story telling, Reader's Theatre, and chanting and singing. Parents are given books to take home to share with their children. France has written that "[t]he most encouraging outcome of the workshop . . . is the interest and pleasure in reading it has generated. . . . [T]he parents reported great increases in the time spent reading at home because of the pleasure it brought them and their children. Since it is at least as important that parents and children want to read as it is that they be able to read, this may be the most significant contribution these workshops can make."

Other features of the program include certificates for parents who complete the workshops and Parent Logs of interactions between parents and children. The Norfolk public television station proposes to run programs in support of the school district efforts to increase parent-child interaction concerning literacy issues. The *American School Board Journal* and the *Executive Educator* have recognized Norfolk's efforts as outstanding curriculum programs.

References

Aaron, I. E. (1987). Enriching the basal reading program with literature. In B. E. Cullinan (Ed.), *Children's literature in the reading program* (pp. 126–138). Newark, DE: International Reading Association.

Adams, M. J. (1990). *Beginning to read: Thinking and learning about print*. Cambridge: MIT Press.

Alexander, F. (1987). California Reading Initiative. In B. E. Collinan (Ed.), *Children's literature in the reading program* (pp. 1126–138). Newark, DE: International Reading Association.

Allington, R. L. (1980). Poor readers don't get to read much in reading groups. *Language Arts, 57*, 872–876.

Allington, R. L. (1983). The reading instruction provided readers of differing reading abilities. *Elementary School Journal, 83*, 548–559.

Allington, R. L., & McGill-Franzen, A. (1989). Different programs, indifferent instruction. In D. Lipsky, & A. Gartner (Eds.), *Beyond separate education: Quality education for all* (pp. 75–98). Baltimore: Paul Brookes.

Anderson, L. M. (1989). Classroom instruction. In M. C. Reynolds (Ed.), *Knowledge base for the beginning teacher* (pp. 100–115). New York: Pergamon Press.

Anderson, L. M. (1989). Learners and learning. In M. C. Reynolds (Ed.), *Knowledge base for the beginning teacher* (pp. 85–99). New York: Pergamon Press.

Anderson, R. C., Hiebert, E. H., Scott, J. A., & Wilkinson, I. A. G. (1985). *Becoming a nation of readers: The report of the commission on reading*. Washington, DC: The National Institute of Education, U.S. Department of Education.

Antler, J. (1987). *Lucy Sprague Mitchell: The making of a modern woman*. New Haven: Yale University Press.

Applebee, A. N. (1978). *The child's concept of story*. Chicago: University of Chicago Press.

Applebee, A. N., Auten, A., & Lehr, F. (1981). *Writing in the secondary school*. Urbana, IL: National Council of Teachers of English.

Applebee, A. N., Langer, J. A., & Mullis, I. V. (1986). *The writing report card: Writing achievement in American schools*. Princeton, NJ: Educational Testing Service.

Atwell, N. (1987). *In the middle: Writing, reading, and learning with adolescents*. Portsmouth, NH: Heinemann.

Au, K., & Jordan, C. (1980). Teaching reading to Hawaiian children: Finding a culturally appropriate solution. In H. Trueba, G. P. Guthrie, & K. Au (Eds.), *Culture and the bilingual classroom* (pp. 91–115). Rawley, MA: Newbury House.

Baghbam, M. (1984). *Our daughter learns to read and write*. Newark, DE: International Reading Association.

Barrs, M. (1990). *The Primary Language Record*: Reflections on issues in evaluation. *Language Arts, 67*, 244–253.

Barrs, M., Ellis, S., Tester, H., & Thomas, A. (1989). *The primary language record: Handbook for teachers*. Portsmouth, NH: Heinemann.

Bereiter, C., & Scardamalia, M. (1985). Cognitive coping strategies and the problem of "inert knowledge." In S. Chapman, J. Segal, & R. Glaser (Eds.), *Thinking and learning skills: Vol. 2. Current research and open questions* (pp. 65–80). Hillsdale, NJ: Erlbaum.

Berthoff, A. E. (1988). *Forming, thinking, writing* (2nd ed.).(with James Stephens). Portsmouth, NH: Boynton/Cook.

Beyer, B. K. (1988 April). Developing a scope and sequence for thinking skills instruction. *Educational Leadership, 45*, 26–30.

Bird, L. B. (1989). The art of teaching: Evaluation and revision. In K. S. Goodman, Y. M. Goodman, & W. J. Hood (Eds.), *The whole language evaluation book* (pp. 15–24). Portsmouth, NH: Heinemann.

Bishop, R. S. (1987). Extending multi-cultural understanding through children's books. In B. E. Cullinan (Ed.), *Children's literature in the reading program* (pp. 60–67). Newark, DE: International Reading Association.

Bishop, R. S. (1990). Walk tall in the world: African American literature for today's children. *Journal of Negro Education, 59*, 556–565.

Bissex, G. L. (1980). *Gnys at wrk: A child learns to write and read*. Cambridge, MA: Harvard University Press.

Bissex, G. L., & Bullock, R. H. (Eds.). (1987). *Seeing for ourselves: Case-study research by teachers of writing*. Portsmouth, NH: Heinemann.

Brandt, R. (1989). On parents and schools: A conversation with Joyce Epstein. *Educational Leadership, 47*(2), 24–27.

Britton, J. (1987). A quiet form of research. In D. Goswani, & P. R. Stillman (Eds.), *Reclaiming the classroom* (pp. 13–19). Upper Montclair, NJ: Boynton/Cook.

Brophy, J. (1983). Conceptualizing student motivation. *Educational Psychologist, 18*, 200–215.

Brophy, J. (1987). On motivating students. In D. C. Berliner, & B. U. Rosenshine (Eds.), *Talks to teachers* (pp. 201–215). New York: Random House.

Brown, A. L., Armbruster, B. B., & Baker, L. (1986). The role of metacognition in reading and studying. In J. Orasanu (Ed.), *Reading comprehension from research to practice* (pp. 49–75). Hillsdale, NJ: Lawrence Erlbaum.

Brown, A. L., Palinscar, A. S., & Armbruster, B. B. (1984). Instructing comprehension—fostering activities in interactive learning situations. In H. Mandl, L.

Stein, & T. Trabasso (Eds.), *Learning and comprehension of text* (pp. 255–285). Hillsdale, NJ: Lawrence Erlbaum.

Brown, C. S., & Lytle, S. L. (1988). Merging assessment and instruction: Protocols in the classroom. In S. M. Glazer, L. W. Searfoss, & L. M. Gentile (Eds.), *Re-examining reading diagnosis: New trends and procedures* (pp. 94–102). Newark, DE: International Reading Association.

Brozo, W. G. (1990). Learning how at-risk readers learn best: A case for interactive assessment. *Journal of Reading, 33*, 522–527.

Bruner, J. (1984). Language, mind, and reading. In H. Goelman, A. Oberg, & F. Smith (Eds.), *Awakening to literacy* (pp. 193–200). Portsmouth, NH: Heinemann.

Busching, B. (1981). Readers theatre: An education for language and life. *Language Arts, 58*, 330–338.

Bussis, A. M., Chittenden, E. A., Amarel, M., & Klausner, E. (1985). *Inquiry into meaning: An investigation of learning to read.* Hillsdale, NJ: Lawrence Erlbaum.

Butler, A., & Turnbill, J. (1984). *Towards a reading-writing classroom.* Rozelle, NSW, Australia: Primary English Teaching Association.

Butler, D., & Clay, M. (1979). *Reading begins at home.* Exeter, NH: Heinemann.

Butler, D., & Clay, M. (1988). *Writing begins at home.* Portsmouth, NH: Heinemann.

Cambourne, B. (1984). Language, learning, and literacy. In A. Butler, & J. Turnbill (Eds.), *Towards a reading-writing classroom* (pp. 5–9). Rozelle, NSW, Australia: Primary English Teaching Association.

Camp, R. (in press). The place of portfolios in our changing views of writing assessment. In R. Bennett & W. Ward (Eds.), *Construction versus choice in cognitive measurement.* Hillsdale, NJ: Lawrence Erlbaum.

Carini, P. F. (1982). *The school lives of seven children.* Grand Forks, ND: University of North Dakota Press.

Carini, P. F. (1986). Building from children's strengths. *Journal of Education, 168*(3), 13–24.

Carr, E., & Ogle, D. (1987). KWL Plus: A strategy. *Journal of Reading, 30*, 626–631.

Cazden, C. B. (1982). Contexts for literacy: In the mind and in the classroom. *Journal of Behavior, 14*, 413–428.

Cazden, C. B. (1983). Adult assistance to language development: Scaffolds, models, and direct instruction. In R. P. Parker, & F. A. Davis (Eds.), *Developing literacy* (pp. 3–18). Newark, DE: International Reading Association.

Cazden, C. B. (1988). *Classroom discourse: The language of teaching and learning.* Portsmouth, NH: Heinemann.

The Children's Book Council/International Reading Association. (1992). *Kids' favorite books: Children's choices, 1989–1991.* Newark, DE: Author.

Chittenden, E. (1990, April). *Authentic assessment, evaluation, and documentation of student performance*. California ASCD Invitational Symposia, San Jose, Riverside.

Cioffi, G., & Carney, J. J. (1983). Dynamic assessment of reading disabilities. *The Reading Teacher, 36*, 764–768.

Chukovsky, K. (1963). *From two to five*. (M. Morton, Trans.). Berkeley, CA: University of California Press.

Clay, M. M. (1976). *What did I write?* Portsmouth, NH: Heinemann.

Clay, M. M. (1979). *Reading: The patterning of complex behaviour*. Portsmouth, NH: Heinemann.

Clifford, J. (Ed.). (1991). *The experience of reading: Louise Rosenblatt and reader-response theory*. Portsmouth, NH: Boynton/Cook Heinemann.

Cohen, D. (1968). The effects of literature on vocabulary and reading achievement. *Elementary English, 45*, 209–13, 217.

Cook, D. (1989). *Strategic learning in the content areas*. Madison, WI: Wisconsin Department of Public Instruction.

Costa, A. L. (1984). Mediating the metacognitive. *Educational Leadership, 42*, 57–62.

Costa, A. L., & Lowery, L. F. (1989). *Techniques for teaching thinking*. Pacific Grove, CA: Midwest Publications.

Cremin, L. (1961). *The transformation of the school: Progressivism in American education, 1957–1976*. New York: Vintage.

Crouse, P., & Davey, M. (1989). Collaborative learning: Insights from our children. *Language Arts, 66*, 756–766.

Cullinan, B., Jagger, A., & Strickland, D. (1974). Language expansion for black children in the primary grades: A research report. *Young Children, 29*, 98–112.

Daly, J. A., Vangelisti, A., & Witte, S. P. (1988). Writing apprehension in the classroom context. In B. A. Raford & D. L. Rubin (Eds.), *The social construction of written communication* (pp. 147–171). Norwood, NJ: Ablex.

Davey, B. (1983). Think aloud—Modeling the cognitive process of reading comprehension. *Journal of Reading, 26*, 38–41.

DeFord, D. (1981). Literacy, reading, writing, and other essentials. *Language Arts, 58*, 652–658.

DeGroff, L. (1990). Informational books: Topics and structure. *The Reading Teacher, 43*, 496–501.

Dewey, J. (1900). *The school and society*. New York: Macmillan.

Dewey, J. (1916). *Democracy and education*. New York: Macmillan.

Dewey, J. (1963). *Experience and education*. New York: Macmillan.

Downing, J. (1979). *Reading and reasoning*. New York: Springer-Verlag.

Durkin, D. (1990). Dolores Durkin speaks on instruction. *The Reading Teacher, 43,* 472–477.

Dyson, A.H. (1986). Transitions and tensions: Interrelationships between the drawing, talking, and dictating of young children. *Research in the Teaching of English, 20,* 379–409.

Dyson, A. H. (1988). Negotiating among multiple worlds: The space/time dimensions of young children's composing. *Research in the Teaching of English, 22,* 355–387.

Edelsky, C., Altwerger, B., & Flores, B. (1991). *Whole language: What's the difference?* Portsmouth, NH: Heinemann.

Educational Testing Service. (1990). BookWhiz™ Princeton, NJ: Author.

Eggleton, J. (1990). *Whole language evaluation.* Hong Kong: Applecross.

Elbow, P. (1983). *Writing without teachers.* New York: Oxford University Press.

Eldredge, J. L., & Butterfield, D. (1986). Alternatives to traditional reading instruction. *The Reading Teacher, 40,* 32–37.

Engle, B. (1990). Keeping Track: An approach to assessment in early literacy. In C. Kamii (Ed.), *Achievement testing in the early grades: The games grown-ups play* (pp. 119–134). Washington, DC: National Association for the Education of Young Children.

Evertson, C. M. (1989). Classroom organization and management. In M. C. Reynolds (Ed.), *Knowledge base for the beginning teacher* (pp. 59–70). New York: Pergamon Press.

Fear, K., Anderson, L. M., Englert, C. S., & Raphael, T. E. (1987). The relationship between teachers' beliefs and instruction and students conceptions about the writing process. In J. E. Readence & R. S. Baldwin (Eds.), *Research in literacy: Merging perspectives.* Thirty-sixth Yearbook of the National Reading Conference (pp. 255–264). Rochester, NY: National Reading Conference.

Feiman-Nemser, S., & Floden, R. E. (1986). The cultures of teaching. In M. C. Wittrock (Ed.), *Handbook of research on teaching* (3rd ed.) (pp. 505–526). New York: Macmillan Publishing Co.

Ferreiro, E., & Teberosky, A. (1982). *Literacy before schooling.* Portsmouth, NH: Heinemann.

Fitzgerald, J. (1987). Revision in writing. *Review of Educational Research, 57,* 481–506.

Flood, J., & Lapp, D. (1989). Reporting reading progress: A comparison portfolio for parents. *The Reading Teacher, 42,* 508–517.

Flood, J., & Lapp, D. (1990). Reading comprehension instruction for at-risk students: Research-based practices that can make a difference. *Journal of Reading, 33,* 490–496.

Flores, B., Cousin, P. T., & Diáz, E. (1991). Transforming deficit myths about learning, language, and culture. *Language Arts, 68,* 369–379.

Forrest, A., Knapp, J. E., & Pendergrass, J. (1976). Tools and methods of evaluation. In Kenton, M. T. (Ed.), *Experiential learning: Rationale, characteristics, and assessment* (pp. 161–188). San Francisco: Jossey-Bass.

Fox, C. (1985). The book that talks. *Language Arts, 62,* 374–384.

France, M. (1989). Personal communication.

Fredericks, A. D., & Rasinski, T. V. (1989). Dimensions of parent involvement. *The Reading Teacher, 43,* 180–182.

Fredericks, A. D., & Rasinski, T. V. (1990). Lending a (reading) hand. *The Reading Teacher, 43,* 520–521.

Fromberg, D. P., & Driscoll, M. (1985). *The successful classroom.* New York: Teachers College Press.

Fulwiler, T. (1980). Journals across the disciplines. *English Journal, 69,* 14–19.

Fulwiler, T., & Young, A. (Eds.). (1982). *Language connections: Writing and reading across the curriculum.* Urbana, IL: National Council of Teachers of English.

Gambrell, L. B. (1990). Introduction to themed issue. *Journal of Reading, 33,* 485–532.

Genishi, C., & Dyson, A. H. (1984). *Language assessment in the early years.* Norwood, NJ: Ablex.

Gere, A. R. (Ed.). (1985). *Roots in the sawdust: Writing to learn across the disciplines.* Urbana, IL: National Council of Teachers of English.

Gerritz, K. (1983). Dear Mrs. McCrea, About that conference next week. . . . *Learning Magazine, 13* (7) p. 46.

Gomez, M. L., Graue, M. E., & Bloch, M. N. (1991). Reassessing portfolio assessment: Rhetoric and reality. *Language Arts, 68,* 620–628.

Good, T. L. (1987). Teacher expectations. In D. C. Berliner, & B. Rosenshine (Eds.), *Talks to teachers* (pp. 159–200). New York: Random House.

Good, T. L., & Brophy, J. E. (1987). *Looking into classrooms* (4th ed.). New York: Harper and Row.

Goodman, K. S. (1986). Basal readers: A call for action. *Language Arts, 63,* 358–362.

Goodman, K. S. (1988). Look what they've done to Judy Blume! The "basalization" of children's literature. *The New Advocate, 1,* 29–41.

Goodman, K. S., Shannon, P., Freeman, Y. S., & Murphy, S. (1988). *Report card on basal readers.* Katonah, NY: Richard C. Owen.

Goodman, Y. M. (1984). The development of initial literacy. In H. Goelman, A. Oberg, & F. Smith (Eds.), *Awakening to literacy* (pp. 102–110). Portsmouth, NH: Heinemann.

Goodman, Y. M. (1985). Observing children in the classroom. In A. Jagger & M. Smith-Burke (Eds.), *Observing the language learner* (pp. 9–17). Newark, DE: International Reading Association.

Goodman, Y. M. (1989). Evaluation of students: [Evaluation of Teachers]. In K. S. Goodman, Y. M. Goodman, & W. J. Hood (Eds.), *The whole language evaluation book* (pp. 3–14). Portsmouth, NH: Heinemann.

Goodman, Y. M. (Ed.). (1990). *How children construct literacy*. Newark, DE: International Reading Association.

Goswani, D., & Stillman, P. R. (Eds.), (1987). *Reclaiming the classroom*. Upper Montclair, NJ: Boynton/Cook.

Graves, D. (1983). *Writing: Teachers and children at work*. Portsmouth, NH: Heinemann.

Harp, B. (Ed.). (1991). *Assessment and evaluation in whole language programs*. Norwood, MA: Christopher-Gordon.

Harste, J. C., Short, K. G., & Burke, C. (1988). *Creating classrooms for authors*. Portsmouth, NH: Heinemann.

Harste, J. C., Woodward, V. A, & Burke, C. L. (1983). *Language stories and literacy lessons*. Portsmouth, NH: Heinemann.

Heald-Taylor, G. (1989). *The administrator's guide to whole language*. Katonah, NY: Richard C. Owens.

Heimlich, J. E., & Pittleman, S. D. (1986). *Semantic mapping: Classroom applications*. Newark, DE: International Reading Association.

Hermann, B. A. (1990). Cognitive and metacognitive goals in reading and writing. In G. S. Duffy (Ed.), *Reading in the middle school* (2nd ed.) (pp. 81–96). Newark, DE: International Reading Association.

Herr, S. (1982). Learning activities for reading (4th ed.). Dubuque, IA: William C. Brown.

Hiebert, E. H. (1980). Peers as reading teacher. *Language Arts, 57*, 877–881.

Hiebert, E. H., & Hutchinson, T. A. (1991). Research directions: The current state of alternative assessments for policy and instructional use. *Language Arts, 68*, 662–668.

Holdaway, D. (1979). *The foundations of literacy*. Sydney: Ashton-Scholastic.

Hubbard, R. (1989). Inner designs. *Language Arts, 66*, pp. 119–138.

Huck, C. S., Hepler, S., & Hickman, J. (1987). *Children's literature in the elementary school* (4th ed.). New York: Holt, Rinehart & Winston.

Huey, E. B. (1968). *The psychology and pedagogy of reading* (rev. ed.). Boston: MIT Press.

Hull, G. A. (1989). Research on writing: Building a cognitive and social understanding of composing. In L. B. Resnick, & L. E. Klopfer (Eds.), *Toward the thinking curriculum: Current cognitive research* (pp. 104–128). Alexandria, VA: Association for Supervision and Curriculum Development.

Irwin, J. W., & Davis, C. A. (1980). Assessing readability: The checklist approach. *Journal of Reading, 24,* 124–130.

Jackson, R. M. (1986). Thumbs up for direct teaching of thinking skills. *Educational Leadership, 43,* 32–36.

Johnson, D. W., & Johnson, R. T. (1987). *Learning together and alone.* Englewood Cliffs, NJ: Prentice-Hall.

Johnson, T. D., & Louis, D. R. (1987). *Literacy through literature.* Portsmouth, NH: Heinemann.

Johnston, P. (1987). Teachers as evaluation experts. *The Reading Teacher, 41*(8), 744–748.

Johnston, P. (1990). Constructive evaluation and the improvement of teaching and learning. *Teachers' College Record, 91,* 1–42.

Johnston, P., & Winograd, P. (1985). Passive failure in reading. *Journal of Reading Behavior, 17,* 279–301.

Jones, B. F., Palinscar, A. S., Ogle, D. S., & Carr, E. C. (Eds.). (1987). *Strategic teaching and learning: Cognitive instruction in the content areas.* Alexandria, VA: Association for Supervision and Curriculum Development.

Juell, P. (1985). The course journal. In A. R. Gere (Ed.), *Roots in the sawdust: Writing to learn across the disciplines* (pp. 187–201). Urbana, IL: National Council of Teachers of English.

Kernan, K. T. (1977). Semantic and expressive elaborations in children's narratives. In S. Ervin-Tripp & C. Mitchell-Kernan (Eds.), *Child discourse* (pp. 91–102). New York: Academic Press.

Kidder, T. (1989). *Among school children.* Boston: Houghton Mifflin.

Kletzien, S. B., & Bedner, M. R. (1990). Dynamic assessment for at-risk readers. *Journal of Reading, 33,* 528–531.

Kohl, H. (1974). *Reading, how to.* New York: Bantam.

Kutz, E. (1992). Teacher research: Myth and realities. *Language Arts, 69,* 193–199.

Lamme, L. L., & Hysmith, C. (1991). One school's adventure into portfolio assessment. *Language Arts, 68,* 629–640.

Langer, J. (1984). Examining background knowledge and text comprehension. *Reading Research Quarterly, 19,* 468–481.

Langer, J. (1984). Facilitating text processing: The elaboration of prior knowledge. In J. Langer & M. T. Smith-Burke (Eds.), *Reader meets author: Bridging the gap* (pp. 149–162). Newark, DE: International Reading Association.

Langer, J. A. (1990a). The process of understanding: Reading for literary and informative purposes. *Research in the Teaching of English, 24,* 229–260.

Langer, J. A. (1990b). Understanding literature. *Language Arts, 67,* 812–816.

Larrick, N. (1987). Literacy starts too soon. *Phi Delta Kappan, 69*, 184–189.

Leu, D. J., & Kinzer, C. K. (1987). *Effective reading instruction in the elementary grades*. New York: Merrill/Macmillan.

Lipman, M. (1988, September). Critical thinking—What can it be? *Educational Leadership, 46*, 38–43.

Lipson, M. Y., & Wixson, K. K. (1989). Student evaluation and basal instruction. In P. N. Winograd, K. K. Wixson, & M. Y. Lipson (Eds.), *Improving basal reading instruction* (pp. 109–139). New York: Teachers College Press.

Lloyd-Jones, R., & Lunsford, A. A. (Eds.). (1989). *The English Coalition Conference: Democracy through language*. Urbana, IL: National Council of Teachers of English.

Marshall, H. H. (1988). Work or learning: Implications of classroom metaphors. *Educational Researcher, 17*(9), 9–16.

Mason, J. M. (1983). An examination of reading instruction in third and fourth grades. *Reading Teacher, 36*, 504–507.

McDiarmid, G. W., Ball, D. L., & Anderson, C. W. (1989). Why staying one chapter ahead doesn't really work: Subject-specific pedagogy. In M. C. Reynolds (Ed.), *Knowledge base for the beginning teacher* (pp. 193–205). New York: Pergamon Press.

Meek, M. (1982). *Learning to read*. London: The Bodley Head.

Morris, B. (1986). Thinking through text. In N. Stewart-Dore (Ed.), *Writing and reading to learn*. Rozelle, NSW, Australia: Primary English Teachers Association.

Mosenthal, J. (1989). The comprehension experience. In K. D. Muth (Ed.), *Children's comprehension of text* (pp. 244–262). Newark, DE: International Reading Association.

Moss, E. (1977). The "Peppermint" Lesson. In M. Meek, M. A. Warlow, & G. Barton (Eds.), *The cool web: The pattern of children's reading* (pp. 140–142). London: The Bodley Head.

Nagy, W. E. (1988). *Teaching vocabulary to improve reading comprehension*. Newark, DE: International Reading Association.

Newman, J. M., & Church, S. M. (1990). Commentary: Myths of whole language. *The Reading Teacher, 44*, 20–27.

Norris, S. & Ennis, R. H. (1989). *Evaluating critical thinking*. Pacific Grove, CA: Midwest Publications.

Norton, D. E. (1991). *Through the eyes of a child: An introduction to children's literature* (3rd ed.). New York: Merrill/Macmillan.

Norton, D. E. (1990). Teaching multi-cultural literature in the reading curriculum. *The Reading Teacher, 44*, 28–41.

Ogle, D. M. (1989). The know, want to know, learn strategy. In K. D. Muth (Ed.), *Children's comprehension of text* (pp. 205–223). Newark, DE: International Reading Association.

Olson, C. B. (1984). Fostering critical thinking skills through writing. *Educational Leadership, 42,* 28–39.

Palinscar, A. S., & Brown, A. L. (1984). Reciprocal teaching of comprehension—fostering and comprehension—monitoring activities. *Cognition and Instruction, 1,* 117–175.

Paul, R. (1987). Critical thinking, moral integrity and citizenship: Teaching intellectual virtues. Paper presented at the Seventh Annual Conference on Critical Thinking and Education Reform, Sonoma State University, Rohnert Park, CA.

Pavlik, R., & Piercy, D. (1989). *Reading activities in the content areas.* Boston: Allyn and Bacon.

Pearson, P. D. (1991, July). *Comprehension: Theory and application.* Presentation at The 1991 Reading Institute, Fordham University, New York.

Pearson, P. D., & Dole, J. A. (1987). Explicit comprehension instruction: A review of research and a new conceptualization of instruction. *The Elementary School Journal, 88*(2), 151–165.

Pearson, P. D., & Valencia, S. (1987). Assessment, accountability, and professional prerogative. In *Research in literacy: Managing perspectives* (pp. 3–16). Thirty-sixth Yearbook of the National Reading Conference. Chicago: Author.

Pellegrini, A. D. (1991). A critique of the concept of at-risk as applied to emergent literacy. *Language Arts, 68,* 380–387.

Peters, C. W. (1990). Content knowledge in reading: Creating a new framework. In G. G. Duffy (Ed.), *Reading in the middle school* (pp. 63–80). Newark, DE: International Reading Association.

Power, B. M. (1989). Beyond "Geddinagrupe": A case study of three first grade collaborators. *Language Arts, 66,* 767–774.

Purcell-Gates, V. (1988). Lexical and syntactic knowledge of written narrative held by well-read-to kindergartners and second graders. *Research in the Teaching of English, 22,* 128–160.

Purcell-Gates, V., & Salinger, T. S. (1991). Access to literacy for young children. In K. M. Borman, P. Swami, & L. P. Wagstaff (Eds.), *Contemporary issues in U.S. education* (pp. 128–141). Norwood, NJ: Ablex Publishing.

Quandt, I., & Selznick, R. (1984). *Self-concept and reading* (2nd ed.). Newark, DE: International Reading Association.

Reimer, K. M. (1992). Multiethnic literature: Holding fast to dreams. *Language Arts, 69,* 14–21.

Resnick, L. B. (1985). Instructional psychology. In T. Husen & T. Postlethwaite (Eds.), *International encyclopedia of education: Research and studies* (Vol. 5)(pp. 2567–2581). Oxford and New York: Pergamon.

Resnick, L. B. (1989). Keynote Address. National Reading Conference Annual Meeting, Austin, Texas.

Rico, G. L. (1983). *Writing the natural way: Using right-brain techniques to release your expressive power.* Los Angeles: J. P. Tarcher, Inc.

Ritty, J. M. (1991). Single-parent families: Tips for educators. *The Reading Teacher, 44,* 604–606.

Rosenblatt, L. M. (1938/1978). *Literature as exploration.* New York: D. Appleton.

Rosenblatt, L. M. (1979). *The reader, the text, and the poem.* Carbondale, IL: Southern Illinois University Press.

Rosenblatt, L. M. (1985). Language, schooling, and society. In S. N. Tchudi (Ed.), *Proceedings of the International Federation of Teachers of English* (pp. 64–80). Portsmouth, NH: Boynton/Cook.

Rosenblatt, L. M. (1989). Writing and reading: The transactional theory. In J. M. Mason (Ed.), *Reading and writing connections* (pp. 153–176). Boston: Allyn and Bacon.

Rosenblatt, L. M. (1991). Literature—S.O.S.! *Language Arts, 68,* 444–448.

Routman, R. (1989). *Transitions.* Portsmouth, NH: Heinemann.

Routman, R. (1991). *Invitations: Changing as Teachers and Learners, K–12.* Portsmouth, NH: Heinemann.

Salinger, T. (1988). *Language arts and literacy for young children.* New York: Merrill/Macmillan.

Salinger, T. (in press). Classroom-based and portfolio assessment for elementary grades. In C. Hedley, D. Feldman, & P. Antonacci (Eds.), *Literacy across the Curriculum.* Norwood, NJ: Ablex.

Salzer, R. T. (1991). TAWL teachers reach for self-help. *Educational Leadership, 48,* 66–67.

Sardy, S. (1985). Thinking about reading. In T. L. Harris & E. J. Cooper (Eds.), *Reading, thinking, and concept development.* (pp. 213–229). New York: The College Board.

Saul, E. W. (1989). "What did Leo feed the turtle?" and other nonliterary questions. *Language Arts, 66,* 295–303.

Sawyer, W. (1987). Literature and literacy: A review of research. *Language Arts, 64,* 33–39.

Shannon, P. (1989). *Broken promises: Reading instruction in twentieth-century America.* Granby, MA: Bergin & Garvey.

Shulman, L. (1986). Paradigms and research programs in the study of teaching: A contemporary perspective. In M. Wittrock (Ed.), *Handbook of research on teaching* (3rd ed.) (pp. 3–36). New York: Macmillan.

Simmons, J. (1990). Portfolios as large-scale assessment. *Language Arts, 67,* 262–268.

Sims, R. (1982). *Shadow and substance*. Urbana, IL: National Council of Teachers of English.

Sims, R. (1984). A question of perspective. *Advocate, 3*, 145–155.

Siu-Runyan, Y. (1991). Learning from students: An important aspect of classroom organization. *Language Arts, 68*, 100–107.

Sloan, G. (1975). *The child as critic*. New York: Teachers College Press.

Sloan, G. (1984). *The child as critic*, 2nd ed. New York: Teachers College Press.

Smith, F. (1988). *Joining the literacy club*. Portsmouth, NH: Heinemann.

Smith, F. (1992). Learning to read: The never-ending debate. *Phi Delta Kappan, 73*, 432–441.

Smith, G. B. (1988). Physical arrangements, grouping, and ethnographic notetaking. In S. M. Glazer, L. W. Searfoss, & L. M. Gentile (Eds.), *Reexamining reading diagnosis* (pp. 169–177). Newark, DE: International Reading Association.

Smith, N. B. (1965). *American reading instruction*. Newark, DE: International Reading Association.

Stanford, G. (1976). *Developing effective classroom groups*. New York: Hart.

Stewart, O., & Tei, E. (1983). Some implications of metacognition for reading instruction. *Journal of Reading, 27*, 36–43.

Stewig, J. W. (1988). *Children and literature* (2nd ed.). Boston: Houghton Mifflin.

Stewig, J. W. (1990). *Read to write: Using children's literature as a springboard for teaching writing* (3rd ed.). Katonah, NY: Richard C. Owen.

Stoll, D. R. (1990). *Magazines for children*. Newark, DE: International Reading Association.

Strickland, D. S. (1987). Literature: Key element in the language and reading program. In B.E. Cullinan (Ed.), *Children's literature in the reading program* (pp. 68–76). Newark, DE: International Reading Association.

Strickland, D., Dillon, R., Funkhouser, Glick, M., & Rogers, C. (1989). Research currents: Classroom dialogue during literature response groups. *Language Arts, 66*, 192–200.

Swartz, R. J., & Perkins, D. N. (1989). *Teaching thinking: Issues and approaches*. Pacific Grove, CA: Midwest Publications.

Taylor, D. (1983). *Family literacy: Young children learning to read and write*. Portsmouth, NH: Heinemann.

Taylor, D. (1989). Toward a unified theory of literacy learning. *Phi Delta Kappan, 70*, 184–193.

Taylor, D., & Dorsey-Gaines, C. (1988). *Growing up literate: Learning from inner-city families*. Portsmouth, NH: Heinemann.

Tchudi, S. N., & Huerta, M. C. (1983). *Teaching writing in the content areas: Middle school/junior high*. Urbana, IL: National Council of Teachers of English.

Teale, W. H. (1984). Reading to young children: Its significance for literary development. In H. Goelman, A. Oberg, & F. Smith (Eds.), *Awakening to literacy* (pp. 110–121). Portsmouth, NH: Heinemann.

Thaiss, C. J. (1986). *Language across the curriculum in the elementary grades.* Urbana, IL: National Council of Teachers of English.

Tierney, R. J., Carter, M. A., & Desai, L. E. (1991). *Portfolio assessment in the reading-writing classroom.* Norwood, MA: Christopher-Gordon.

Torbe, M., & Medway, P. (1981). *The climate for learning.* Montclair, NJ: Boynton/Cook.

Trelease, J. (1985). *The read-aloud handbook.* New York: Penguin.

Trousdale, A. M. (1990). Interactive story-telling: Scaffolding children's early narratives. *Language Arts, 67,* 164–173.

Tunnell, M. O. (1986). The natural act of reading: An affective approach. *The Advocate, 5,* 156–164.

Valencia, S. W., McGinley, W., & Pearson, P. D. (1990). In G. G. Duffy (Ed.), *Reading in the middle school* (2nd ed.) (pp. 124–153). Newark, DE: International Reading Association.

Veatch, J. (1968). *How to teach reading with children's books* (2nd ed.). New York: Richard C. Owen.

Vygotsky, L. S. (1962). *Thought and language.* Cambridge, MA: MIT Press.

Wang, M. C., & Palinscar, A. S. (1989). Teaching students to assume an active role in their learning. In M. C. Reynolds (Ed.), *Knowledge base for the beginning teacher* (pp. 71–84). New York: Pergamon Press.

Weaver, C. (1988). *Reading process and practice: From socio-psycholinguistics to whole language.* Portsmouth, NH: Heinemann.

Weaver, C., & Groff, P (1989). *Two reactions to the report card on basal readers.* Bloomington, IN: ERIC Clearinghouse on Reading and Communication Skills.

Weis, J., & Steward-Dore, N. (1987). Writing and reading to learn together. In N. Steward-Dore (Ed.), *Writing and reading to learn* (pp. 67–80). Rozelle, NSW, Australia: Primary English Teaching Association.

Welty, E. (1983). *One writer's beginnings.* New York: Warner Books.

Wiggins, G. (1989). Teaching to the (authentic) test. *Educational Leadership, 46*(7), 41–49.

Winograd, P. N., & Bridge, C. A. (1986). The comprehension of important information in written prose. In F. Bauman (Ed.), *Teaching main idea comprehension.* Newark, DE: International Reading Association.

Winograd, P. N., & Paris, S. G. (1988–89). A cognitive and motivational agenda for reading instruction. *Educational Leadership, 46*(4), 30–36.

Winograd, P. N., Wixson, K. K., & Lipson, M. Y. (Eds). (1989). *Improving basal reading instructions.* New York: Teachers College Press.

Wixson, K. K., Bosky, A. B., Yochum, N., & Alvermann, D. E. (1984). An interview for assessing students' perceptions of classroom reading tasks. *The Reading Teacher, 37*, 346–352.

Wolf, D. P. (1989). Portfolio assessment: Sampling student work. *Educational Leadership, 46*, 35–40.

Wood, K. D. (1984). Probable passages: A writing strategy. *The Reading Teacher, 37*, 496–499.

Zumwalt, K. (1989). Beginning professional teachers: The need for a curricular vision of teaching. In M. C. Reynolds (Ed.), *Knowledge base for the beginning teacher* (pp. 173–184). New York: Pergamon Press.

CHILDREN'S BOOKS CITED IN THE TEXT

Balestino, P. (1989). *The skeleton inside you*. New York: Crowell.

Benchley, N. (1969). *Sam the minuteman*. New York: Harper Junior Books.

Benchley, N. (1972). *Small wolf*. New York: Harper & Row.

Brenner, B. (1978). *Wagon wheels*. New York: Harper & Row.

Brown, M. W. (1942/1972) *The runaway bunny*. New York: Harper & Row.

Carle, E. (1971). *Do you want to be my friend?* New York: Harper & Row.

Carlson, N. (1989). *I like me!* New York: Viking.

Clapp, P. (1968). *Constance: A story of early Plymouth*. New York: Lothrop, Lee and Shepard.

Colman, H. (1978). *Tell me no lies*. New York: Crown.

Forbes, E. (1946). *Johnnie Tremain*. Boston: Houghton Mifflin.

Fox, P. (1973). *Slave dancer*. New York: Bradbury.

Fritz, J. (1972). *And then what happened, Paul Revere?* New York: Coward.

Haugaard, E. C. (1963). *Hakon of Rogen's saga*. Boston: Houghton Mifflin.

Haugaard, E. C. (1965). *A slave's tale*. Boston: Houghton Mifflin.

Hoban, R. (1960) *Bedtime for Frances*. New York: Harper (and other books in the Frances series).

Horenstein, H. (1989). *Sam goes trucking*. Boston: Houghton Mifflin.

Janeczko, P. B. (1990). *The place my words are looking for*. New York: Bradbury Press.

L'Engle, M. (1962). *A wrinkle in time*. New York: Farrar, Straus, & Giroux.

L'Engle, M. (1973). *The wind at the door*. New York: Farrar, Straus, & Giroux.

L'Engle, M. (1978). *A swiftly tilting planet*. New York: Farrar, Straus, & Giroux.

Lobel, A. (1970). *Frog and Toad are friends*. New York: Harper (and other books in the Frog and Toad series).

Macaulay, D. (1990). *Black and white*. Boston: Houghton Mifflin.

MacLachlan, P. (1985). *Sarah, plain and tall*. New York: Harper.

Mayer, M. (1968). *There's a nightmare in my closet*. New York: Dial.

McDonald, J. (1989). *Mail-order kid*. New York: Putnam.

Norton, M. (1953). *The borrowers*. San Diego: Harcourt (and other books in the Borrowers series).

Paterson, K. (1989). *Park's quest*. New York: Lodestar.

Ryder, J. (1977). *Fireflies*. New York: Harper & Row.

Saville, L. (1988). *Horses in the circus ring*. New York: Dutton.

Simon, S. (1988). *How to be an ocean scientist in your own home*. New York: Lippincott.

Sutcliff, R. (1978). *Sun horse, moon horse*. New York: Dutton.

Tolkien, J. R. R. (1984). *The hobbit*. Boston: Houghton Mifflin. (See also other books by this author.)

Viorst, J. (1972). *Alexander and the terrible, horrible, no good, very bad day*. New York: Atheneum.

White, E. B. (1945). *Stuart Little*. New York: Harper & Row.

White, E. B. (1952). *Charlotte's web*. New York: Harper & Row.

White, E. B. (1970). *The trumpet of the swan*. New York: Harper & Row.

Wiseman, B. (1970). *Morris the Moose goes to school*. New York: Harper & Row (and other books in the Morris series).

Zims, H. S. (1952). *What's inside me*. New York: William Morrow. (See also other books by this author.)

Index

ISBN 0-675-21328-2

9 780675 213288